Introduction to
Feminist Legal Theory

D1262134

Introduction to
Feminist Legal Theory

MARTHA CHAMALLAS
Professor of Law
University of Pittsburgh

ASPEN LAW & BUSINESS
A Division of Aspen Publishers, Inc.
Gaithersburg   New York

Permissions
Aspen Law & Business
1185 Avenue of the Americas
New York, NY 10036

Printed in the United States of America

Library of Congress Cataloging-in-Publication Data

Chamallas, Martha.
    Introduction to feminist legal theory / by Martha Chamallas.
        p.   cm.
    Includes bibliographical references and index.
    ISBN 0-7355-0045-2
    1. Feminist jurisprudence.   2. Women—Legal status, laws, etc.—
United States.   I. Title.
K349.C49   1998
340'.082—dc21   98-30396
                                                                CIP

About Aspen Law & Business
Legal Education Division

In 1996, Aspen Law & Business welcomed the Law School Division of Little, Brown and Company into its growing business—already established as a leading provider of practical information to legal practitioners.

Acquiring much more than a prestigious collection of educational publications by the country's foremost authors, Aspen Law & Business inherited the long-standing Little, Brown tradition of excellence—born over 150 years ago. As one of America's oldest and most venerable publishing houses, Little, Brown and Company commenced in a world of change and challenge, innovation and growth. Sharing that same spirit, Aspen Law & Business has dedicated itself to continuing and strengthening the integrity begun so many years ago.

ASPEN LAW & BUSINESS
A Division of Aspen Publishers, Inc.
A Wolters Kluwer Company

Dedication

For Peter and Beth

Summary of Contents

Contents

CHAPTER 4

The Difference Stage (1980s)   47

CHAPTER 5

The Diversity Stage (1990s)   85

CHAPTER 9

Applied Feminist Scholarship—
Motherhood and Reproduction

CHAPTER 10

Conclusion

Preface

Introduction to Feminist Legal Theory is designed principally for students who have made some commitment to study feminist legal theory, by signing up for a course by that name or a related course on gender and law. This text functions as a paperback treatise and as a guide to exploring the connections between feminism and law. It examines many of the substantive topics that feminists have written extensively about, discusses the major cases in the field, and shows how feminism has influenced the shape of legal categories and doctrines since the 1970s. It should help students understand some of the more difficult and theoretically sophisticated law review articles assigned for their courses. It works well as a companion text to the major casebooks in the area. My students have also used the text to help them choose paper topics and to study for final exams.

FEATURES

This book illuminates the central debates of the past three decades and explains the basic concepts and vocabulary of feminism in a legal context. The chronological narrative of the development of feminist legal theory presented in the initial chapters of this book gives readers who are new to the field a sense of its history. The book offers a concise overview of a dynamic field, paying particular attention to how feminist legal theory intersects with other new schools of thought, such as critical race theory and gay and lesbian legal studies. The citations in this book were carefully chosen to allow readers to locate prominent authors and articles commonly regarded as exemplary and important to the overall development of the field. Without attempting to reduce the whole of feminist legal theory to a few basic themes, writers, and narratives, I have tried to provide enough content and context to represent the contours of the field.

Introduction to Feminist Legal Theory is written to be accessible to readers with no background in feminist theory, including those who are simply curious about the subject. As a law professor who has offered a cluster of related courses: Feminist Legal Theory, The Legal Control of Sexual Conduct, and Women and the Law, I have often been approached by law students, graduate students from other disciplines, faculty colleagues, judges, and practitioners who tell me they are intrigued by my field and sense that feminist legal theory contains something new and potentially valuable for them. Others express a desire to discover the ways in which their lives as women might relate to the study or practice of law, particularly because the law is so often depicted as gender-neutral and unconnected to politics and cultural conflicts. At times, male students and colleagues have confided that they wished there were a text that would give them some background and insight into feminist legal theory to expand their knowledge beyond the context of contentious debates in the classroom and the faculty lounge about date rape, sexual harassment, or abortion rights.

Introduction to Feminist Legal Theory is a concise and compact summary of the field. It can be used to compare legal feminism to other schools of thought—for example, whether law and economics, critical race theory, or law and literature, and can enrich fields of study such as women's history, women and politics, or feminist philosophy. I particularly hope that it will be of value to scholars and judges who wish to infuse feminist perspectives into their scholarship and judicial opinions, as well as by lawyers who wish to argue that basic legal concepts such as fairness, justice, and autonomy, should take on new meanings.

ACKNOWLEDGMENTS

In the several years I have worked on this book, I have received help from so many different people and institutions that it is simply not possible to acknowledge everyone who supported this project. In the early stages, I gained valuable insights from students and colleagues at the University of Iowa College of Law and its Women's Studies Program. In particular, I wish to thank the law students and graduate students in my Feminist Legal Theory courses and my seminars on Legal Control of Sexual Conduct. I also learned a great deal from my colleagues at Iowa, particularly Sally Kenney, Linda Kerber, Mary Lou Fellows, Sue Lafky, and Barbara Schwartz, and I am grateful for the summer stipends provided by the College of Law.

Preface

At the University of Pittsburgh School of Law, I benefited from detailed comments provided by my students in Feminist Legal Theory and from the careful and intelligent research assistance of Lisa Bleier, Drew Ciancia, and Heather Zink. My colleagues Jody Armour, Peter Alexander, Vivian Curran, David Herring, Margaret Mahoney, and Lu-in Wang also deserve my thanks for their valuable feedback and moral support. Carolyn Jones provided crucial help to me in writing the section on feminism and taxation. I am particularly indebted to Douglas Scott, who spent nearly two years reading feminist and critical theory, pointing me in the right direction, and helping me formulate my views.

Special thanks go to Kate Bartlett and Stephanie Wildman for reviewing the manuscript, and especially to Judith Resnik for her suggestions for adding new material to the text. Their thoughtful reading of the text helped me to revise and strengthen the book and to discover more about this fast-growing field. During the editorial process, Jessica Barmack and A.C. Willment were particularly good at their jobs and improved the organization and style of the book. I am also especially grateful to Carol McGeehan, who supported this project from the very beginning.

Finally, I want to thank Peter Shane, my spouse, colleague, and (sometimes) Dean, for everything.

Introduction to
Feminist Legal Theory

INTRODUCTION

A. THE CONTOURS OF FEMINIST LEGAL THEORY

There is little mystery to the attraction of feminist legal theory. Many people are drawn to the subject because of its capacity to get beneath the surface of the law. As an intellectual field, feminist legal theory goes beyond rules and precedents to explore the deeper structures of the law. Particularly for students, practitioners, and scholars who are critical of conventional legal categories, feminist legal theory offers ways of understanding how and why the law might have come to take its present shape and an appreciation of the human conflicts and diverse interests that often underlie even the most ordinary of legal standards.

Feminist legal theory responds to a basic insight about life and law. It proceeds from the assumption that gender is important in our everyday lives and recognizes that being a man or a woman is a central feature of our lives, whether we are pleased or distressed by the thought of gender difference. Feminist legal theory takes this approach into the study of law by examining how gender has mattered to the development of the law and how men and women are differently affected by the power in law. This concentrated focus on gender and the law is particularly appropriate at this point in our history when matters of sex and law are perpetually in the headlines. There is no better orientation to hot legal topics such as sexual harassment, domestic violence, and pay equity than taking a course on feminist legal theory.

As a field of law attuned to perspective and the influence of experience on our understanding of events, feminist legal theory also addresses important questions related to the construction of personal identity. In my fifteen years of teaching feminist legal theory and related courses to law students and graduate students from other disciplines, I have found that women are disproportionately attracted to these offerings. Perhaps this is because the courses pay close attention to women's experiences and do not pretend that the victim's, defendant's, or judge's gender is always irrelevant to the outcome of a legal dispute. Few courses in the law school curriculum have a similar capacity to excite, illuminate, and enrage. For some students, the course changes their lives.

The subject matter that forms the central core of feminist legal theory is the exploration of women's subordination through the law. In this context, the use of the term "subordination" by feminist writers is meant to convey the systemic nature of women's inequality. Many of the feminist scholars whose writings are discussed in this book have concluded that gender bias constitutes a pervasive feature of our law, rather than merely representing isolated instances of abuse of law. In a variety of contexts, feminist scholars have dissected legal doctrines and the language of court opinions and statutes to find hidden mechanisms of discrimination and uncover the implicit hierarchies that are contained within a body of law. This book will be an eye-opener for readers who thought that sex discrimination could have only one meaning, namely, the explicit different (or disparate) treatment of men and women under the law. In this book, I go beyond discussing problems of disparate treatment to explore bias that takes the form of gender stereotyping, devaluation of women and their activities, and the use of biased prototypes that distort women's injuries and experiences.

The theme of social change figures prominently in this introduction to feminist legal theory. For the most part, feminist legal scholars tend to be advocates of change and, particularly in the past three decades, have proposed large and small reforms of the law and the legal system in the name of gender equality. We have reached a stage at which we can reflect on the larger meanings of some of these changes. By tracing how feminists have agitated for recognition of new legal causes of action, extension of legal rights, and greater enforcement of existing laws, this book gives readers a foundation for evaluating the potential for feminism to transform the law. In some cases we will see that change does not always mean progress, as feminist scholars demonstrate how basic gender hierarchies can survive attempts at reform and how patterns of inequality are reproduced in different and updated forms. A good deal of feminist theory grapples with choice of strategies and with pragmatic calculations about coming up with the best change for a particular moment.

We have reached a point where feminist legal theory is a fairly commonplace offering in the law school curriculum. Most law schools have a course of this kind, whether called "Feminist Legal Theory," "Feminist Jurisprudence," or "Gender and Law." Such a course typically investigates legal doctrines, discourses, institutions, and culture through a feminist lens. However, students often come to the course with little idea of what to expect in terms of content or major themes. Particularly, students are often surprised by the great diversity among feminist legal writers. They learn that feminist legal writers differ in almost every conceivable respect: their particular visions of a just society, their strategies for change, their assumptions about human nature, and their judgments about the use of law as a method of social change. For this area of study, it is useful to speak in the plural; to talk in terms of feminist theories, feminist perspectives, feminist ideals.

I wrote this book with my students in feminist legal theory uppermost in my mind. It is intended to demystify the subject and provide a foundation for more specialized readings assigned throughout the course, whether the course is primarily focused on scholarly writings or case analysis. The text is designed so it can either be read at the very beginning of the semester as an overview of the entire course or be assigned in sections in conjunction with relevant readings. My goal is to make this very dynamic and often misunderstood subject accessible to readers who may not have a background in feminist or critical theory and who are not familiar with specialized anti-discrimination law doctrines.

I also hope that the book will be useful as an introduction to feminist legal theory for practitioners and judges who have never had the opportunity to take such a course, but who nevertheless confront difficult issues of gender and social inequality in their work. Particularly for lawyers who graduated from law school before the mid-1980s, the very idea of feminist legal theory may be both intriguing and perplexing. I wish to satisfy a bit of their curiosity and to allow them an entry point into the vast feminist legal literature that too rarely finds its way outside academia. Finally, I hope the book will be of value for researchers and students in women's studies and related fields. In the world of feminist theory, legal scholars have been very active and are beginning to gain considerable attention outside law schools. This book helps such interdisciplinary scholars to understand how feminist themes play out in the legal context and to locate sources and writers in their particular areas of interest.

The study of any new field of inquiry is often a daunting prospect, particularly a field as politically and emotionally charged as feminist legal theory. My goal is to ease "first day" anxieties by offering a compact text that provides a critical base of information. In terms of content, this book concentrates on introducing the reader to the somewhat specialized vocabulary of feminist legal theory, through both definitions and concrete examples. I have paid particular attention to identifying prominent themes explored in feminist legal writings, in the hope of providing a sense of what it means to say that an analysis or perspective on the law is feminist or is informed by feminism. Although the limits of space prevent me from citing and discussing many excellent articles and books I have read in the course of researching this book, I have attempted at least to introduce readers to many of the major writers in the field and to explain why their work is important to the larger field of inquiry. This presentation of the themes and writers in feminist legal theory is by its nature highly selective. For the most part, I have limited my discussion to legal developments in the United States and to U.S. writers, telling only the narrower story of how feminist legal theory has evolved in this country. My major objective is to aid in comprehension, without attempting to be comprehensive.

This book is also designed to provide context. The prominent themes in feminist legal theory, such as the interplay between equality and difference and the hidden bias in objectivity, offer a backdrop for understanding the significance of leading cases and legislative action relating to women and gender. As most law students have discovered early in their careers, the holding of an individual case rarely tells us what the case is really about, without a theoretical framework to make sense of the law in context. In this book, I have also endeavored to place the various brands or schools of feminist legal thought in historical context, focusing on some of the crucial political and cultural developments that have marked the last three decades. My narrative of the developments of feminist legal theory, for example, ties the scholarship to debates over the Equal Rights Amendment (ERA) and affirmative action, and to conflicts and changes within the feminist movement.

The book is probably most useful for readers who wish to "locate" or "situate" a particular writer or article within a broader intellectual context. Even for those of us who are inclined to mistrust rigid categorization and are wary of the arrogance that often accompanies the construction of labels and categories, the location process can be the key to acquiring a deeper understanding of a writer's ideas or viewpoint.

It should come as no surprise that in a new and fluid field such as feminist legal theory, there is no clear boundary setting it off from other intellectual movements that have flourished in law in the last generation. For quite some time, moreover, both academics and activists have taken an intense interest in exploring the intersection of different forms of discrimination and oppression—in seeing, for example, how racism and sexism operate in similar and dissimilar ways, and how even feminist-inspired legislation or rulings can overlook the importance of sexual orientation. For these reasons, a considerable portion of this book explores the points of connection or links between feminist theory and allied discourses in the law, particularly critical race theory and gay and lesbian legal studies. These connections illuminate feminist legal theory because they allow us to see how analogous themes emerge in these other intellectual movements, broadening our more general understanding of the social and cognitive forces behind inequality. Identifying the connections between feminism and allied schools of thought also underscores that feminist legal theory, like all other fields, is constantly shifting and redefining itself.

Finally, although this book is an introduction to feminist legal theory and not a defense of feminist legal theory, at various points in the text I have alerted readers to the some of the varieties of criticism leveled at the field and at the work of particular feminist scholars. I believe that connecting feminist legal theory to its critics has the beneficial effect of forcing feminists to state their positions more clearly and forcefully. It also helps us to see how a difference in starting points and basic commitments can alter both what we describe as the law and our aspirations for what the law should be.

B. ORGANIZATION OF THIS BOOK

This book introduces feminist legal theory through two paths. After a brief description of five of the basic methods or "moves" of feminist analysis, I analyze the development of feminist legal theory chronologically. In chapters 2 through 5, I examine the three major stages of feminist legal theory that have emerged since 1971, when the United States Supreme Court first invalidated a gender-based law in *Reed v. Reed*.[1] The stages roughly correspond to the last three decades: the *Equality Stage* of the 1970s; the *Difference Stage* of the 1980s; and the *Diversity Stage* of the 1990s.

These chronological chapters provide an overview of the major themes in feminist scholarship and the debates which have inspired the growth and refinement of feminist legal theory. In them, I describe the various schools of feminist legal thought, identifying the prominent features of liberal, radical, cultural, and postmodern feminist writings. These initial chapters also contain explanations of many of the key terms and theoretical concepts used in recent feminist scholarship. I place concepts such as "women's agency," "gender essentialism," and "multiple perspectives" into the chronological development of feminist legal theory and show how this new vocabulary expands the core of feminist theory to include more diverse groups of women. I also summarize the arguments of opponents of feminist legal theory in order to locate the basic points of disagreement between feminists and their most visible critics.

The first path ends with a chapter discussing trends outside feminist legal theory. To place feminist legal theory in context, Chapter 6 discusses two significant allied intellectual movements—critical race theory and gay and lesbian studies—that sometimes converge with feminist legal theory to produce a broader body of critical scholarship.

The second path into feminist legal theory focuses on substantive areas that are of particular importance to feminist scholars. To gain an understanding of what the law means for women in their daily lives, feminist theory has had to address three broad topics: money, sex, and family. These chapters provide a more in-depth summary and analysis

---

[1] 404 U.S. 71 (1971).

of specific areas, and they concentrate on applied, as opposed to theoretical, feminist scholarship.

Chapter 7 surveys applied feminist research on the economic subordination of women, examining women's access to material resources in several contexts, including as homemakers, as employees, as litigants in civil disputes and as taxpayers.

In Chapter 8, some of the vast literature on women's sexual exploitation and women's sexuality is canvassed. The chapter covers writings about rape, sexual harassment, and domestic violence. It also explores the phenomenon known as "heterosexism," the cultural preference given to male/female sexual relationships and the corresponding denigration of same-sex relationships, especially same-sex marriage.

Feminist analysis of motherhood and reproduction is the subject of Chapter 9. The chapter looks at the scholarship on such contentious topics as welfare reform, abortion, and single motherhood.

The final chapter offers a retrospective on the growth of feminist legal theory and speculates on the future.

Each of the chronological and substantive chapters has a dual objective: first, to describe the contours of feminist scholarship; second, to assess its impact on the law, whether in reshaping legal doctrine, generating new causes of action or providing direction for the passage of legislation. The feminist influence on legal doctrine is sometimes clearly visible, through, for example, a court's citation of feminist articles or the endorsement in litigation of positions advocated by women's organizations. At other times, the influence of feminism is inseparable from other intellectual and cultural trends. This book concentrates on major themes in feminist legal theory and related discourses, making connections to the practice and interpretation of law in the most prominent cases.

CHAPTER 1

Thinking Like a Feminist

Most legal writers or practitioners who identify themselves as feminists are critical of the status quo.[1] The root of the criticism is the belief that women are currently in a subordinate position in society and that the law often reflects and reinforces this subordination. Whatever their differences, feminists tend to start with the assumption that the law's treatment of women has not been fair or equal and that change is desirable. This stance separates feminists from researchers who study gender and law with the implicit assumption that the law has not produced or reproduced systematic gender inequity. This nonfeminist gender-oriented scholarship often simply describes gender differences or traces the impact of law on subgroups of men and women. Feminist legal scholarship is more oppositional; it assumes there is a problem and is suspicious of current arrangements, whether they take the form of different standards for men and women or purportedly neutral, uniform standards that nevertheless work to women's disadvantage.

---

[1] *See* Linda Lacey, Introducing Feminist Jurisprudence: An Analysis of Oklahoma's Seduction Statute, 25 Tulsa L.J. 775, 777-79 (1990). A smaller group of scholars who regard themselves as feminists do not share this view about the inequity of the status quo. Their "feminism" derives more from a professed commitment to equality of the sexes and a focus on women in their research. Included in such a group would be conservative critics of feminists such as Phyllis Schlafly, as well as more mainstream scholars who occasionally turn their attention to women and the law. *See* Gary Lawson, Feminist Legal Theories, 18 Harv. J.L. & Pub. Pol'y 325, 326-30 (1995). In this book, I focus primarily on feminist scholars who see a need for substantial changes in law and in the larger culture.

Unlike most other courses in the curriculum, feminist legal theory often requires an initial defense. The debate centers on the word "feminism," a hotly contested term with multiple meanings. For the most part, legal subjects tend to be described using neutral categories, unmodified by any particular viewpoint or methodological orientation. Feminist legal theory, however, is distinguished by its explicit reliance on feminism as the guiding force behind its inquiry into law. It owes its existence to the second wave of the women's movement, which began in the late 1960s. Although other legal subjects also have a history and are tied to particular cultural developments—for example, courses on the law of cyberspace, or about new reproductive technologies—feminist legal theory stands out because of its unapologetic connection to a specific political movement and its clear focus on women.

Criticism of the law from a feminist standpoint is a major undertaking. Feminist critiques can take many forms; they can consist of thick descriptions, causal analyses, or advocacy of reform. Clare Dalton's definition of feminism as it relates to the study of law lists some of the possible directions that feminist critiques may take:

> Feminism is . . . the range of committed inquiry and activity dedicated first, to *describing* women's subordination—exploring its nature and extent; dedicated second, to asking both *how*—through what mechanisms, and *why*—for what complex and interwoven reasons—women continue to occupy that position; and dedicated third, to change.[2]

Dalton's definition captures the different emphases of feminist legal writing, even on a single topic. For example, the feminist literature on domestic violence illustrates the three main components of Dalton's definition. First, feminists have sought to describe the *nature* and *extent* of domestic violence. They have not only gathered statistics about the prevalence of domestic violence but have sought a deeper understanding through narratives of battered women and firsthand accounts of those who have worked in women's shelters. The picture of domestic violence generated by these stories contrasts sharply with the conventional wisdom that regards fights between husband and wives as normal and maintains that families should be left alone to work out

---

[2] Clare Dalton, Where We Stand: Observations on the Situation of Feminist Legal Thought, 3 Berkeley Women's L.J. 1, 2 (1988-89) (emphasis added).

their disputes. The feminist narratives reveal a dynamic of domestic violence, a pattern of abuse, which includes not only punching, shoving and other forms of physical violence, but a complex of actions that one commentator calls a "regime of private tyranny."[3] The thick descriptions contained in feminist writings show how batterers often isolate their wives or partners, cut off support from family or friends, and secure submission by destroying a woman's confidence. The new feminist images are useful not only to persuade legislatures and courts to amend laws regarding domestic violence, but to change the cultural understanding of the phenomenon itself.

Second, feminist scholarship has explored *how* and *why* domestic violence continues to be a major contributor to women's subordinate status. For example, inaction by the police and prosecutors was early identified as one mechanism that allows domestic violence to thrive. Feminists argued that the criminal laws against assault and battery are simply not enforced in the domestic context and that the concept of "family privacy" has been used to justify nonintervention. Some feminist scholarship sought out the deeper structural and psychological supports for domestic violence. Women's economic dependence on men was cited as a major impediment to women's freedom, while the term "learned helplessness" was used to describe the devastating psychological impact that years of violence can have on victims. Because many women value intimate relationships and may still love a violent man, feminist scholars explained that a woman need not be a masochist to hesitate to leave an abusive relationship.[4]

Finally, in their writings and political activism, feminists have advocated *changes* in the legal system and the broader society to decrease the incidence of domestic violence and help victims of abuse. Mandatory arrest laws, special provisions for protective orders, and recovery of tort damages from abusive partners all represent reforms in formal legal doctrine inspired by the feminist advocacy. Feminists also argued for the creation of supportive institutional structures, including women's shelters and the provision of domestic violence advocates who help a victim find her way through a labyrinthian legal bureaucracy. Most recently, there has been an attempt to have domestic violence

---

[3] Jane Maslow Cohen, Regimes of Private Tyranny: What Do They Mean to Morality and for the Criminal Law?, 57 U. Pitt. L. Rev. 757 (1996).

[4] *See* Christine A. Littleton, Women's Experience and the Problem of Transition: Perspectives on Male Battering of Women, 1989 U. Chi. Legal F. 23.

treated as unethical conduct that signifies a person's lack of qualifications for positions of public trust or honor.

Dalton's description of the range of feminist inquiries is expansive in that it includes both highly theoretical and practical work, personal narrative and quantitative research. The contemporary emphasis on feminist "theory" does not mean that only abstract scholarship is valued. In fact, more than other schools of thought, feminist theories are apt to emphasize the importance of concrete changes in society and to stress the interaction between theory and practice. Theory tends to be valued not for its own sake, but for its capacity to give meaning to women's experience and to allow women to articulate their experiences more fully.

A.   FIVE OPENING MOVES

A good place to begin the study of feminist legal theory is to reflect on what it might mean to "think like a feminist"—to approach legal issues from a feminist stance or perspective. Law students are familiar with what has often been described as the goal of the first year of law school: getting students to "think like a lawyer." This initiation into the discipline offers few answers but emphasizes the kind of questions to which lawyers pay the most attention. Early on, law professors tell their students that mastering the specific content of the courses is not as important as learning the techniques of the lawyer: in particular, exposure to the case method, attention to factual details, separating the relevant from the irrelevant, and tracing out the logical implications of rules or principles. In a similar vein, there are some recurring techniques and insights that can help initiate students in the study of feminist scholarship. Although there is no uniform methodology or approach, feminist scholars often deploy a few recurring "moves" in their analyses, moves that help to place women at the center rather than the margins of the study of law. The following five moves are intended to give some sense of the scope and preoccupations of the critical study of law as it is engaged in by feminists. Throughout this book, we will see how these moves appear and reappear in both theoretical and applied feminist scholarship.

A. Five Opening Moves

1. Women's Experience

A recurring theme in much feminist scholarship is the importance of women's experience. This emphasis can be traced to the consciousness-raising groups of the late 1960s and early 1970s, where women were encouraged to express their subjective responses to everyday life and discovered that their personal problems also had a political dimension. As a methodology, validation of personal experience has much to offer marginal groups who lack the power to have their understanding of the world accepted as the way things are. Consciousness-raising, for example, simultaneously exposed the depth of women's oppression and the systematic nature of male domination. Women began to name their grievances and reinterpret reality in a critical fashion.

Patricia Cain's definition of feminist legal scholarship centers on this grounding in women's experience.

> Feminist legal scholarship seeks to analyze the law's effect on women as a class . . . [T]he analysis is formed by a distinctly feminist point of view, a point of view that is shaped by an understanding of women's life experiences. This understanding can come either from living life as a woman and developing critical consciousness about that experience or from listening carefully to the stories of female experience that come from others . . . [L]egal scholarship is not feminist unless it is grounded in women's experience.[5]

The emphasis on women's experience is especially useful to identify exclusions in the law, particularly injuries that have not been recognized by courts or legislatures or have been minimized because women's experience is not adequately expressed in the law. When used in combination with political activism, this methodology can sometimes lead to recognition of new legal causes of action.

The story of the recognition of sexual harassment is perhaps the best example of the grassroots development of a legal claim grounded in women's experience. Although sex discrimination in employment had been outlawed as early as 1964, it was not until the mid-1970s that sexual harassment was given a name and challenged as a form of sex discrimination in employment, equivalent to unequal pay or discrimi-

---

[5] Patricia A. Cain, Feminist Legal Scholarship, 77 Iowa L. Rev. 19, 20 (1991).

natory job assignments based on sex. In her influential book on the subject,[6] Catharine MacKinnon recalls that the term "sexual harassment" was first used in 1975 by a women's advocacy organization in connection with the case of Carmita Wood. Wood was an administrative assistant at Cornell University who finally quit her job after being subjected to a pattern of lewd sexual behavior by her supervisor.

Today we would describe Wood's response to her harassment as a "constructive discharge," meaning that the intolerable working conditions left Wood no real choice but to quit. At that time, however, harassing conduct tended to be dismissed as harmless flirtations. A transformation in the cultural meaning of such conduct occurred when women workers began to express their negative responses to touching, jokes, propositions and other sexualized conduct at work and explain why they felt powerless to complain. Starting with women's experience, from women's perspective, feminists were able to cast sexual behavior in a different light: to argue that what was pleasurable or inconsequential from the harasser's viewpoint was disturbing and serious when seen from the eyes of the target.

Cain's description of the "feminist point of view" emphasizes women's experience because she believes this source of knowledge should inform feminist scholarship. Like most feminist scholars, however, Cain does not believe that only those persons who experience discrimination or oppression firsthand can ever hope to understand it. In Cain's account, women and men who have not personally experienced sex discrimination can nevertheless gain an understanding of it by listening closely to the stories of others and avoiding the temptation to conclude that the speaker is not intelligent enough or perceptive enough to get it right. Although this definition does not preclude men from doing feminist scholarship, in fact, most feminist legal scholars are women, and many incorporate personal stories in their work.

2.   *Implicit Male Bias*

The focus on women's experience often leads to the question of how that experience could have been suppressed or ignored, especially

---

[6] Catharine A. MacKinnon, *Sexual Harassment of Working Women: A Case of Sex Discrimination* 250 n.13 (1979).

A. Five Opening Moves

since women constitute a numerical majority of the population and no longer labor under the formal legal disabilities that kept them from exercising their rights as citizens in the past. Many feminists address this dilemma by seeking to uncover male bias in rules, standards, and concepts that appear neutral or objective on their face. Rules designed to fit male needs, male social biographies, or male life experiences have been described as "androcentric" or "phallocentric."[7] Implicit male bias can be revealed by examining the real life impact of laws on women as a class, paying particular attention to how even noncontroversial legal concepts and standards tend to disadvantage women. In this usage, bias refers not simply to practices deliberately intended to hurt women, but also to practices which have an unintended negative impact or effect. This technique of tracing out the gender implications of a social practice or rule is sometimes referred to as asking "the woman question" because it places women at the center of the inquiry, even when the rule or practice in question appears to have little to do with gender.[8]

An example of implicit male bias can be found in the standard definitions of full-time and part-time work. It is commonly accepted that the standard work week is 40 hours and that anyone who works less than 35 hours per week is appropriately classified as a part-time worker. In today's workplace, most part-time workers are at a serious disadvantage relative to full-timers: they usually receive no pro rata fringe benefits, many types of jobs are closed to them, and they may even be paid at a base rate lower than full-time workers doing the same job. The great majority of part-time workers are also women. In contrast to more mainstream studies of the workplace, a feminist analysis of the part-time workforce questions the neutrality of the 40-hour standard in part because its effect is disadvantageous to women workers as a class.[9] The standard of 40 hours, it seems, is not a magic number but reflects the average amount of time that *men* work. The standard for everyone is thus premised on the norm for only part of the working

---

[7] A particularly lucid and comprehensive description of androcentric standards in the law and in the larger society is given by Sandra Lipsitz Bem, *The Lenses of Gender: Transforming the Debate on Sexual Inequality* 39-79, 183-91 (1993).

[8] *See* Katharine T. Bartlett, Feminist Legal Methods, 103 Harv. L. Rev. 829, 837-49 (1990).

[9] I analyze this example in Martha Chamallas, Women and Part-Time Work: The Case for Pay Equity and Equal Access, 64 N.C. L. Rev. 709, 713 (1986).

population. The 40-hour standard may look objective, because it is applied alike to male and female workers. What is hidden, however, is that under the standard, men's experience is privileged, and far more women than men are adversely affected by the definition of full-time work.

The implicit male bias in the part-time work standard is not surprising if we consider that the standard is man-made. It originated when there were many fewer women in the labor force and only a tiny percentage of women occupied management positions. This kind of systematic structuring of institutions to reflect the viewpoint and position of those in power is most often invisible. In fact, male-centered standards derive their force from being uncritically accepted as universal in nature. Challenging them is particularly difficult once they have gained legitimacy as an "objective" way of categorizing people and organizing people's activities and work.

The feminist critique of objectivity and androcentrism in the law can be seen in almost all substantive contexts. A forceful version of the critique comes from Catharine MacKinnon, who claims that implicit male bias pervades every facet of modern life:

> [V]irtually every quality that distinguishes men from women is . . . compensated in this society. Men's physiology defines most sports, their needs define auto and health insurance coverage, their socially designed biographies define workplace expectations and successful career patterns, their perspectives and concerns define quality in scholarship, their objectification of life defines art, their military service defines citizenship, their presence defines family, their inability to get along with each other—their wars and rulership—defines history, their image defines god, and their genitals define sex. For each of their differences from women, what amounts to an affirmative action plan is in effect, otherwise known as the structure and values of American society.[10]

Feminist scholarship responding to implicit male bias in the law is sometimes *deconstructive*, that is, it shows at what particular points the standards are male-centered and how they fail to take account of the situation of women. It can also be *reconstructive*, insofar as it is aimed at developing more inclusive standards that fairly represent the diverse interests of all those affected by the law.[11]

---

[10] Catharine A. MacKinnon, Difference and Dominance: On Sex Discrimination, in *Feminism Unmodified: Discourses of Life and Law* 36 (1987) (footnotes omitted).

[11] *See* Robin West, Jurisprudence and Gender, 55 U. Chi. L. Rev. 1, 58-72 (1988).

A. Five Opening Moves

3. Double Binds and Dilemmas of Difference

In contrast to the popular media, which often depict women as having already attained equality with men, feminist scholarship is far more skeptical about what passes for progress. After more than two decades of sustained feminist criticism of law, feminists are troubled by the resiliency of sexism in society and have not been able to forge a consensus about how to approach or solve many of the critical problems women face. One reason there is so much debate among feminists about strategies for challenging sexism in the law is that, as a subordinated group, women are often confronted with "double binds," or as the philosopher Marilyn Frye puts it, "situations in which options are reduced to a very few and all of them expose one to penalty, censure or deprivation."[12] Frye sees the double bind as one of the "most characteristic and ubiquitous features of the world as experienced by oppressed people . . ." Being caught in a double bind or "catch-22" means that women constantly face dilemmas in which they are forced to predict which less-than-ideal course of action will prove to be the least hazardous.

The case of Ann Hopkins against Price Waterhouse[13] presents a classic example of a double bind. Hopkins was an ambitious female manager in a large accounting firm who consistently outperformed men on a number of conventional standards, such as generating high-paying clients, working extra-long billable hours, and gaining client approval. She nevertheless was denied a partnership in the firm because the male partners objected to her lack of social graces and her unfeminine style. For their taste, she was too aggressive, abrasive, and macho. The double bind for Hopkins arose because even if she had been able to soften and feminize her appearance and style, she might still not have made partner. The problem is that in male-dominated settings such as elite accounting firms, feminine women are often regarded as lacking the competitiveness, technical competence, and ambition to make the grade. Either course of action was precarious for Hopkins because there is no predetermined script for success for women in such contexts.

[12] Marilyn Frye, *The Politics of Reality: Essays in Feminist Theory* 2 (1983).

[13] *Price Waterhouse v. Hopkins*, 109 S. Ct. 1775 (1989). For a fuller discussion of the case and its implications for feminist theory, *see* Martha Chamallas, Listening to Dr. Fiske: The Easy Case of *Price Waterhouse v. Hopkins*, 15 Vt. L. Rev. 89 (1990).

In the short run, Hopkins was able to evade the double bind. She prevailed on her Title VII claim of sex discrimination when the United States Supreme Court ruled that it was unlawful to demand that a woman (but not a man) be feminine and yet still possess the traditional masculine traits associated with partners in large accounting firms. Hopkins's predicament, however, demonstrates the double bind of professional women who are required to conform simultaneously to conflicting stereotypes.

At a broader level, Martha Minow has theorized about the double bind that faces reformers who want to correct for past exclusions by opening institutions to "different" groups of people.[14] The dilemma stems from the fact that most large institutions follow practices and policies saturated with implicit male bias. Simply to follow these "neutral" rules and ignore gender reproduces patterns of exclusion and paradoxically assures that gender will continue to matter in the world. However, to pursue a different strategy and implement an "affirmative action" program that focuses explicitly on gender also may backfire. The danger of taking gender into account is that it will stigmatize the group as different and inferior, and thereby reinforce gender difference. This "dilemma of difference" means that neither ignoring nor highlighting gender will necessarily translate into positive gains for women. Instead, feminists find themselves grappling with how fundamentally to alter the way people think about difference and how to resist the cultural tendency to equate difference with inferiority.

4.   Reproducing Patterns of Male Domination

A phenomenon related to the double bind and identified by feminist scholars as contributing to the resiliency of sexism is the reproduction—in altered or updated forms—of patterns of male dominance. The theme of some recent feminist scholarship can be described as "the more things change, the more they stay the same." In fields as diverse as employment law and family law, feminists have looked behind claims of progress to uncover important continuities in women's subordinate status. The point often made is that change is

[14] Martha Minow, *Making All the Difference: Inclusion, Exclusion and American Law* 20 (1990).

A. Five Opening Moves

not inherently progressive and that even substantial shifts in rhetoric and rules may not bring about major improvements in women's lives.

In the realm of employment, for example, feminists have long sought ways to integrate occupations as a way of improving the status and pay of women workers who tend to be concentrated in predominantly "female" jobs. Challenging gender hierarchy in employment has been especially tricky, however, because "gains" in integrating occupations can easily be offset by counter-trends, including the reconfiguration of jobs. Barbara Reskin, a sociologist who specializes in occupational segregation, has questioned the conventional wisdom that great progress has been made in women's employment status.[15] Her empirical research indicates that the apparent trend toward sex integration of occupations is misleading because there is also a trend toward sex segregation of jobs within occupations, with the more elite jobs being held predominantly by men. For example, women's entry into the field of pharmacy has been confined largely to the retail sector, while men work in the more lucrative and more prestigious commercial, research, and academic settings. Reskin's research also shows that what might at first seem to be "integration" of an occupation may actually be the beginning of job shifting, that is, changing a male occupation into a predominantly female occupation, with lower pay and less autonomy. Feminization has occurred in fields that have already started to deteriorate in status.[16] The net result may be that even as women successfully enter formerly male-dominated fields, they remain disadvantaged as workers relative to men.

Reva Siegel's scholarship on domestic violence also emphasizes how the law has managed to continue to immunize this type of abuse of women, despite substantial reforms in formal doctrine.[17] The early legal doctrine of "chastisement" officially gave husbands the right to use a "reasonable" degree of force to compel their wives to submit to their authority. When this right of force was abolished, however, courts developed the doctrine of "family privacy" to justify their refusal to intervene in cases charging domestic violence. The new rhetoric of pri-

[15] Barbara F. Reskin, Bringing the Men Back In: Sex Differentiation and the Devaluation of Women's Work, 2 Gender & Soc'y 58 (1988).

[16] Barbara F. Reskin & Patricia Roos, *Job Queues, Gender Queues: Explaining Women's Inroads into Male Occupations* 11-15 (1990).

[17] Reva B. Siegel, "The Rule of Love:" Wife Beating as Prerogative and Privacy, 105 Yale L.J. 2117 (1996). Siegel is discussed infra at pp. 260-62.

vacy had the effect of continuing the older regime of male prerogative, albeit in gentler, less direct terms. Feminist scholarship such as Siegel's historical study recognizes the possibility that massive changes can occur over time without fundamentally altering basic gender hierarchies. The emphasis is on uncovering how male domination is reproduced and how new rationales and discourses develop to justify the continuing gender disparities.

5. Unpacking Women's Choice

In contemporary society, women's inequality presents a paradox. Many who would endorse gender equality as an ideal nevertheless resist the idea that discrimination is the principal cause of women's inequality. Instead, women's subordinate status is often ascribed to women's own choices, and women are held responsible or blamed for their own disadvantages. The old notion that women are not intelligent enough or lack the moral accountability to be leaders in business, politics, or the academy has been replaced by justifications centered on women's choice. This explanation of women's disadvantage is particularly prominent in the discourse on women in the workplace. The conventional wisdom is that because women place more importance on their families, they voluntarily choose to subordinate their career and job aspirations for the sake of their children or their partners. This rationale allows employers to make the paradoxical claim that women actually prefer lower-paying jobs or jobs that offer little opportunity for advancement.

A growing body of feminist scholarship is devoted to unpacking the concept of "choice" and investigating the constraints under which women commonly make choices. The very use of the word "choice" implies that the actor has alternatives, and often suggests that the choice represents the actor's authentic preference. Moreover, in law, responsibility is commonly placed on the person who chooses. An employer, for example, will typically not be responsible for the disparate choices of male and female workers because the sex-linked pattern is thought not to be caused by the employer's own actions. Instead, the law typically presupposes that women's choices derive either from biological imperatives, especially the desire to nurture, or early socialization, which supposedly motivates women to pursue traditionally female activities as adults.

B. Summary

Feminists who resist this emphasis on choice often point to the role that institutional structures and culture play in shaping women's choices. The counter-theory is that choices are not made in a vacuum, and that in making choices, women are influenced by the opportunities presented to them and the dominant cultural attitudes of those with whom they interact. Scholars such as Vicki Shultz explain how certain blue-collar jobs are still regarded as "masculine" and inappropriate for women.[18] This cultural coding of jobs is reinforced by the persistent and often virulent harassment of women who try to break through gender barriers. Absent some affirmative indication by employers that women are welcome and will be supported in nontraditional work—through, for example, a special training and recruitment program for women—it is likely that the percentage of women in such jobs will remain extremely low, that women will "choose" not to enter this line of work or will quit once they realize what they face.

This account of why women are unrepresented in blue-collar work places less emphasis on women's motivations and orientations before they enter the workplace and more emphasis on experiences women have as adult workers. This shift in emphasis complicates the notion of choice, making it a function of present opportunities and contexts as well as preexisting preferences. The shift also means that forces outside the psyche of the individual woman—employer policies, legal programs, employee training—help shape a woman's decisions and bear some responsibility for the patterns that emerge. The critical stance toward choice liberates feminists to recognize women's *agency*, that is, the capacity for self-direction, without denying or minimizing the distinctive constraints placed on women in a male-dominated society.

B. SUMMARY

The five *moves* described above are theoretical tools that legal feminists have found useful to critique legal doctrines and categories

[18] Vicki Shultz, Telling Stories About Women and Work: Judicial Interpretations of Sex Segregation in the Workplace in Title VII Cases Raising the Lack of Interest Argument, 103 Harv. L. Rev. 1749, 1802 (1990).

in each of the three *stages* of feminist legal theory. As I will define them, the stages reflect broader cultural and political struggles that emerged most prominently in each of the three decades under study, particularly the right of access to formerly male-dominated institutions, the treatment of pregnant women and mothers under the law, and the connection between gender discrimination and discrimination based on race and sexual orientation. During each stage, the five theoretical moves enabled feminists to think more deeply about the basic concepts of equality, difference, and diversity that continue to shape law and legal discourse in this area.

As we discuss the chronological development of the field, the reader will see how these five moves have animated feminist scholarship and activism, regardless of the school of feminist thought most prominent at the moment. For example, the emphasis on women's experience stimulated equality-oriented feminists in the 1970s to work toward integrating male-dominated institutions because they understood that segregation limited women's chances for success in public life. In the 1980s, feminists emphasizing gender domination and gender difference again drew upon women's experience to call attention to the myriad forms of violence directed at women, in the domestic as well as the public sphere. By the 1990s, black and lesbian feminists in particular were able to reflect upon their own experiences with the women's movement to develop an internal critique of the feminist agenda and assumptions of feminist theory.

Similarly, in each historical period, feminists have uncovered implicit male bias in "neutral" rules and struggled with ways around the double bind in a wide range of contexts. They have engaged in a recurring debate over strategies as they find their individual choices limited and recognize that even feminist-inspired legal reform may be overtaken by traditionalist forces and absorbed into new patterns of gender hierarchy.

CHAPTER 2

Three Stages of
Feminist Legal Theory

In the past three decades, the field of feminist legal theory has grown so rapidly that it defies neat categorization. The words we use to describe this body of work have changed, as have the boundaries between feminist scholarship and other critical inquiry. However, as an introduction to the field, I have found it most useful to divide feminist legal theory into three stages tracking the three decades of intensive developments: the *Equality Stage* of the 1970s, the *Difference Stage* of the 1980s, and the *Diversity Stage* of the 1990s.[1] I must caution that the stages are oversimplifications, indicating only when certain themes or theoretical orientations emerged or became visible. They may not even represent the predominant feminist influence in the law or legal scholarship at the time. Thus, for example, throughout the periods discussed in this book, equality thinking has dominated in the courts and legislatures, with the newer trends toward difference and diversity having only limited influence beyond academia. Moreover, in each stage, there were individual scholars whose work seemed to fit better in another stage; for instance, even in the 1970s, when most scholarship

---

[1] These stages very closely resemble Patricia A. Cain's demarcation lines in Feminist Jurisprudence: Grounding the Theories, 4 Berkeley Women's L.J. 191, 198-205 (1989-90). In constructing her stages, Cain tracked Clare Dalton's analysis in Where We Stand: Observations on the Situation of Feminist Legal Thought, 3 Berkeley Women's L.J. 1 (1987-88). For a periodization and taxonomy of feminist legal theory that also covers developments in North America and Europe, see Carol Smart, Feminist Jurisprudence, in *Law, Crime & Sexuality* 162 (1995).

stressed the similarity between men and women, some feminists emphasized the diversity among women.

It is important to remember that the three stages of feminist legal theory do not exist in nature or history. They are constructions by scholars that enable us to organize and make sense of the diverse and sometimes contradictory arguments of feminist scholarship. Readers familiar with the development of feminist theory in other fields will not find the three stages surprising.[2] The field of feminist legal theory is by no means autonomous; it has absorbed and responded to theoretical developments from feminist writers in women's studies, history, philosophy, economics, sociology, psychology, and literary and cultural studies. Legal feminism has borrowed heavily from these other quarters, sometimes taking years to incorporate themes that interdisciplinary scholars outside the law have already explored.

The major themes of the Equality Stage are by now so familiar that they are sometimes thought to encompass the only meaning of feminism in law. During this time, the emphasis was on women's similarity to men. This generation of feminists concentrated primarily on dismantling the intricate system of sex-based legal distinctions which had been established purportedly to protect women. Equality theorists argued that protection through the law was harmful to women because it served to restrict women's lives to the home and family. The claim was simply stated and understood: Because women were the same as men in all relevant respects, they deserved access to all public institutions, benefits and opportunities on the same terms as men. The most prominent discourse of the 1970s concerned individual rights, particularly the right of nontraditional women to engage in male-dominated activities. Its central message was that gender should be irrelevant to the distribution of legal benefits and burdens and that persons should be treated as individuals, not as members of a class. Feminists of this era were reluctant to dwell on any differences that might exist between men and women. Because for so long sexual differences had been uncritically accepted as natural, biologically based, and inalterable, feminists were inclined to deny difference and to insist that social change was possible and desirable.

---

[2] Some of the well-known texts that describe different schools and/or stages in feminist theory are: Alison M. Jagger, *Feminist Politics and Human Nature* (1983); Rosemarie Tong, *Feminist Thought: A Comprehensive Introduction* (1989); Alison M. Jagger & Paula S. Rothenberg, *Feminist Frameworks* (2d ed. 1984).

Chapter 2. Three Stages of Feminist Legal Theory

Equality advocates are often associated with the school of thought known as *liberal feminism*. Liberal feminists share a commitment to individual autonomy and choice and insist that these freedoms be afforded to women as well as men. Liberal feminists have sometimes been called "assimilationists" because their arguments tend not to challenge the standards, rules, or structures themselves, but focus instead on equal access within their framework. More so than other feminist orientations, liberal feminism can be translated into legal reform, generally requiring only incremental changes and expansion of current structures to make room for women.

In law schools during most of the 1970s, the term "feminist legal theory" or "feminist jurisprudence" was not yet in use.[3] Feminists were more apt to describe themselves as women's rights advocates, women's liberationists, or egalitarians. These terms seemed to fit better with 1970s equality themes than did the term "feminist" with its more distinctive and oppositional tone. Moreover, in this formative decade, arguments made by feminists to courts and in law reviews were still too new, and oriented toward the practice of law, to be thought of as a legal theory or as jurisprudence. To be sure, the early feminist legal scholars were often influenced by feminist theory from other disciplines, particularly the new women's studies movement. However, it was not until the 1980s that theorizing about the relationship between gender and law became a major project for feminist academics. Course titles then changed from "Sex-Based Discrimination," to "Feminist Legal Theory" and "Gender and the Law."

At that time, feminist legal theorists turned to considering the concept of difference. The enthusiasm for legal reform along equality lines gradually gave way to a realization that this effort would not cure the substantive inequality that beset most women's lives. The 1980s brought to the forefront of discussion the feminization of poverty, the gender gap in politics, the "glass ceiling," and other phenomena, which made it clear that, in many ways that mattered, men and women were different. Like many other social commentators, feminists ques-

---

[3] The phrase "feminist jurisprudence" purportedly was first used in 1978 at a conference celebrating the 25th anniversary of women graduates of Harvard Law School. *See* Patricia A. Cain, supra note 1, at 193. Some writers prefer the term "feminist legal theory" because it does not carry the quasi-scientific connotations of the term "jurisprudence."

tioned both the idea that gender was irrelevant and the ideal of a gender-blind society.

Feminists theories of the 1980s began to emphasize the various ways that men and women were different. Recognizing gender differences, however, did not mean accepting those differences as inherent or inalterable. Instead, most difference theorists of the 1980s were also social constructionists; that is, they located the source of gender difference in cultural attitudes, ideology, socialization, or organizational structures.

An important project of 1980s feminism involved revising the concept of "equality" to mean something other than "identical treatment" of men and women. Feminists theorized that if men and women did not start from the same position, identical treatment of each group might never produce meaningful equality. In practical terms, this meant that to be treated as equals, women whose lives differed from those of men paradoxically needed to be treated differently. Rather than requiring women to act more like men to achieve equality, feminist theorists argued that the norms themselves should be changed. Questioning implicit male norms in law and society allowed feminists to go beyond assimilation and to set an agenda for legal change premised on women's distinctive needs.

The 1970s equal-rights approach was best suited to handling disputes involving characteristics shared by men and women. However, when biological differences such as pregnancy were involved, the traditional equality principle ("treat likes alike") faltered. Debates among feminists over the best way to confront discrimination against pregnant workers proved to be a catalyst for broader theoretical discussions. The 1980s emphasis on difference also made it possible for feminists to take up such important issues as pregnancy and sexual violence, including rape, sexual harassment, domestic violence, and pornography. These topics had not been fully analyzed by liberal feminists who had concentrated more on economic issues of access.

Feminist legal scholarship in the 1980s was more diverse and less practically oriented than it had been in the prior decade. Although the existence of differences between men and women was a major theme, not all scholars focused on the same manifestations of difference. Some emphasized the difference in power among men and women and speculated on how male domination was accomplished. Dominance theorists developed a critique of liberalism, including liberal feminism. They argued that rather than increasing women's power, well-established concepts such as privacy, objectivity, and individual rights actually operated to legitimate the status quo. This more radical brand of feminist legal theory called for a major transformation of the law to eradicate the domination of women as a class. A principal project of radical feminism as applied to law described how the legal system had failed to protect women's bodily integrity. The anti-pornography campaign that developed during this period, for example, drew links between portrayals of women as sex objects and the prevalence of sexual violence and sex discrimination.

The influence of cultural (sometimes called "relational") feminism was also felt in the 1980s. More so than other schools of feminist thought, this group of theorists both recognized and celebrated women's differences from men. The starting point for this branch of difference feminism was to articulate the ways women often tended to approach problems, view the world, and construct their identity. Feminists debated how women's "different voice"—with its concern for human relationships and for the positive values of caring, nurturing, empathy, and connection—could find greater expression in law. In contrast to liberal feminism's de-emphasis of the mothering role, cultural feminists sought ways to support maternal and other traditional activities associated with women.

The feminist law curriculum expanded in the 1980s, with new offerings on sexuality, sexual violence, and feminist jurisprudence. The more theoretical feminist critiques also provided a path of entry into the first-year curriculum, challenging traditional courses in criminal law, torts, contracts, and property as inadequate and biased. Similar to the initiative in liberal arts disciplines, feminists in law schools embarked on a dual strategy of creating distinctively feminist offerings and mainstreaming feminism into the standard curriculum.

In the 1990s, feminist preoccupation with comparing the situation of men and women began to be eclipsed by a new focus on diversity among women. Recent critiques of liberal, radical, and cultural feminism have stressed that women are a huge and dramatically diverse group. The hallmark of the scholarship of the Diversity Stage is its attention to differences among women. This shift was impelled by powerful critiques by women of color and lesbians who claimed that they had been left out of the now-classic feminist analyses. While claiming to speak for "women" in general, many feminist writers failed to grasp that their work had little relevance for women who were not white, middle-class, and heterosexual. The 1990s feminist critics of feminism emphasized the dangers of essentialism—the assumption that there is some essential commonality among all women—whether it be women's oppression by men or women's different voice.

The anti-essentialist writings of the 1990s start from the premise that the lived (real-life) experiences of women differ depending on such factors as race, class, ethnicity, physical disability, and sexual orientation. Given this complexity, it makes sense to replace the goal of devising one overreaching feminist strategy with the less grand objective of considering legal policies from the perspectives of different groups of women. In the Diversity Stage, feminists have become used to the idea that they are likely to disagree and that coalitions are necessary to produce legal reforms.

The salience accorded to differences other than gender also generated new theories about the interaction of various kinds of oppression in society. Theorists tried to explain how race, class, and gender intersected in multiple ways to create distinctive forms of discrimination for specific subgroups of women. These theories of multiple oppression meant that the traditional focus of anti-discrimination law on discrete, mutually exclusive kinds of discrimination needed to be re-examined. For example, if the situation of African-American women was to be fully addressed, the habit of thinking about "women and minorities" would have to be broken. Such conceptual dichotomies tended to focus attention on white women and black men, subtly erasing black women from the equation. In the Diversity Stage, feminists have aspired to embrace a "both/and" rather than "either/or" mindset, thereby avoiding the temptation to reduce people's experience to only one aspect of personal identity or only one form of oppression.

Treating oppression in discrete boxes, moreover, tended to obscure how different forms of discrimination may be mutually reinforcing. In this period, gay men and lesbians argued for a broader definition of sex discrimination that would cover harassment and discrimination based on sexual orientation. The term "heterosexism" was coined to describe the ideology that privileges heterosexual relationships over same-sex ones, underlining the historically male-dominated character of heterosexual relationships.

Paralleling the move to studying multiple forms of oppression, feminist scholarship in the 1990s became more attuned to the complex nature of personal identity and attempted to present women simultaneously as both victims of oppression and agents of their own destiny. The focus on sexual violence, particularly the account given by dominance feminists in the 1980s, generated complaints from many quarters that feminism had become fixated on victimization and did not adequately account for women's ability to resist, make choices, and contribute to the cultural meaning attached to gender in society. The "both/and" strategy was again deployed to develop new accounts of women's behavior, showing how women are often forced to make strategic choices within constraining structures. This more nuanced account of women's agency and victimization also highlighted differences among women: Not only is discrimination experienced differently by different groups of women, but women use a variety of coping mechanisms to deal with discrimination, ranging from forthright resistance, to co-optation, to avoidance.

The shift in the 1990s to a theory of multiple oppression led to the blurring of demarcation lines between the various allied intellectual movements. Just as feminists were required to take race into account in constructing their agendas and analyzing problems, scholars from the critical race school could not ignore the role of gender in shaping racism. The law school curriculum reflected this convergence with the introduction of offerings on stereotyping, critical perspectives, and a textbook on power, privilege and the law.

The present period is also marked by particularly trenchant critiques of feminism, coming not only from writers who disagree with most feminist aims but also from self-declared feminists who believe that the direction of feminist scholarship in the last decade has undermined women's quest for equality. Some of the younger feminist critics entered the debate at a time when liberal feminism was under intense scrutiny. They longed for simpler times when the feminist agenda was unitary, focused on equality, and not so clearly linked to politics of race and sexual orientation. One purpose of this book is to provide just enough context and history to the study of feminist legal theory to encourage a new generation of feminists to take a broader and more complex view of the movement and its influence on law.

Before we turn to look more closely at the Equality Stage which began in the 1970s, it is important to note that the narrative of the development and growth of feminist legal theory in the United States presented in this book is but one of many stories that can be told about the connection between feminism and the law. A longer view would start over 150 years ago with the Declaration of Sentiments unveiled at the Seneca Falls Convention in 1848, and would describe how first-wave feminists focused heavily on the legal constraints of their time, such as laws that prevented married women from enjoying the ordinary rights of citizens to own property and to retain the wages from their labor. Like the feminists who followed them more than a century later, they devoted considerable efforts to agitating for legal reforms, knowing that the legal structure itself was part of a system that endorsed and enforced gender inequality. As with contemporary feminists who have been intensely engaged with (some might even say preoccupied by) legal issues in the last three decades, these earlier generations of women's rights advocates appreciated that they must confront the law if they were to understand and transform women's social and economic status. A formidable challenge that continues into the present has been finding ways to harness the power of law to construct gender equality, rather than to perpetuate patterns of gender subordination.

CHAPTER 3

The Equality Stage (1970s)

Feminist legal theory is a relatively new field. Usually, scholars date its inception to the early 1970s, when women's rights advocates first mounted an organized legal campaign against sex discrimination in the courts. As is true of most social or political movements, however, the groundwork for this burst of energy in the early 1970s had been laid in an earlier era. Statutes mandating equal pay for equal work and prohibiting sex discrimination in employment had been passed by the mid-1960s, and every state had a commission on the status of women. Most importantly, by 1970, a sizeable number of women were studying law (approximately 10 percent of the total number of law students) and the percentage of licensed practitioners who were female was finally growing after years of languishing at approximately 2 percent.[1] This was the first time in history that women had a sufficient presence in legal institutions to argue for their own cause. They also had the benefit of legal precedents established in response to the black civil rights movement in the 1960s. Throughout this early period, a basic strategy was to analogize unequal or discriminatory treatment of women to racial discrimination.

---

[1] In 1970, 2.8 percent of attorneys licensed to practice law were women. This was very close to the figure of 2.5 percent in 1951. By 1980, women's representation in the profession had risen to 8.1 percent. Barbara Curran, *The Lawyer Statistical Report* 10 (American Bar Foundation) (1984).

A. THE ELIMINATION OF SEX-BASED CLASSIFICATIONS

The legal controversy that best captures the activism of the 1970s was the movement to pass the Equal Rights Amendment (ERA). The ERA was passed by both Houses of Congress in 1972 and sent to the states for ratification. Until its ultimate defeat in 1982, the amendment was a central feature of the feminist agenda, so much so that the term "ERA" was sometimes used synonymously with the term "women's liberation." The basic thrust of the ERA was that, in virtually all respects, men and women were similar and ought to receive similar treatment under the law. Even though the lives led by men and women were often quite different, ERA proponents stressed the right of the individual to choose not to conform to prevailing customs and argued that "[t]he law owes an obligation to treat females as persons, not statistical abstractions."[2] This mandate for legal equality of the sexes was sometimes taken to mean that the ERA would somehow make sex irrelevant and that America would become a unisex society.

As a matter of legal interpretation, however, it was doubtful that the ERA would have accomplished the kind of thoroughgoing social changes envisioned by some of its supporters and feared by its opponents. Like the Fourteenth Amendment, the ERA was limited in scope to actions of the government and did not affect private discrimination by employers, banks, insurance companies, or other nongovernmental entities. Most scholars explained that the ERA's primary effect would be to invalidate statutes and common law rules that drew *explicit* distinctions between men and women. One irony about the unsuccessful campaign for the ERA is that much of what the ERA would have accomplished did in fact come about in the 1970s, through other means, principally a more expansive interpretation of the Equal Protection Clause of the Fourteenth Amendment. Despite the amendment's defeat, the public discourse surrounding the ERA energized the feminist movement and provided much of the impetus for acceptance of the equal rights agenda in Congress, state legislatures, and the courts.

[2] Barbara A. Brown, Thomas I. Emerson, Gail Falk, & Ann E. Freedman, The Equal Rights Amendment: A Constitutional Basis for Equal Rights for Women, 80 Yale L.J. 871, 889 (1971).

A. The Elimination of Sex-Based Classifications

One of the most visible figures in the 1970s legal activism for women's rights was Ruth Bader Ginsburg, who subsequently became the second woman to serve on the United States Supreme Court. While on the Columbia law school faculty, Ginsburg directed the Women's Rights Project of the American Civil Liberties Union (ACLU).[3] In that position, she was the chief architect of the litigation strategy that built the foundation of contemporary sex discrimination law. She carefully selected several of the cases that challenged the Supreme Court's long-standing view that there was nothing wrong with having explicit gender lines in the law.

Prior to the progression of cases which began with *Reed v. Reed*[4] in 1971, the law was riddled with sex-based distinctions: Gender determined not only who received alimony (only women) or who was eligible for the draft (only men), but virtually every facet of life subject to legal regulation. The law embraced the *separate spheres* ideology that relegated women to the private sphere of the home and family, while men dominated the public spheres of work, politics, and intellectual life. Separate spheres is more aptly regarded as an ideology than as a description of reality because it did not accurately reflect the lives of many women—particularly minority women and working-class women—who had long worked outside the home to support themselves and their families.[5] Instead, separate spheres reflected the dominant culture's ideal of the woman's role, even while denying the "right" of many women to lead lives consistent with this image. Consistent with the dominant ideology, explicit gender lines in the law went largely unnoticed and unchallenged because lawyers and judges accepted them as reflecting natural differences between the sexes.

The gender lines in statutes and the common law were typically grounded in stereotypes about the different roles, abilities, and interests of the sexes. Sometimes the stereotypes were easy to fathom from the structure of the legal scheme. For example, the age of majority was often different for males and females: Under state law, women might be classified as adults at age 18, while men did not attain that

---

[3] *See* Dr. Ruth B. Cowan, Women's Rights Through Litigation: An Examination of the American Civil Liberties Union Women's Rights Project, 1971-1976, 8 Colum. Hum. Rts. L. Rev. 373 (1976).

[4] 404 U.S. 71 (1971).

[5] *See* Linda K. Kerber, Separate Spheres, Female Worlds, Woman's Place: The Rhetoric of Women's History, 75 J. Am. Hist. 9 (June 1988).

status until age 21. The sex/age differential reflected the conventional belief that girls matured faster than boys and needed less time to prepare themselves for their adult roles as wives and mothers. Although on its face this generalization may not have seemed demeaning to women, the statutory scheme put women at a disadvantage in both a practical and an ideological sense. As a practical matter, girls were at a disadvantage in securing a higher education. Because legally they were adults at 18, young women had no right to require their parents to support them during their college years. The younger age of maturity also sent an ideological message that girls were destined to lead domestic lives and that fewer societal resources needed to be invested in their development.

Sometimes the gender-based generalization was less obvious from the face of the law and tracing out the implications of a gender classification was more complicated. When I was a law student in the early 1970s, my favorite example of an unfathomable gender-based distinction was an obscure provision in the Louisiana Civil Code that dictated that in the event of death by a common conflagration (e.g., a fire in which both husband and wife perish), the law presumed that the man survived longer than the woman. My professor explained that the provision probably stemmed from the belief that women were the "weaker" of the two sexes and that, in a crisis, the woman would succumb faster than the stronger male. This dubious proposition had some very serious effects, in addition to discounting women's ability for physical survival. Because under the law the survivor takes all, the presumption meant that all of the couple's estate would be inherited by the man's family. Through the use of explicit gender lines, the law stereotyped and stigmatized women by presuming that all women would exhibit certain habits, desires and traits. In most cases, moreover, explicit gender lines worked to women's material disadvantage.

The campaign against gender classifications waged by Ginsburg and the Women's Rights Project was remarkably successful. Within only five years (1971-76), the Supreme Court changed its direction and began to regard gender lines as problematic. The Equal Protection Clause of the Fourteenth Amendment was interpreted to invalidate gender classifications in a wide variety of contexts, with the result that there are now few explicit gender lines in statutes. The states were told that they could no longer presume that men deserved to be appointed as administrators of estates over competing claims by women, or that only men's contributions to Social Security would yield survivor's ben-

A. The Elimination of Sex-Based Classifications

efits to children or spouses, or that only men had a civic obligation to serve on juries. Although, unlike race, gender was never held to be a suspect classification, the Court's approach to gender-based distinctions—known as "intermediate scrutiny"—made most classifications hard to sustain, especially if they were not consciously designed to aid women in nontraditional areas.

Many of the gender cases decided by the Supreme Court involved male plaintiffs.[6] The strategy of the Women's Rights Project was to attack gender stereotypes across the board, even when the gender line might appear to be of advantage to women. Many public benefit schemes, for example, were built on the assumption that wives, but not husbands, were economically dependent on their spouses for support. Following this assumption, the laws typically accorded automatic benefits to female survivors, but required male survivors to prove their dependency, often by means of stringent financial tests. These schemes were successfully challenged as discriminatory in part because of their indirect effects: The reasoning was that because employed women could not count on their families being provided for in the event of their death or disability, their efforts as workers were valued less than the efforts of similarly situated male workers. The presumption of dependency reflected a model of the husband as breadwinner and the wife as homemaker. Even though this model did accurately describe many families at that time, it was objectionable because it served as a self-fulfilling prophecy and was unfair to families whose lives did not fit the gendered norm. The 1970s rejection of gender-based classifications reflected an individualistic philosophy which disfavored even rational generalizations that left no room for unconventional patterns. The Supreme Court cases of this era countered the separate spheres ideology by providing support for employed women and de-emphasizing women's maternal and domestic roles. What were once regarded as benign forms of "protection" were recast as forms of gender discrimination.

These developments in constitutional law are commonly referred to as having established a system of "formal" equality, in the sense of requiring that the form of the law be gender neutral—that, on its face, the law make no distinction between the sexes. In the 1990s, for-

---

[6] *See* David Cole, Strategies of Difference: Litigating for Women's Rights in a Man's World, 2 L. & Inequality 33 (1984).

mal equality is more often criticized as inadequate, rather than heralded as a major advance in women's rights. Critics make the points that formal equality did little to change the reality of most women's lives and that the early emphasis on gender classifications was misplaced. They also sometimes say that the Ginsburg strategy primarily benefits men and does not present a sufficiently radical challenge to the status quo.

For its day, however, the attack on gender classifications was quite oppositional and it is only the passage of time that tends to hide the human significance of these "formal" legal disputes. The first major victory—*Reed v. Reed*—illustrates this point.[7] On the surface, the case simply held that Idaho could not automatically appoint men over women as administrators of the estates of persons who died without a will. This right to compete with men on a gender-neutral basis for letters of administrators was admittedly not high on the list of feminist priorities, and it probably did not affect large numbers of women.

Beneath the surface, however, *Reed* was not so gender neutral. The case involved a family tragedy that called into question the rights of mothers and fathers. Sally Reed and Cecil Reed had separated when their son Richard was a young child. Sally Reed was awarded custody during Richard's "tender years," but custody was transferred to Cecil Reed when Richard became a teenager, according to the custom in Idaho. After he was released into his father's custody, Richard got into trouble, became depressed, and ultimately committed suicide. His "estate" consisted of a near-worthless used car. Sally Reed challenged the gender presumption in the law not because she stood to gain financially, but because she did not want Cecil to have the satisfaction of being declared the administrator of his son's estate. By representing Sally Reed in the Supreme Court, Ginsburg gave a mother the right to argue that she deserved recognition as a responsible parent and that she should not have to watch on the sidelines while others settled her son's affairs after his death. *Reed* demonstrates how even the demand for formal equality may challenge traditional gender relations and is not devoid of substance.

---

[7] This account of the case is taken from Deborah L. Markowitz, In Pursuit of Equality: One Woman's Work to Change the Law, 11 Women's Rts. L. Rep. 73, 77-81 (1989).

B.   EQUAL ACCESS TO JOBS AND EDUCATION

The practical impact of the equality thinking of the 1970s was to gain access for women to formerly male-dominated domains, including blue-collar jobs, the professions, the sciences, and Ivy League universities. During this period, Title VII's[8] ban on sex discrimination in employment began to be enforced in earnest. Comparatively few jobs were considered eligible for the bona fide occupational qualification (BFOQ) defense, which allowed employers to limit a job to one sex only. Echoing the Supreme Court's dislike for stereotypes, the Equal Employment Opportunity Commission (EEOC)—the federal agency enforcing Title VII—issued guidelines that warned employers not to refuse to hire an individual based on stereotyped characterizations of the sexes, such as "women employees have higher turnover rates" or "women are incapable of performing strenuous jobs."[9] After years of ambivalence, the EEOC also took a position against protective labor legislation, which had prohibited women from working at night or had limited the number of hours women could work per week.[10] The agency concluded that the "protection" offered women amounted to unlawful sex discrimination because it did not take into account the capacities, preferences, and abilities of *individual* women.

The early Title VII cases tested whether the courts would defer to employers' judgments about which jobs were inappropriate for women. Lorena Weeks, for example, had worked for the telephone company for 19 years before she put in a bid for the job of "switchman." Although Weeks was the most senior employee bidding for the job, the company and the union argued that the job should not go to any women because it was too strenuous, required lifting more than 30 pounds, and often called for duty during the late night hours, when the switchman worked alone. Judge Frank Johnson, who had gained a reputation as a civil rights supporter on race issues, ruled for Weeks

---

[8] The section of the 1964 Civil Rights Act prohibiting employment discrimination on the basis of race, color, sex, national origin, and religion is known as "Title VII."

[9] *See* EEOC Guidelines on Discrimination Because of Sex, 29 C.F.R. § 1604.2(a)(1)(i).

[10] *Id.* at § 1604.2(b)(1).

stating that she had the right to decide for herself "whether or not to take on unromantic tasks."[11]

The philosophy underlying decisions such as that in *Weeks* was that men and women were similar in most relevant respects. Differences among men and differences among women were as significant as the differences between men and women. In this view, the image of over-lapping curves depicted the situation of the sexes more accurately than the phrase "opposite sex."

The 1970s was also a time of widespread sex integration of higher education, particularly at the graduate school level. During the decade, women's enrollment in medical school increased from 11 to 26 percent; in law schools, from 10 to 34 percent. The number of Ph.D.s earned by women rose from 16 to 30 percent.[12] The move to co-education was strong. Elite institutions like Yale, Dartmouth, and Princeton admitted their first integrated undergraduate classes.

Sex segregation was not the only form of discrimination that had faced college-bound women prior to the 1970s. Opportunities were also stunted by a system of restrictive quotas that reserved most of the places in elite universities to men. Harvard, for example, admitted four men for every one woman admitted to Radcliffe.[13] These quotas made it harder for women to gain admission and typically resulted in classes in which women were markedly more qualified than men in the same college. Upon graduation from college, women discovered that they were still expected to take secretarial jobs and were not allowed to compete with their male classmates for professional or management positions. It was not uncommon for a Wellesley graduate to spend a year gaining secretarial skills at Katherine Gibbs School for Women in Boston before entering the job market. The paradox of highly educated women being prevented from using their education in careers was accepted as natural. It also gave educators an excuse not to spend edu-

---

[11] *Weeks v. Southern Bell Telephone & Telegraph Co.*, 408 F.2d 228, 236 (5th Cir. 1969).

[12] These statistics are taken from J. Ralph Lindgren & Nadine Taub, *The Law of Sex Discrimination* 289 (1988).

[13] Pauli Murray, Economic and Educational Inequality Based on Sex: An Overview, 5 Val. U. L. Rev. 237, 250 (1971) *citing* Hearings on Section 805 of H.R. 16098 Before the Special Subcomm. on Education of the House Comm. on Education and Labor, 91st Cong. 2d Sess. 643 (1970).

cational resources on women who would, after all, probably end up as housewives.

The changing patterns in the 1970s could be attributed in part to a loosening of institutional resistance to women's participation in traditionally male enclaves and in part to women themselves rejecting stereotypes that they were psychologically unsuited for these fields. The common practice of employing more stringent admissions standards for women than men came under constitutional attack, as did the exclusion of women from public institutions. In contrast to employment, however, the courts and Congress never fully repudiated "separate but equal" in the context of education, as the recent legal battles over women's access to male institutions like The Citadel and Virginia Military Institute (VMI) have demonstrated.[14] The women's movement did, however, clearly call into question the presumption that education was wasted on women because they would only become housewives or secretaries.

In education and employment, the theme of equal access was most prominent. The primary strategy was to desegregate public institutions, particularly elite male-dominated institutions. Occasionally, men would seek to enter women's jobs or educational institutions, like the lawsuits brought by men to be hired as flight attendants. However, because women generally did not occupy positions of power and wealth, men had less interest in gaining access to women's domains.

C. EQUALITY IN THE FAMILY

The equality theme was not as easy to transport to the context of the family. Women, of course, had never been excluded from the family as they had from public institutions. Thus there was no equal-access

---

[14] Only in 1996 did the Supreme Court rule that the Equal Protection Clause required VMI to admit women, while noting that Virginia did not provide a comparable single-gender institution for women. *United States v. Virginia*, 116 S. Ct. 2264 (1996). The male-only policy at The Citadel was held unconstitutional in *Faulkner v. Jones*, 66 F.3d 661 (4th Cir. 1995).

strategy, comparable to that in the public sector, that would quickly create new opportunities for women. To create equality in the family meant addressing the source of women's disadvantage—their subordination to male family members who, as husbands or fathers, had been assigned the status of "head and master" of the family.

Prior to the women's movement in the late 1960s, the subordination of women within the family was well hidden. The cultural myths of the 1950s had attributed to women the power behind the throne. It was commonly thought that wives, not husbands, really decided how the children would be raised and how to spend the family's income. The message was that women should consider themselves fortunate if they were not "forced" to work outside the home.

The image of the happy and fulfilled housewife was first dispelled in 1963 by Betty Friedan in *The Feminine Mystique.* That book exposed "the problem that has no name," referring to the frustrations and dissatisfaction of suburban middle-class women whose lives were taken up by trivial concerns of housekeeping and consumerism. Well-educated women in particular began to question why they were forced to choose between motherhood and a career, and argued that they should "have it all," in much the same way that men seemed able to combine work and family. With this new emphasis on combining work and family, feminists in the 1970s needed a strategy for change within the family that would restructure the relations of men and women and set women free from some of the burdens of domestic life.

Many feminists at this time envisioned a family in which men and women would share equally in all aspects of family life—housework, child care, and earning a living. In law, this desire for equal sharing of domestic responsibilities led some feminists to support equal, nongender-based standards for divorce, child custody, and distribution of marital property. This was the era in which no-fault divorce gained wide acceptance. No-fault replaced a fault-based system of divorce that had allowed only the innocent spouse to sue for divorce, and which punished the guilty spouse (most often the husband) for adultery, desertion, or other immoral conduct. Because of the economic dependence of most married women, some feminists were skeptical about the benefits of no-fault from the beginning. However, the reconceptualization of divorce law did have the advantage of rejecting an antiquated image of marriage, one in which dependent, powerless

C. Equality in the Family

wives had to rely on the coercive powers of law to keep husbands from straying. In theory, no-fault divorce offered both spouses a dignified exit and respected their choice to end the marriage.

With respect to child custody, the most significant development of the Equality Stage was the abandonment of the "tender years" presumption. This doctrine had accorded a preference for a mother to be granted custody of her young children, if she was found to be a fit parent. In the vast majority of cases, fathers did not seek custody of their children upon divorce and unwed fathers only rarely resorted to the law to assert parental rights. The tender years presumption thus operated most prominently in that relatively small percentage of cases in which fathers contested mothers' claims. Once the separate spheres ideology was discredited, it was no longer persuasive to argue that women were naturally better suited to rear children, and thus the rationale for the presumption was undermined. Most states responded by instructing courts to use the gender-neutral "best interests of the child" standard and to compare the parents as individuals in the specific context of the case.

Although women stood to lose more often under the new rules, many feminists hoped that a gender-neutral legal regime would encourage men's participation in child care and indirectly result in greater acceptance of women in the workplace, once both parents found that they had to "juggle" their time between jobs and families. In retrospect, the hope that gender neutrality in family law would somehow produce gender equity in workplace structures and spousal relationships may seem naïve. The working mother who would spend her "second shift" caring for children and cleaning the house was not yet a popular media image. At the time, feminists did not yet fully appreciate the futility of trying to devise a uniform strategy to counter the different forms of women's subordination. More often, rather than investigating the distinctive ways in which women were oppressed within the family, arguments proceeded on the assumption that women actually exercised more power in the family than men did, and that it was only fair to require equalization in the domestic sphere to justify women's claims to equality in the larger society. The equality theme that had proved so powerful a critique in employment and education had more backfire potential for women when applied to the family.

D.   PRIVACY AND THE LEGAL REGULATION
OF SEXUAL CONDUCT

Ironically, the most important judicial case for women in the 1970s did not rest explicitly on equality principles. *Roe v. Wade* (1973)[15] afforded women the right to seek an abortion in the first trimester of a pregnancy, free from legal restrictions or regulations. Rather than relying on the Equal Protection Clause, the Court based its decision on the constitutional right to privacy, a concept that was interpreted to give individuals greater freedom with respect to important decisions involving procreation and childrearing. The rationale of *Roe* fit nicely with the 1970s feminist emphasis on individual choice and autonomy. Since the late 1960s, access to legal abortions had been high on the feminist agenda for social change. In practical terms, the right to choose allowed women the chance to stay in school, retain jobs, and pursue careers on the same terms as men, at least if they had enough money to pay for abortions. On a more symbolic level, *Roe* legitimized the desire of some women not to become mothers or to choose to limit the size of their families. Perhaps more so than any other single change in this era, abortion rights challenged separate spheres ideology by permitting employed women to control their fertility, and signaling that the claim of access to the public sphere could be realized for greater numbers of women.

Prior to *Roe* and the liberal era of the 1970s, the law had taken a harshly punitive view toward nonmarital sex. Fornication and sodomy were outlawed and most states denied contraceptives to unmarried persons. Pregnant, unmarried high school students were frequently forced to drop out of their regular school program or were denied the right to participate in extracurricular activities. The parties to the illicit sexual encounter were not the only ones punished in the effort to discourage nonmarital sex. The sins of the parents were visited upon illegitimate children, who were denied rights of inheritance and support. Most prominently, persons who did not conform to traditional norms of heterosexual behavior were subject to legal repression. Gay men and lesbians were commonly branded as "immoral" persons who deserved to lose their jobs or other social benefits.

---

[15] 410 U.S. 113 (1973).

E. Feminist Scholarship During the Equality Stage

The movement to liberalize legal regulation of sexual conduct co-incided with, and was reinforced by, the feminist movement for equality in the 1970s. An important feminist theme of this time was that marriage and motherhood should not be treated as compulsory for all women. The liberal notion of privacy advocated legal immunity for the acts of consenting adults in private, and counseled tolerance of sexual behavior that caused no tangible harm to third parties. Together, these two ideological currents supported significant changes in the law that made it easier for some women to resist tradition.

E.   FEMINIST SCHOLARSHIP DURING THE EQUALITY STAGE

During the Equality Stage, the impetus for legal change came primarily from feminist practitioners. Many of the major scholars often associated with the Equality Stage and liberal feminism were not only "academic" feminists in the sense that they made their reputations solely through writings in law journals. Rather, their experiences in courtrooms or legislative hearings provided the material for their later scholarship. Sylvia Law represented women in cases concerning abortion and health. Nadine Taub ran the sex discrimination clinic at Rutgers. Wendy Williams testified before Congress and helped draft the pregnancy amendments to Title VII. The women's rights scholarship of the 1970s also had a distinctively practical bent. It was too soon to theorize extensively either about the significance of reforms already made or the shape that feminist challenges should take in the future.

Perhaps the most important published works in the 1970s were two major casebooks on sex-based discrimination,[16] which were responsible for introducing courses on women and the law or sex-based discrimination into the law school curriculum for the first time. This meant that a new generation of law students, particularly women law students, would be exposed to the "big picture" and would have the

---

[16] Barbara Allen Babcock, Ann E. Freedman, Eleanor Holmes Norton, Susan D. Ross, *Sex Discrimination and the Law* (Little, Brown and Co. 1975); Kenneth M. Davidson, Ruth Bader Ginsburg, Herma Hill Kay, *Sex-Based Discrimination* (West Publishing 1974).

opportunity to reflect on how the law treated women in a variety of important contexts, principally under the Constitution, in employment and education, within the family, and in the criminal law. Before this development, women or women's issues were rarely mentioned in law courses, or at best were relegated to the margins of a few courses. It was not unusual for the discussion of equal rights for women to take up less than one class hour in constitutional law and be ignored in virtually all other courses, except perhaps for family law.

A major shift took place in the realm of scholarship toward the end of the decade: The new field of feminist legal theory became dominated by women writers, rather than men. In 1969, probably the best known book on the subject was Leo Kanowitz's *Women and the Law.* The law review article that had a great impact in the early 1970s was the definitive article on the ERA, written by Thomas Emerson in 1971, jointly with three women law students from Yale.[17] As women became more established on law faculties, some chose to write about issues of gender discrimination and slowly began to bring a firsthand account of these issues to a legal audience. Not surprisingly, there is a close connection between the sexual integration of the legal academy and the development of feminist legal theory.

F.   THE IMPACT OF LIBERAL FEMINISM ON LAW

Although liberal feminism is often described in negative terms in contemporary scholarship, there is little doubt that its impact has been significant and still represents the dominant feminist influence in the law. A recent example of liberal feminist influence on the law can be seen in the opinion of the majority of the United States Supreme Court in *J.E.B. v. Alabama,*[18] holding that peremptory challenges based on gender are unconstitutional. Peremptory challenges are strikes given to parties in a civil or criminal action to exclude a particular

---

[17] Barbara A. Brown, Thomas I. Emerson, Gail Falk & Ann E. Freedman, The Equal Rights Amendment: A Constitutional Basis for Equal Rights for Women, 80 Yale L.J. 871 (1971).

[18] 511 U.S. 127 (1994).

juror based on the party's hunch or intuition that the juror will be biased or unfair to their side. *J.E.B.* was a paternity case in which the state had used its peremptories to strike all the men from the jury, apparently acting on the prosecutor's belief that women jurors would be more sympathetic to a mother's attempt to establish the legal responsibility of the father. The Court relied on precedents outlawing the use of race-based peremptories and ruled that it was impermissible to strike jurors on the basis of stereotypes or hunches about how women (or men) will decide cases. In the majority's view, using sex stereotypes to strike a juror stigmatized the potential juror by presuming that he or she was not capable of individualized, independent decision making and harkened back to the day when women were excluded altogether from juries because they were presumed too different from men to be trusted to make moral decisions.

J.E.B. is a classic decision in the liberal feminist mode. The Court minimized any differences that might exist between how men as a group, as compared to women as a group, might react to a charge of rape, paternity, or sexual harassment and concluded that individual differences overwhelmed any gender-based tendencies. The Court wished to avoid endorsement of a practice that exacerbated gender-consciousness, lest it contribute to a mentality that relegated women to a separate and unequal status. Additionally, like so many of the cases in the 1970s, the precise holding in *J.E.B.* benefited a man in the name of sexual equality. Interestingly, the only woman on the Court at that time, Justice Sandra Day O'Connor, wrote a separate opinion to express her discomfort with the sameness approach of the majority, stating that "one need not be a sexist to share the intuition that in certain cases a person's gender and resulting life experience will be relevant to his or her view of the case."[19]

Perhaps because its influence has been so pervasive in the law, scholars sometimes assert that liberal feminism no longer has the capacity to generate gains for women. This is an overstatement. Despite the changes in the last 25 years, formal equality theory still can pose a challenge to deeply ingrained legal practices. For example, my research on tort damages has revealed that courts routinely rely on gender-based generalizations when they calculate the important ele-

---

[19] *Id.* at 149.

ment of loss of future earning capacity.[20] An award for loss of future earning capacity compensates for the ability to earn money when an injury has impaired a plaintiff's earning power. Particularly when a young woman is injured and has no track record of earnings, economists appearing as expert witnesses at the trial will often rely on gender-based tables based on past economic patterns for women. Such tables project that women will work fewer years than men and will earn less money for doing the same type of work. Litigators and judges often uncritically accept these explicitly gender-based projections, despite the fact that they dramatically reduce awards for women, magnify past and present employment discrimination, and assume that women will exhibit the same patterns of labor force participation as in previous generations. Perhaps because this gender-based generalization is hidden from view under a maze of statistics, there is little recognition as yet of its capacity to devalue the earning potential of women and to deprive women of fair compensation for their injuries. This is one instance where applying the individualistic vision of liberal feminism would produce a tangible gain for women.

---

[20] Martha Chamallas, Questioning the Use of Race-Specific and Gender-Specific Economic Data in Tort Litigation: A Constitutional Argument, 63 Fordham L. Rev. 73 (1994).

CHAPTER 4

The Difference Stage (1980s)

Feminist legal theory came of age in the 1980s. It seems ironic that in a period characterized by a resurgence of political conservatism and backlash against the women's liberation movement, feminism in the legal academy would thrive. However, during this time feminist scholars were called upon to respond to a claim that there was no longer a pressing need for their work. A persistent theme pervaded popular culture: The women's movement had been successful, equality had been achieved, and sex discrimination was a thing of the past. For the most part, feminists disputed this claim by arguing that "true" or "real" or "meaningful" equality was far from being accomplished. Instead, they argued that there was a need to dig deeper to uncover the roots of sexual inequality and to articulate a feminist vision that went beyond identical treatment to men. Much of the theorizing in the 1980s attempted to explain why the liberal feminist approach of the Equality Stage was inadequate, particularly that the inclusion of women into male-dominated sites was not the exclusive meaning of equality.

A. THE DEBATE OVER EQUAL V. SPECIAL TREATMENT

The United States Supreme Court unwittingly provided the impetus for the maturation of feminist legal scholarship. Shortly after the

Court began using the Equal Protection Clause to strike down explicit sex classifications, it decided the infamous case of *Geduldig v. Aiello*.[1] *Geduldig* challenged the exclusion of pregnancy from California's disability benefits program for state workers. Virtually all other disabilities except pregnancy were covered, including elective procedures, such as cosmetic surgery, and sex-specific procedures, such as prostatectomies and circumcisions. Intuitively, this singling out of pregnancy for unfavorable treatment seemed like a clear instance of sex discrimination because, of course, only women could become pregnant. Moreover, in the United States, in marked contrast to many European nations, employers had failed to accommodate pregnant workers. After giving birth, women often found that their jobs had been given to others and that their seniority or other employee benefits had been forfeited because they interrupted work to have a child.

The *Geduldig* Court concluded that there was no discrimination, not because California's plan was reasonable or cost-justified, but because it did not regard pregnancy discrimination as tantamount to gender discrimination. For the Court, the exclusion of pregnancy was a "far cry from cases like *Reed v. Reed*"[2] because it did not involve "discrimination based upon gender as such."[3] Instead, the Court described pregnancy as an "objectively identifiable physical condition with unique characteristics"[4] and refused to find a constitutional violation absent some additional showing that California was deliberately hostile toward women employees. This ruling signaled the Court's willingness to allow real (i.e., biological) differences to justify disparate treatment of the sexes. Because men and women were not similarly situated with respect to pregnancy, the Court never reached the issue of whether women had been treated equally. The Court reasoned that there was no Equal Protection violation because "[t]here is no risk from which men are protected and women are not."[5]

The response to *Geduldig* and related rulings was intense and negative. One commentator stated that criticizing *Geduldig* had become

---

[1] 417 U.S. 484 (1974).
[2] *Id.* at 496 n.20.
[3] *Id.*
[4] *Id.*
[5] *Id.* at 496-97.

A. The Debate Over Equal v. Special Treatment

"a cottage industry."[6] Most important, a bill was introduced in Congress—which became the Pregnancy Discrimination Act of 1978 (PDA)—to prohibit pregnancy discrimination by employers and to overrule *Geduldig* in the context of employment. The theory underlying the PDA was that pregnancy should be treated like any other temporary physical disability. The "equal treatment" approach of the PDA requires that pregnant employees receive the same benefits and privileges that other employees (male or female) receive when disability affects their capacity to work. From a conceptual standpoint, a great value of this equal treatment approach to pregnancy was that, even though real differences were at stake, it was still possible to use equality analysis to aid women. The simple move of analogizing pregnancy to other disabling conditions demonstrated that it was not logically necessary to treat pregnancy as a "unique" condition warranting distinctive treatment. This move presented the equality issue differently than it had been framed by the Supreme Court. The philosophy implicit in the PDA was that, given that both men and women could become temporarily disabled, it would be unfair to cover all men's disabilities while affording women only partial coverage by excluding pregnancy.

The equal treatment approach to pregnancy discrimination, however, had its drawbacks. Under the PDA, employers were required only to treat pregnant employees as well as they treated others with temporary disabilities. Many employers, particularly those in highly competitive industries such as retail sales, employed a high percentage of women and tended to offer few benefits to any of their employees when it came to sick and disability leaves, guaranteed rights of reinstatement, and other fringe benefits. For the huge class of predominantly female temporary and part-time workers, moreover, there were often no fringe benefit programs of any kind. Thus, as a practical matter, the PDA left large numbers of women employees unprotected. For women in these marginalized jobs in the "secondary labor market," equality with men was an empty benefit. Additionally, on a more symbolic level, many resisted equating pregnancy to disability, preferring to think of pregnancy as an "ability" that women possessed. They were put off by what they regarded as the PDA's emphasis on the negative aspects of pregnancy.

[6] Sylvia A. Law, Rethinking Sex and the Constitution, 132 U. Pa. L. Rev. 955, 983 (1984).

One corrective to the inadequacy of the PDA's equal treatment approach was to mandate special protection for pregnant employees. Several states took the initiative to pass legislation requiring employers to guarantee women their jobs after they returned from maternity leave, and to award at least unpaid disability leave to women during the period they were unable to work due to pregnancy and childbirth. This "special treatment" legislation differed from the PDA in that it did not matter how the employer treated other employees with temporary disabilities. The protection went exclusively to pregnant employees and thus exclusively to women.

The tension between the equal treatment and the special treatment approaches came to a head in the case of *California Federal Savings & Loan Ass'n v. Guerra*.[7] In *Cal Fed* employers tested the legality of a California "special treatment" law requiring unpaid pregnancy leave and reinstatement after childbirth. The feminist community split on the issue.[8] The American Civil Liberties Union (ACLU) and the National Organization for Women (NOW) sided with the employer which took the position that legislation mandating special treatment was inconsistent with the PDA and void under the Supremacy Clause, which gives precedence to federal over state law. A coalition of women's groups from California argued to sustain the law, offering yet another spin on the equality argument. For these feminists, "special" treatment was appropriate because it served to put employed women on an equal footing with employed men. They argued that without guaranteed leave, mothers would not have the same opportunity as fathers to have families and retain their jobs. Rather than compare pregnant women to disabled workers, the coalition reshaped the argument to compare mothers to fathers.

The United States Supreme Court upheld the California legislation, ultimately holding that the PDA constituted a floor of protection for workers, rather than a ceiling for benefits. This interpretation left states free to require reinstatement and unpaid leave for pregnant workers, even if employers did not give those benefits to other disabled workers. The most noticed portion of Justice Marshall's opinion for the majority was his characterization of California's law as a "statute that allows women, as well as men, to have families without losing

<hr>

[7] 479 U.S. 272 (1987).

[8] *See* Christine A. Littleton, Does it Still Make Sense to Talk About "Women," 1 UCLA Women's L.J. 15, 26 (1991).

A. The Debate Over Equal v. Special Treatment

their jobs."[9] The feminist case for nonidentical treatment of men and women had found a receptive audience with liberal members of the Supreme Court.

For the development of feminist legal theory, *Cal Fed* had significance beyond the context of the legal treatment of pregnancy. The debate over equal versus special treatment forced feminists to articulate more precisely what they meant by "equality." The fatal flaw with *Geduldig* was its implicit assumption that women were entitled only to those benefits that men already received. Feminists from both camps criticized this reasoning as embracing a male norm. The Court in *Geduldig* was able to exclude pregnancy discrimination from its definition of gender discrimination only because it took men's needs and men's experiences as its starting point. Using the male worker as the standard meant that women could not suffer actionable discrimination if the source of their disadvantage came from identical treatment (i.e., no pregnancy benefits for any worker). The problem for feminist theorists thus became: How could they fashion arguments to reject the male norm and to broaden the notion of equality to encompass the needs and experiences of both sexes?

Without discounting the depth of the division that surfaced among feminists in the debate over pregnancy, I would stress that both camps renounced the male norm and disagreed as much about strategy as fundamental theory. Equal treatment feminists such as Wendy Williams who championed the PDA criticized *Geduldig* for treating pregnancy as a unique condition, an "extra, an add-on to the basic male model for humanity."[10] As a strategic matter, however, Williams objected to the special treatment approach because of the backlash that might occur when pregnant workers received better treatment than their disabled male co-workers and the license it seemed to give to state legislatures to interfere in matters affecting reproduction. As a liberal feminist, Williams feared that unless women refused to accept special treatment, state legislatures and employers would again be tempted to stereotype all women workers as potential mothers and thus undermine the gains that these women had made in the previous decade. Special treatment feminists such

---

[9] 479 U.S. at 289.

[10] Wendy W. Williams, Equality's Riddle: Pregnancy and the Equal Treatment/Special Treatment Debate, 13 N.Y.U. Rev. L. & Soc. Change 325 (1984/85).

as Linda Krieger[11] and Christine Littleton[12] also based their position on a critique of the male norm. They argued that not only did use of the male norm make gender-specific injury such as pregnancy discrimination invisible as a legal injury, but it was particularly harmful to those women, specifically working-class and single mothers, whose lives diverged most sharply from the male model. As a strategic matter, moreover, it made sense to concentrate on the needs of the majority of women who were not professionals and who were in marginalized female-dominated jobs.

Critique of implicit male norms is such a prominent feature of contemporary feminist legal scholarship that it is easy to forget that this conceptual move has its historical roots in the feminist debate over pregnancy. Teasing out implicit male bias is now a standard technique applied to rules that, though neutral on their face, have a disproportionate negative impact on women as a group, as well as to pregnancy classifications whose effect is felt exclusively by women. The 1970s emphasis on the harmfulness of gender-based generalizations and stereotypes was augmented considerably by the 1980s recognition that even identical treatment of men and women could sometimes result in discrimination.

There was, however, never any clear resolution of the question as to whether similar or dissimilar treatment of men and women should be preferred as a strategy. It is interesting to note that after *Cal Fed* was decided, feminist forces joined together to lobby Congress for passage of the Family and Medical Leave Act, which was finally signed into law in 1993. This gender-neutral law requires large employers to offer all parents of newborns and adopted children a total of three months of unpaid leave in the first year following birth or adoption. In some respects, the FMLA seems the ideal solution to the equal-versus-special treatment dilemma because, by giving both mothers and fathers time to care for their infants, it accommodates the workplace to women's pregnancies without sending the message that child care is an exclusively female activity. However, the current legislation still leaves many women workers unprotected by exempting small and midsized employ-

---

[11] Linda J. Krieger & Patricia N. Cooney, The Miller-Wohl Controversy: Equal Treatment, Positive Action and the Meaning of Women's Equality, 13 Golden Gate U. L. Rev. 513 (1983).
[12] Littleton, supra note 8.

ers and providing no benefits for lower-income women who cannot afford to take unpaid leave.

B.   THE EMERGENCE OF DOMINANCE FEMINISM

The unearthing of implicit male norms in the law was greatly intensified by feminist scholars of the 1980s who leveled their criticism at both traditional legal standards and liberal feminism. The contrast between equality-type feminists and 1980s radical feminists was often dramatic. While Wendy Williams sought to "squeeze the male tilt" out of the law, Catharine MacKinnon attempted to demonstrate how the legal system was fundamentally opposed to women's interests and designed principally to perpetuate male dominance. MacKinnon is probably the most influential feminist legal theorist of the contemporary era. Her book *Feminism Unmodified*,[13] a collection of her speeches from 1981 to 1986, may be the most widely read text in the field.

Trained as both a political scientist and a lawyer, MacKinnon approached the question of women's legal status by first considering women's relationship to the state. In an early essay, she compared her brand of feminist theory to Marxist theory, explaining that "[s]exuality is to feminism what work is to Marxism: that which is most one's own, yet most taken away."[14] The significance of this comparison is that, for MacKinnon, the appropriation of women's sexuality by men and the male-dominated state was as central to feminist theory as capitalist appropriation of the labor of the working class was for Marxist theory. This emphasis on sexuality set MacKinnon apart from liberal feminists. MacKinnon's work centers on the domination of women in the sexual sphere, highlighting rape, sexual harassment, and pornography. These topics had tended to be neglected by liberal feminists who concentrated more on economic issues. MacKinnon contended that the sexual use and abuse of women was the principal mechanism by which women's subordination was perpetuated.

---

[13] Catharine A. MacKinnon, *Feminism Unmodified: Discourses on Life and Law* (1987).

[14] Catharine A. MacKinnon, Feminism, Marxism, Method, and the State: An Agenda for Theory, 7 Signs: J. Women in Culture & Soc'y 515 (1982).

Liberal feminists may have shied away from analyzing sexuality and sexual abuse because it was an area in which women were thought to be different from men. The conventional wisdom was that only men were capable of rape and that most men tended to be more aggressive than women in initiating and pursuing sexual relationships. The difference in men's and women's sexual behavior was often traced to biology, reflecting a "biology is destiny" philosophy that liberal feminists feared would surface again to justify discriminatory legal treatment of women.

MacKinnon flatly rejected the view of sexuality as a biological given that differentiated the sexes. Instead, in her view, sexuality itself was socially constructed, that is, given its meaning by prevailing social practices and ideology. Following Simone de Beauvoir's insight that "one is not born, one rather becomes a woman,"[15] MacKinnon contended that our male-dominated society, aided by male-dominated laws, had constructed women as sexual objects for the use of men. She argued that

> femaleness means femininity, which means attractiveness to men, which means sexual attractiveness, which means sexual availability on male terms. What defines woman as such is what turns men on. Good girls are "attractive," bad girls "provocative." Gender socialization is the process through which women come to identify themselves as sexual beings, as beings that exist for men.[16]

In this view, what passed as women's sexuality was a product of male domination and not an authentic expression of women's sexual desire. Moreover, what seemed to be a sexual difference was more appropriately regarded as a manifestation of domination.

MacKinnon first applied her dominance theory to the workplace and was instrumental in establishing the cause of action for sexual harassment. Before the mid-1970s, there was no word to describe the phenomenon of sexual harassment. What we now regard as sexual harassment was largely invisible as a harm. Harassing conduct was most often dismissed as harmless and as the inevitable byproduct of mixing the sexes at work. One reason it may have taken so long to recognize sexual harassment as a harm is that it has no precise analogue in the

---

[15] Simone de Beauvoir, *The Second Sex* 249 (Knopf, 1970).
[16] MacKinnon, supra note 14, at 530-31.

B. The Emergence of Dominance Feminism

experience of men. Unlike other forms of employment discrimination, such as denials of promotions, wage discrimination, or discriminatory termination, all of which men frequently suffer, the great majority of sexual harassment victims are women.

In her 1979 book,[17] MacKinnon blended particularized accounts of women's experiences of sexual harassment with a novel legal argument for prohibiting harassment as a violation of women's civil rights. Central to her argument was how women's inferior status in the workplace was reinforced by the social meaning of women's sexuality. Particularly in feminized, pink-collar jobs, MacKinnon contended that employees were "set up" for sexual harassment. Often part of a woman's job was to be pleasing to the boss, to be attractive, and to project the appearance of sexual availability. It was not surprising that supervisors and male co-workers in these sexualized environments propositioned women, made offensive comments about their physical appearance, and engaged in other forms of verbal and physical harassment. MacKinnon's argument was straightforward and powerful: Because sexual harassment was a central mechanism for perpetuating women's inferior status in the workplace, it ought to be regarded as sex discrimination. Although the courts never fully adopted her dominance thesis, MacKinnon's work on harassment had a great impact. The two categories of harassment she delineated in her book (*quid pro quo* and hostile environment) were later embraced by the EEOC and provided the basic doctrine for organizing litigation in this area.

When MacKinnon applied her theory of sexuality and dominance to the law of rape, she fastened on the concept of "consent" as the means by which the law institutionalized male dominance. Consent plays a very important function in liberal jurisprudence because it separates lawful (consensual intercourse) from unlawful sex (rape). Starting in the late 1970s, feminist writers had begun to object to the definition of consent used in rape prosecutions. The traditional version of consent in the law of rape maintained that a woman consented to intercourse if she did not offer physical resistance. Thus, if a woman was too afraid to resist, she had never been taught to fight back, or for some other reason she offered no physical resistance, this could prevent the man's behavior from being classified as rape. For MacKinnon, this equation of "lack of physical resistance" with "consent" was

---

[17] Catharine A. MacKinnon, *Sexual Harassment of Working Women* (1979).

the critically important conceptual move. MacKinnon claimed that, despite appearances, the law actually tolerated forced sex. Rather than regarding any use of force as unacceptable, the law set "[t]he level of acceptable force" at "just above the level set by what is seen as normal male sexual behavior, including the normal level of force."[18] The neutral sounding concept of consent was unpacked to reveal its male bias. For MacKinnon, forced sex was tolerated because women had been constructed as sexual beings who desired to be forced. This social construction of women's sexuality led to a biased view of consent that had immunized countless rapes, particularly date and acquaintance rapes perpetrated by white men.

MacKinnon's view of the prevalence of forced sex also led her to be less than enthusiastic about the newly won right of abortion in *Roe v. Wade*. She refused to disentangle abortion from the context of women's sexuality. In a pre-AIDS era essay,[19] MacKinnon began with the proposition that most women do not control the conditions under which they have sex. She argued that many women may be reluctant to use birth control because of its social meaning, namely, signaling a woman's sexual availability. If women become pregnant under such constraining conditions, their choice to abort is not as free as it would be if women had equal power to control sex. For MacKinnon, even the privacy doctrine of *Roe v. Wade* embraced the male point of view because, ironically, it facilitated women's heterosexual availability. She cynically observed that "[t]he availability of abortion removes the one remaining legitimized reason that women have for refusing sex besides the headache."[20]

In addition to contesting the concepts of consent and privacy, MacKinnon attacked another liberal mainstay, the concept of objectivity. Objectivity in the law, like objectivity in journalism or other endeavors, is frequently associated with evaluations or assessments that do not reflect or express a particular point of view; in MacKinnon's words, objectivity can best be described as "point-of-viewlessness."[21] For example, the objective, reasonable person standard in tort law is not

---

[18] Catharine A. MacKinnon, *Toward a Feminist Theory of the State* 173 (1989).

[19] Catharine A. MacKinnon, Privacy v. Equality: Beyond *Roe v. Wade* (1983), in *Feminism Unmodified: Discourses on Life and Law* 93-102 (1987).

[20] *Id.* at 99.

[21] MacKinnon, supra note 18, at 162.

B. The Emergence of Dominance Feminism

linked to the perspective either of the defendant or of the plaintiff, but supposedly encourages the jury to reach its verdict free from partisan influences.

Presaging a prominent theme of many later feminist and postmodern scholars, MacKinnon questioned the very existence of objectivity. She argued that what passes for objective analysis is often the viewpoint of the dominant group, hidden from our view because the speaker possesses the power to have his version of reality accepted as truth. In the context of rape, for example, the law had incorporated a male version of reality that presumed consent from nonresistance, and which supposed that a woman might still want to have intercourse even if she said "no," or cried, or otherwise expressed her lack of desire. In MacKinnon's analysis, women's sense of violation and injury did not factor prominently into the law's purportedly objective definition of consent, despite the fact that the criminal law was supposed to prevent victimization and protect individuals from violence and force. The feminist critique of objectivity marked a departure from the tenets of liberal feminism, which had staked its case on insisting that the law be neutral and sought to minimize sexual differences rather than highlight them.

In the realm of constitutional law, MacKinnon argued for an entirely new approach to equal protection. She located the source of the problem in the Court's emphasis on "difference." Traditional equal protection doctrine requires that "likes be treated alike" and that only similarly situated persons have the right to demand equal treatment. For MacKinnon, the focus on difference legitimated sex discrimination because in so many important contexts (especially sexuality and reproduction), women had been constructed as different from men. She argued that what should be crucial to constitutional analysis should not be the existence of difference, but the prevalence of domination. In fact, difference was often a telltale sign of dominance, as illustrated by MacKinnon's retelling of the story of the origin of man:

> Here, on the first day that matters, dominance was achieved, probably by force. By the second day, division along the same lines had to be relatively firmly in place. On the third day, if not sooner, differences were demarcated, together with social systems to exaggerate them in perception and in fact, *because* the systematically differential delivery of ben-

efits and deprivations required making no mistake about who was who. Comparatively speaking, man has been resting ever since.[22]

Acceptance of the dominance approach would substantially change the doctrinal tests currently used in constitutional analysis. Under the current equal protection analysis, the law may withstand a constitutional challenge if differential treatment of women is based on real (not stereotyped) differences between the sexes. MacKinnon would have the courts focus instead on whether the law serves to perpetuate the subordination of women. This more explicitly political test confronts the issue of women's inferior status directly and attempts not to use men's experience and men's needs as the standard by which the treatment of women is judged. Perhaps most importantly, MacKinnon's approach does not require identical treatment of men and women: The dominance approach is concerned with substantive rather than formal inequality, recognizing that identical treatment of people in unequal positions can result in injustice.

MacKinnon's dominance approach found considerable appeal among many feminist writers in the 1980s. Ruth Colker, for example, argued for adoption of an anti-subordination approach to constitutional law that would encompass not only gender but race-based discrimination, deciding the constitutionality of measures by whether they deepened power disparities among groups or made it less likely that systematic discrimination would be dismantled in the future.[23] Kathryn Abrams proposed a new MacKinnon-like approach to sexual harassment claims alleging a hostile environment, one that would judge the legality of conduct by whether it had the capacity to create a fear of sexual coercion on the part of women workers or conveyed a dismissive message about the value and worth of women employees.[24] Even liberal feminists such as Sylvia Law argued for a selective adoption of the dominance approach to test laws affecting reproductive bi-

---

[22] Catharine A. MacKinnon, Difference and Dominance: On Sex Discrimination (1984), in *Feminism Unmodified: Discourses on Life and Law* 40 (1987).

[23] Ruth Colker, Anti-Subordination Above All: Sex, Race and Equal Protection, 61 N.Y.U. L. Rev. 1003 (1986).

[24] Kathryn Abrams, Gender Discrimination and the Transformation of Workplace Norms, 42 Vand. L. Rev. 1183 (1989).

B. The Emergence of Dominance Feminism

ology, where the traditional emphasis on difference had proven so unavailing to women.[25]

Feminist criticism of MacKinnon and of dominance feminism began to mount, however, when MacKinnon teamed up with Andrea Dworkin in a campaign against pornography. The two scholar-activists targeted pornography because they regarded pornography as a particularly pernicious form of sexual subordination. The earlier generation of equality feminists had tended to tolerate pornography, taking the liberal view that sexual explicitness in films and books did not produce any tangible harm and perhaps even provided a cathartic outlet in a repressive society. Before MacKinnon and Dworkin drafted model ordinances in Minneapolis and Indianapolis to provide for a civil rights cause of action against pornography, there was little recognition of pornography as a woman's issue. The law of obscenity—the term used to describe sexually explicit material not protected by the Constitution—was largely a discourse centering on moral decency, offensiveness and freedom of speech, with little mention of sexual equality or sexual violence.

MacKinnon's anti-pornography ordinance defined pornography in women-centered terms as the "graphic sexually explicit subordination of women."[26] Both hard-core and soft-core pornography were covered within its sweeping definition, including depictions of women as "sexual objects who experience pleasure in being raped" and presentations of women as "sexual objects for domination, conquest, violation, exploitation, possession, or use, or through postures or positions of servility or submission or display." MacKinnon argued that such a broad attack on pornography was warranted because pornography was central to the social construction of sexuality. She maintained that through pornography, dominance and inequality were eroticized. The ordinances were based on the proposition that "[p]ornography works by making sexism sexy."[27] MacKinnon argued that pornography forges a connection between sexual hierarchy and male orgasm. "Pornogra-

---

[25] Sylvia A. Law, Rethinking Sex and the Constitution, 132 U. Pa. L. Rev. 955, 1008-1013 (1984).

[26] The Indianapolis anti-pornography ordinance is reproduced in *American Booksellers Ass'n, Inc. v. Hudnut*, 771 F.2d 323, 324 (7th Cir. 1985).

[27] Catharine A. MacKinnon, Pornography as Defamation and Discrimination, 71 B.U. L. Rev. 793, 802 (1991).

phy does not work sexually without hierarchy. If there is no inequality, no violation, no dominance, no force, there is no sexual arousal."[28] In MacKinnon's view, men transport what they learn in pornography about the nature of women to their everyday interactions, resulting in a higher incidence of sexual violence and abuse, as well as sex discrimination generally, particularly sexual harassment. Further, because the use of pornography for masturbation promotes a "one-sided sex"[29] in which women are objects who lack human subjectivity, the effect is to dehumanize women as a class and to reinforce a sexist ideology that ultimately produces a second-class status for women.

Many feminists, however, were not persuaded by MacKinnon's account of pornography and feared that censorship of pornography might prove worse for women than the status quo. In 1984, a group of feminist academics, writers, artists, and activists formed the Feminist Anti-Censorship Task Force (FACT), a coalition to oppose dominance-based anti-pornography laws.[30] They filed an amicus brief in a case challenging the Indianapolis ordinance and asked the court to strike down the ordinance as a violation of free speech. A major source of their disagreement with the dominance account of pornography was its assumption that women were victimized by sex and its failure to recognize that, for some women, sex and sexual fantasy might be experienced as liberating. The FACT brief argued that the anti-pornography ordinance played into Victorian notions of women as asexual beings and "resonates with the traditional concept that sex itself degrades women . . ." It echoed liberal concerns for choice by protesting that the ordinance implied that "individual women are incapable of choosing for themselves what they consider to be enjoyable, sexually arousing material without being degraded or humiliated." Most significantly, FACT told the court of their concern that, in the hands of conservative judges, the ordinance would likely be interpreted in punitive ways against lesbians, gay men, and other sexual minorities whose sexual practices could easily be found to be degrading or subordinating or an affront to the dignity of traditionally minded people.

---

[28] Catharine A. MacKinnon, Not a Moral Issue (1983), in *Feminism Unmodified: Discourses on Life and Law* 160 (1987).

[29] MacKinnon, supra note 27, at 802.

[30] *See* Kathryn Abrams, Sex Wars Redux: Agency and Coercion in Feminist Legal Theory, 95 Colum. L. Rev. 304, 321-324 (1995).

B. The Emergence of Dominance Feminism

The federal court of appeals substantially agreed with FACT's position and struck down the Indianapolis ordinance as a violation of the First Amendment in the 1985 case of *American Booksellers Ass'n v. Hudnut*.[31] Despite the importance of the issue and the political controversy it had generated, the United States Supreme Court did not weigh in on the debate, choosing instead to summarily affirm the lower court's holding of unconstitutionality without issuing an opinion. MacKinnon's dominance approach, however, had greater success in Canada. The Canadian statutory definition of pornography was modeled after MacKinnon's ordinance and was ultimately sustained by the Supreme Court of Canada.[32]

The anti-pornography debate exposed divisions in feminist thought that went deeper than the strategic differences that had separated feminists in the equal-versus-special treatment debate over pregnancy. The tension between women's victimization and what would later be described as women's agency was most prominent. Dominance theory emphasized victimization and left little room for women to describe how they had taken actions to shape their lives and create their own identity. The critics of the anti-pornography movement stressed women's capacity for finding pleasure in sex and their ability to interpret sexual images in positive ways. More so than in the equality discussions of the 1970s, a lesbian voice could be heard in the anti-pornography debates cautioning feminists not to base their positions on the experience of heterosexual women alone.

The controversy over the Indianapolis ordinance also highlighted a paradox for feminist legal theorists and activists concerning reliance on the state to achieve feminist goals. Despite her radical view of the state as embodying and perpetuating male dominance, MacKinnon championed statutory reforms to combat sexual harassment and pornography. Implementation inevitably meant involvement of the state, particularly through the rulings of judges and administrators. There was no escaping the fact, for example, that a largely white, male, and nonfeminist judiciary would be called upon to decide what qualified as sexual harassment or pornography. This lack of control over the unintended effects of feminist-inspired reforms complicated debates

---

[31] 771 F.2d 323 (7th Cir. 1985), *aff'd mem.*, 475 U.S. 1001 (1986).
[32] *Regina v. Butler*, 89 D.L.R. 4th (S.C.C. 1992).

over strategy and may help to explain why pornography remains a highly divisive issue among feminists today.

C.   CULTURAL FEMINISM MEETS THE LAW

At approximately the same time that MacKinnon was publishing her important essays on sexuality and dominance, the influence of Carol Gilligan and her genre of cultural feminism also surfaced in legal discourse. Gilligan is a developmental psychologist who studies moral development, particularly among adolescent girls. Her first book, *In a Different Voice*,[33] sparked an unusual volume of interdisciplinary feminist commentary, with what has seemed to be an equal number of followers and critics. The book was so popular that sometimes the school of thought is called "different voice" feminism and used interchangeably with the terms "cultural feminism" or "relational feminism."

Gilligan's research investigated how men and women make moral choices and solve moral dilemmas. In her field, pivotal research on the stages of human moral development had been done by Lawrence Kohlberg of Harvard University, where Gilligan received her Ph.D. Remarkably, Kohlberg had devised his study and built his theory using an all-male sample. Like so many scholars prior to the 1970s, however, Kohlberg did not report his findings as valid only for describing men's moral development. Instead, it was simply assumed that the research could be generalized and adequately represented *human* moral development. Not surprisingly, men generally scored higher on Kohlberg's six-stage scale than women, who tended not to advance beyond stage three, a stage characterized by seeing morality as a question of interpersonal relations, by caring for and pleasing others.

Struck by this rather graphic example of use of the tacit male norm, Gilligan set out to rectify Kohlberg's "enormous design flaw"[34] by devising studies that not only would include women, but would pay

[33] Carol Gilligan, *In a Different Voice: Psychological Theory and Women's Development* (1982).
[34] Feminist Discourse, Moral Values, and the Law—A Conversation, 34 Buff. L. Rev. 11, 39 (1985) (remarks of Carol Gilligan).

C. Cultural Feminism Meets the Law

close attention to how women made moral decisions, including their choice of language. Gilligan's most famous study—known by the name of two of the respondents, Amy and Jake—involved posing one of Kohlberg's standard moral dilemmas to 11-year-old boys and girls, who were later interviewed at age 15. In the "Heinz" dilemma, the respondents are told that Heinz cannot afford to buy a drug that will save the life of his dying wife and that the druggist refuses to lower the price. They are then asked one question: Should Heinz steal the drug?

Jake is confident that the druggist should steal the drug. He approaches the dilemma as if it were a "math problem with humans" and bases his conclusion on the abstract belief that "a human life is worth more than money." Amy's response is far more ambivalent, described by one legal scholar as fighting the hypothetical.[35] Amy equivocates by stating that she doesn't think that Heinz should steal the drug because "there might be other ways besides stealing it, like if he could borrow the money or make a loan or something . . ."[36] but neither does she believe that Heinz's wife should die. Amy also worries about the consequences of a theft: "If he stole the drug, he might save his wife then, but if he did, he might have to go to jail, and then his wife might get sicker again, and he couldn't get more of the drug, and it might not be good."[37] Finally, Gilligan describes Amy as having confidence that "if Heinz and the druggist had talked it out long enough, they could reach something besides stealing."[38]

Gilligan interpreted Jake's and Amy's responses as representing two very distinctive voices or reasoning processes. Jake speaks a language of rights. He abstracts the moral problem from the interpersonal relationships and then balances the rights in a hierarchical fashion (life over property) to reach a certain conclusion. His response was characterized by Gilligan as the voice or ethic of justice, corresponding closely to the reasoning process most prominent in legal decision making. Jake's response also scores well on Kohlberg's scale because he employs a logic of universal ethical principles.

The logic of Amy's response was far more difficult for Gilligan to articulate, primarily because mainstream psychological theory had

[35] Carrie Menkel-Meadow, Portia in a Different Voice: Speculations on a Woman's Lawyering Process, 1 Berkeley Women's L.J. 39, 46 (1985).
[36] Gilligan, supra note 33, at 28.
[37] Id.
[38] Id. at 29.

tended to rate Amy's response as immature and incoherent. Gilligan, however, made sense of Amy's response by claiming that Amy placed greater value on relationships. Amy's primary concern was not to prioritize the rights of the various parties, but to seek a solution that would cause the least harm to all involved. Amy also did not approach the problem by abstracting the salient categories of analysis, but remained embroiled in the particulars of the interpersonal situation. She approached the dilemma contextually and was willing to let the druggist and Heinz work out a mutually satisfying solution, without dictating the result. Gilligan named Amy's approach the "ethic of care," perceiving it as a "different voice" from Jake's and Kohlberg's approach to moral reasoning. Gilligan invoked the imagery of the web to characterize Amy's interconnected approach to the world; Jake's hierarchical orientation was captured by the image of the ladder.

In the rapid-fire reaction to Gilligan's work by the popular media and in academia, many writers casually equated the ethic of care with women and the ethic of justice with men, reducing the "different voice" to "women's voice." In fact, the gender correlation Gilligan found in her research was more complex: Most people, male and female, used both voices or orientations in defining and resolving problems. Nearly all the male respondents (57 out of 60, or 95 percent of the sample), however, tended to focus on the justice voice, while a large proportion of the women (approximately 60 percent) emphasized the care voice.[39] Significantly, Gilligan also found that, as girls developed, they often learned to couch their responses in the justice language and to suppress their different voice, unless they were somehow urged to reveal what they really thought.

One reason Gilligan's research may have been simplistically cited as providing proof of polarized gender differences is that Gilligan did not dwell on the question of the possible origins of the different voice. Conservative readings of her work—what Mary Jo Frug called "crude Gilliganism"[40]—assumed that women's different voice had its origin in biological differences between the sexes and sought to use the research to justify gender disparities in a wide variety of contexts. To the extent that she discussed origins, however, Gilligan seemed to embrace a feminist psychoanalytic explanation of the formation of gen-

---

[39] Feminist Discourse, supra note 29, at 47-48 (remarks of Carol Gilligan).

[40] Mary Jo Frug, Progressive Feminist Legal Scholarship: Can We Claim "A Different Voice"?, 15 Harv. Women's L.J. 37, 50 (1992).

C. Cultural Feminism Meets the Law

der differences, most often associated with the work of Nancy Chodorow. Chodorow attributes gender differences not to the differences in male and female anatomy, but to the fact that women are generally responsible for early child care.[41] This theory posits that girls tend to identify with their mothers and to form a feminine personality centered on affiliation, empathy and connection. Boys, however, experience a sense of separation from their primary caretaker at an earlier age and develop a masculine gender identity that is threatened by intimacy. The crucial implication of such a psychoanalytical model is that patterns of gender identity could change if men would participate more extensively in caring for infants and young children.

However closely linked the different voice is to women, Gilligan's obvious respect for the different voice makes it appropriate to characterize her work as an example of cultural feminism. As a theoretical orientation, cultural feminism celebrates the distinctive contributions women make to society, particularly women's capacity for nurturing, empathy, and preservation of relationships. This positive vision of women's culture goes beyond acknowledging differences between men and women, and argues for a revaluation of the activities and attributes commonly associated with women and femininity. Thus, for example, Gilligan's objective was not simply to demonstrate that the different voice had not been heard or had been discounted by psychologists in the construction of moral theory. She also argued in favor of transforming the moral domain by bringing the two voices together in an inclusive way that required changing both orientations. More so than liberal or radical feminism, which tends to focus on gender-based inequities and harms, cultural feminism aims at changing men and society by stressing female virtues. Clare Dalton has suggested that cultural feminism usually draws upon a core image or archetype of woman as "Mother," in contrast to radical feminism's preoccupation with woman as "Sexual Subordinate."[42]

Feminist legal scholars were quick to apply different voice feminism to legal topics. The resemblance between Jake's hierarchical orientation and dominant legal discourse made Gilligan's methodology a useful tool to critique the law and to suggest alternative analyses and solutions. Some of these applications took feminist theory into areas

[41] Gilligan, supra note 33, at 7-8.

[42] Clare Dalton, Where We Stand: Observations on the Situation of Feminist Legal Thought, 3 Berkeley Women's L.J. 1, 7-8 (1987-88).

of the law that had not been traditionally gender-coded—that is, not thought to be of special concern to women. For example, Leslie Bender set out to re-evaluate tort law. She speculated on how the "no duty to rescue" doctrine might be reexamined from a cultural feminist perspective to uncover the full extent of the damage done when a person refuses to aid a stranger.[43] In Bender's reconceptualization, even a stranger should be regarded as a person who is interconnected with others and whose well-being substantially affects the lives of others. She argued that the Jake-like "no duty to rescue" rule placed too high a premium on the abstract value of personal autonomy, decontextualized the issue, and discounted the relational injuries suffered. Taking Gilligan's theories into the law of evidence, Kit Kinports argued that a feminist revision of evidentiary privileges would tend to be less hierarchical and would, for example, extend the doctor/patient privilege to nurses, rape counselors, and other less prestigious professionals who encourage their clients to disclose private confidences.[44] Inspired by Gilligan and relational feminists from other disciplines, Judith Resnik questioned the abstract ideal of impartiality and detachment in the process of judging and developed a more nuanced, contextual description of the work of judges, which included recognition of the pain inflicted by adjudication.[45]

Perhaps the legal scholar most active in importing cultural feminism to the law was Carrie Menkel-Meadow who focused her research on the legal profession and the adversary system.[46] Menkel-Meadow questioned whether the growing numbers of women in the legal profession might change the way lawyers behave, particularly their tendency to seek binary results, with one party declared the winner and the other the loser. As a proponent of the emerging field of law known as alternative dispute resolution, she used cultural feminist theory to suggest how greater emphasis on cooperation, preservation of relationships, and attention to process might produce legal reforms that could

[43] Leslie Bender, A Lawyer's Primer on Feminist Theory and Tort, 38 J. Legal Educ. 3, 33-36 (1988).

[44] Kit Kinports, Evidence Engendered, 1991 U. of Ill. L. Rev. 413, 443-44 (1991). The Supreme Court has recently extended the psychotherapist's privilege to licensed social workers. *See Jaffee v. Redmond,* 518 U.S. 1 (1996).

[45] Judith Resnik, On the Bias: Feminist Reconsiderations of the Aspirations for Our Judges, 61 S. Cal. L. Rev. 1877 (1988).

[46] Menkel-Meadow, supra note 35.

C.   Cultural Feminism Meets the Law

benefit not only women lawyers and their clients but the legal profession as a whole. Menkel-Meadow's scholarship also challenged male-defined measures of success, which regard large-firm and corporate practice as the most prestigious kinds of law practice. She argues that many women (and some men) have developed alternative definitions of success which place greater weight on achieving a balance between work and family, "doing socially useful work or having meaningful relationships at work with clients and co-workers."[47]

The most provocative article of this era in the cultural feminist mode was probably Robin West's Jurisprudence and Gender.[48] West made the sweeping claim that modern legal theory was "essentially and irretrievably masculine." She contended that the critical premise underlying both conservative and liberal versions of modern jurisprudence was the "separation thesis," the belief that the individual was first and foremost physically separate and apart from all others. It then followed that autonomy and freedom would rank high among the values fostered by law and that the most recognizable type of harm would be threats from outside aggressors. According to West, however, women and their values were nowhere represented in contemporary jurisprudence. West claimed that the basic separation premise was "patently untrue of women" and argued that women are materially connected to others through critical experiences, notably pregnancy, heterosexual penetration, menstruation (by signaling the potential for pregnancy), and breast-feeding. According to West, the value that women cherished above all was intimacy, while their greatest fear was injury produced by separation. West regarded feminist theory as responding to this "connection thesis," particularly cultural feminism's emphasis on attachment, responsibility to others, empathy and relationships. Even MacKinnon's brand of radical feminism tacitly embraced the connection thesis in West's schema. Through its emphasis on sexual exploitation, radical feminism acknowledged the importance women placed on their connections to men and was able to comprehend the special harm of "invasion or intrusion" caused when men disregarded women's subjective wishes relating to their bodily integrity.

---

[47] Carrie Menkel-Meadow, Exploring a Research Agenda of the Feminization of the Legal Profession: Theories of Gender and Social Change, 14 L. & Soc. Inquiry 289, 307-08 (1989).

[48] Robin West, Jurisprudence and Gender, 55 U. Chi. L. Rev. 1 (1988).

West's broad indictment of jurisprudence was accompanied by a plea for a greater volume of feminist scholarship grounded in women's subjective experience. She argued that until women were able to articulate their joy and suffering in a language not foreign to their experiences, and to have those experiences understood by men, feminist legal reforms would appear to be irrational. The agenda West set for feminist legal scholarship bore a striking resemblance to Gilligan's project in *In A Different Voice*:

> We need to flood the market with our own stories until we get one simple point across: men's narrative story and phenomenological description of law is not women's story and phenomenology of law. We need to dislodge legal theorists' confidence that they speak for women, and we need to fill the gap that will develop when we succeed in doing so.[49]

West's article was the subject of heated debate among feminists, primarily because she traced the origin of sexual differences to biology and built her elaborate theory around the physical events of female pregnancy and heterosexual intercourse. West displayed little of Gilligan's scholarly caution about linking the different voice to women and, like so many nonfeminist theorists, West can be faulted for exaggerating the significance of pregnancy and childbirth. Nonetheless, Jurisprudence and Gender was important to the development of feminist theory because of West's audacity in taking on the whole body of legal theory and her construction of a useful taxonomy to organize the divergent strains of feminist legal criticism that the 1980s produced.

D. CONFRONTING THE DANGERS OF CULTURAL FEMINISM

Cultural feminism did not have much time to settle into the legal domain before feminist critics began to expose the dangers of the dif-

---

[49] *Id.* at 65.

D. Confronting the Dangers of Cultural Feminism

ferent voice approach. Perhaps the most recurring criticism was that the portrait of women painted by cultural feminism too closely resembled the Nineteenth Century stereotyped portrait of Woman as naturally emotional, domestic, and nurturing. Joan Williams argued that relational feminists had updated the separate spheres ideal to "reclaim the compliments of Victorian gender ideology while rejecting its insults."[50] Her point was that although Twentieth Century cultural feminists rejected the image of women as passive and dependent, they still clung to the maternal virtues of care and nurturing. According to Williams, Gilligan and her adherents were not tapping into what men and women were really like, but were engaged in a process of rehabilitating cultural images of femininity and domesticity, a dangerous process that could backfire and resurrect barriers to women's inclusion in public and economic spheres.

Many critics of Gilligan also mistrusted the authenticity of women's different voice. MacKinnon, for example, interpreted the different voice as the "voice of the victim," explaining that women who live under conditions of gender subordination have never had the freedom to develop their own voice, position, or perspective.[51] In their view, the "feminine" perspective Gilligan uncovered is principally a coping mechanism, an adaptation to male domination. Such a recasting of the different voice maintains that women place a high importance on caring and sensitivity, not as an expression of their individual identity and personality but because "the important men in their lives insist on being taken care of."[52] Rather than celebrating the different voice, feminist critics of Gilligan renewed the debate over the origins of difference, and remained skeptical about claiming difference without first analyzing the impact of domination.

The case most often cited as proof of the dangers of cultural feminism is *EEOC v. Sears, Roebuck & Co.*,[53] a major Title VII class action against the nation's largest retailer. Suing on behalf of female employees and applicants, the EEOC claimed that Sears discriminated by denying women jobs as commission sales representatives. *Sears* challenged

---

[50] Joan C. Williams, Deconstructing Gender, 87 Mich. L. Rev. 797, 807 (1989).

[51] Feminist Discourse, Moral Values, and the Law—A Conversation, 34 Buffalo L. Rev. 11, 27 (1985) (remarks of Catharine A. MacKinnon).

[52] Clare Dalton, Where We Stand: Observations on the Situation of Feminist Legal Thought, 3 Berkeley Women's L.J. 1, 10 (1987-88).

[53] 628 F. Supp. 1264 (N.D. Ill. 1986), *aff'd*, 839 F.2d 302 (7th Cir. 1988).

a familiar pattern of job segregation and stratification: Women accounted for 75 percent of the noncommission sales force, but only 27 percent of the new hires for commission sales. The disparity was important because median hourly wages for commission sales jobs were about twice as high as those of noncommission salespersons.

For its part, the EEOC put on an elaborate statistical case to demonstrate that Sears should have recruited and selected more women from its largely female pool of noncommission sales workers. Sears countered by arguing that the gender disparity in its workforce was not the product of discrimination, but the result of women's own choices. Sears's principal defense was that women lacked interest in commission sales because of the nature of the jobs and product lines sold. Sears portrayed commission sales in masculine terms, arguing that women feared and disliked the "dog-eat-dog" competition, pressure and risks that the jobs entailed. Sears also contended that women felt uncomfortable selling "hard lines" of merchandise, such as automotive supplies, furnaces, fencing, and roofing, typically sold on a commission basis. By contrast, Sears constructed an image of noncommission sales work as more feminine and claimed that women preferred this kind of work because it was more friendly and involved less pressure and lower risk. According to Sears witnesses, women also preferred selling small-ticket, soft lines of merchandise like cosmetics, children's clothing, and linens, which were sold on a noncommission basis.

The unique aspect of the *Sears* defense was its use of the testimony of Dr. Rosalind Rosenberg, a feminist historian, to bolster its claims about gender differences. Citing Gilligan and other scholars, Rosenberg asserted that historically, women and men have had different interests and motivations regarding work. She portrayed women as voluntarily subordinating work to family needs, as "more relationship centered" than men, "more interested than men in the cooperative, social aspects of the work situation," and "less competitive."[54] Offered as expert testimony, Rosenberg's generalizations about women workers legitimized job segregation, gave a fresh face to domestic stereotypes about women, and used cultural feminism to defeat women's claims to equal employment opportunity. The EEOC rebutted Rosen-

---

[54] Offer of Proof concerning the testimony of Rosalind Rosenberg, 11 Signs: J. Women in Culture & Soc'y 757-66 (1986).

berg's account with expert testimony by Alice Kessler-Harris, a feminist historian who stressed women's willingness to do nontraditional work when opportunities presented themselves. The judge, however, found the conservative version of women's distinctive interests to be more credible, and ruled for Sears.

For many feminists, *Sears* exemplified how easily cultural feminist claims of gender difference can be appropriated to defend the status quo and may be ineffective in challenging the value assigned to women's activities and feminine traits. The nuanced different voice identified by Carol Gilligan and the rich diversity in women's culture described by feminist social historians were missing from Rosenberg's testimony. Perhaps these complexities could never be adequately presented in an adversarial proceeding where the object is to declare one side the winner and the other the loser.

E.   CROSS-FERTILIZATION AND BLENDED FEMINIST THEORIES

Perhaps the most lasting legacy of the Difference Stage of the 1980s was to imprint both dominance feminism and cultural feminism onto contemporary feminist legal theory. By the late 1980s, feminist scholars felt the need to grapple simultaneously with power and cultural differences, rather than simply align themselves with one or another feminist camp. Although I still find it helpful to "locate" scholars by ascertaining, for example, whether they cite Gilligan with approval or disapproval, most recent feminist scholarship is more aptly described as "blended," showing the influence of the three major strands of feminist thought—liberal, radical, and cultural feminism.

Christine Littleton's "equality of acceptance" model is a good illustration of a blended approach.[55] Littleton starts from the proposition that whether they are regarded as biologically based or socially constructed, gender differences should not be ignored or eradicated. In this respect, she shares the cultural feminist recognition and cel-

---

[55] Christine A. Littleton, Reconstructing Sexual Equality, 75 Cal. L. Rev. 1279 (1987).

ebration of gender difference. Her main point, however, is that gender differences of any sort should not be used to justify inequality. The emphasis should be on "eliminating the unequal consequences of sex differences,"[56] paying close attention not to formal constructs but to the "lived-out experience of all members of the community."[57] Littleton's "acceptance" model posits an ideal in which "gender differences, perceived or actual, [are] costless relative to each other, so that anyone may follow a male, female, or androgynous lifestyle according to their natural inclination or choice without being punished for following a female lifestyle or rewarded for following a male one."[58] This aspect of her model shows the influence of dominance feminism with its focus on power and on women's experience of subordination, and its concern that gender difference can easily translate into gender disadvantage. Finally, Littleton's proposal retains equality as a central concept and envisions men and women together engaging in a "sexually integrated debate about a more appropriate value system."[59] Despite her trenchant critique of male norms, Littleton still seems to embrace a liberal vision of individuals freed from gender role constraints and does not lose sight of the common desires of men and women, even in such areas as procreation where difference seems most prominent.

F.   FEMINISM AND CRITICAL LEGAL STUDIES

The intellectual roots of dominance feminist and cultural feminist legal theory came principally from discourses outside the law. In search of frameworks to critique the deep structures and ideology of law, feminists legal scholars in the 1980s drew heavily upon fields such as women's studies, women's history, social history, and feminist scholarship in sociology, anthropology, psychology, and literary criticism. Another major influence on many feminist scholars in the difference stage was Critical Legal Studies (CLS), a left-wing school of thought

---

[56] *Id.* at 1296.
[57] *Id.* at 1297.
[58] *Id.*
[59] *Id.* at 1303.

F. Feminism and Critical Legal Studies

that gained momentum within the legal academy in the early 1980s. During this period, groups of academic women calling themselves "fem-crits" formed to produce work that incorporated, yet contested, many of the central features of Critical Legal Studies. It is hard to classify much of the feminist critical scholarship of the mid- to late 1980s. The body of work does not fit comfortably within either dominance or cultural feminism, even though an individual scholar, such as Carrie Menkel-Meadow, may be identified both as a fem-crit and a cultural feminist. In retrospect, it is easier to see the feminist critical scholarship as a bridge to the 1990s, as the precursor of the postmodern and anti-essentialist scholarship of the Diversity Stage.

One hallmark of Critical Legal Studies was its forceful critique of liberalism. For CLS scholars, liberalism's emphasis on individual autonomy and the separation of law and politics was a major impediment to radical social change. Many of the members of the CLS school were white male law professors who shared a radical political outlook developed through their involvement in the anti-Vietnam War student movement. They were highly critical of the status quo and tended to see law as a means through which powerful elements in society legitimated their control. Their rich and eclectic body of work changed and developed during the 1980s, influenced by such diverse philosophical strains as legal realism, Marxism, post-structuralism, and deconstructionism.

From the start, feminists played a role in the development of CLS. By the mid-1980s, however, feminists within CLS began to criticize the movement for marginalizing the concerns of women and for embracing hierarchical procedures and masculine styles of discourse that tended to exclude or silence many women. In a move reminiscent of the split by women's liberationists from male-dominated radical organizations in the late 1960s, the fem-crits began holding their own seminars and exchanging papers.[60] This produced a feminist "take" on many of the jurisprudential debates that interested CLS scholars.

CLS scholarship is noted for its belief in the indeterminacy of legal rules and the internally contradictory nature of legal rights. In a highly simplified form, the indeterminacy claim is that legal rules are too specific to yield definite answers in the law, given that the next

---

[60] Carrie Menkel-Meadow, Feminist Legal Theory, Critical Legal Studies, and Legal Education or "The Fem-Crits Go to Law School," 38 J. Legal Educ. 61 (1988).

case is always distinguishable. On the other hand, legal standards and principles are notoriously general and leave ample room for a variety of conflicting interpretations. Students early in their study of law often notice the manipulable quality of legal rules. CLS scholars, however, typically go beyond the observation that the law is uncertain and regard the indeterminacy of legal principles as built into our structure of legal reasoning. Most importantly, once the indeterminacy of rules is acknowledged, it is easier to unmask the political quality of legal decision making. In the CLS analysis, the law's rhetoric of objectivity and neutrality is deceptive, because it hides political and cultural conflict. In this view, policy considerations do not merely enter into legal decisions that are otherwise governed by legal rules, principles and precedent. The legal reasoning process itself is laden with political judgment.

Despite their left-leaning political views, CLS scholars have often been highly skeptical of the value of legal rights. CLS adherents have argued that, rather than serving as a tool for liberation and equality, "rights analysis" has the opposite effect, that of reinforcing the status quo. They see the penchant for abstract discussion of rights as a substitute for concrete political action, serving to keep victimized groups passive and dependent on the state for protection. In the United States, moreover, rights have taken on a highly individualistic quality. Rights are conceived of as something that individuals possess, in much the same way they possess tangible property. Courts rarely recognize rights of social groups or communities. In the CLS critique, the individualistic nature of rights exacerbates their indeterminate quality; one individual's right can often just as easily be viewed as the violation of another individual's right.

Frances Olsen's work on the topic of statutory rape[61] is a good example of the CLS skepticism of legal rights, combined with a dominance feminist perspective on sexuality. The centerpiece of her critique is the 1981 Supreme Court case of *Michael M v. Superior Court of Sonoma County,*[62] upholding the constitutionality of California's gender-specific statutory rape law. The law made it a crime for a male to have sexual intercourse with a woman under the age of 18. Under this specific statute, only the male was punished. His underage female partner escaped prosecution. Moreover, the law did not prescribe the

[61] Frances Olsen, Statutory Rape: A Feminist Critique of Rights Analysis, 63 Tex. L. Rev. 387 (1984).
[62] 450 U.S. 464 (1981).

same harsh penalties for an older woman who had sex with an under-age male.

The Supreme Court upheld the law on the ground that men and women were not similarly situated in this context, and thus, identical treatment was not warranted. The plurality and the concurring Justices accepted the rationale that the gender-based law was a legitimate way to deter teenage pregnancy. They reasoned that the underage girls did not need the deterrence of the criminal law to refrain from intercourse because the threat of pregnancy was deterrence enough. They deemed it appropriate to subject males to criminal prosecution for this type of consensual intercourse, however, because it served to "equalize" the deterrence borne by each sex. Even the dissenting Justices focused on the deterrent value of the law, despite the fact that there are few prosecutions for statutory rape compared to the vast number of teenage pregnancies. The dissenters reasoned, however, that the law should also punish the underage girl, thereby doubling the incentive for the couple to refrain from engaging in sex.

Most feminist commentators disliked the result of *Michael M* and tended to agree with the dissenters that men and women should be treated equally, even if that imposed a hardship on some young women. Echoing liberal feminist objections to "special treatment," they worried that exempting women from statutory rape penalties would perpetuate the stereotype of young women as passive victims in sexual matters who lacked the capacity to consent. In the aftermath of the Supreme Court "loss," few feminist writers used a dominance feminist framework to support the result in *Michael M*, even though there was a forceful argument to be made that the social conditions under which many young women were pressured into having sex were exploitive. Under such analysis, statutory rape laws might be viewed as compensating for the inadequacy of forcible rape laws, where prosecutors generally refuse to proceed unless there is evidence of substantial physical force by the defendant and active resistance by the victim.

Olsen disagreed with both the plurality and the dissent in *Michael M* and argued that even the feminist commentary failed to articulate the full dimension of the political issues surrounding statutory rape. In Olsen's analysis, starting from the proposition that "women's rights ought to be respected" got women nowhere. Like so many important issues involving sexuality, the California law posed a dilemma for feminists: At the same time it reinforced debilitating stereotypes of women as victims, it provided a measure of concrete protection against sexual exploitation. Moreover, because the law essentially made women (but not men) under the age of 18 "taboo" for sexual intercourse, it restricted their sexual freedom, while allowing men of the same age to "experiment" with older women without being subject to criminal prosecution. Thus, a young woman's right to be free from sexual exploitation was purchased at the expense of her rights to sexual freedom and to be treated as an individual free from the negative effects of stereotypes. The dissenters' solution of punishing underage women was unlikely either to decrease their exploitation or increase their freedom.

Olsen argued that rights analysis offered feminists no definitive way to "solve" the rights conflict. She believed that the Supreme Court and most feminist commentators had been hindered by rights discourse from directly confronting the difficult question of which strategy was best to pursue. Instead of arguing for one superior solution, Olsen constructed a list of the various advantages and disadvantages associated with different versions of statutory rape laws. For example, a more desirable gender-neutral system, which many states had already adopted, was to decriminalize sex between teenagers but to outlaw sex between older persons and teenagers of both sexes. This alternative protected women from exploitive sex with older men, gave them the same freedom to have sex with their peers as young men had, and linked capacity to age rather than gender. A law so drafted, however, provided no protection to girls who were sexually exploited by boys closer to their age.

In examining the various proposals, Olsen identified her ultimate objective as empowering women. Closely aligned with MacKinnon's anti-subordination theory, Olsen asked whether, on balance, a specific proposal would empower women, not whether it would invade a particular right. Olsen suggested a novel approach to enforcement of statutory rape laws, giving the underage woman control over the decision whether to prosecute. Under this approach, a woman who regarded the sexual encounter as exploitive could press charges. The woman might, however, characterize the sex as consensual and have no desire to prosecute. In Olsen's view, giving individual women this option was a way of simultaneously protecting against exploitation and safeguarding sexual freedom. The suggestion also cleverly demonstrated the nonfeminist character of current laws, because it is highly unlikely that Olsen's vision of a gender-specific law that made criminal prosecutions turn on the decisions of young women would ever be enacted. Olsen nevertheless wanted feminists to imagine an approach that addressed both the harm of social control of women's sexuality and the sexual victimization of women.

Despite Olsen's doubts about the value of abstract rights discourse for legal analysis, she was not willing to give up on rights completely. For Olsen, claiming rights has a positive emotional dimension for women because it enables individuals to assert their self-worth and their sense of entitlement. Particularly since women have traditionally been denied rights to individual autonomy in the family because of power exercised by fathers and husbands, they have something to gain from insisting on individual rights. Indeed, the unwillingness to abandon "rights-talk" is often cited as a salient difference between critical feminist and white male CLS scholarship. Some feminists, for example Patricia Williams, stress the symbolic value of rights for disempowered people. Williams has argued that, for black people, the conferring of rights signals "a respect . . . that elevates one's status from human body to social being."[63] Even when black people knew that their rights would not protect them from injustice, Williams claims, they nevertheless "believed in them so much and so hard that we gave them life where there was none before."[64]

Feminists have also argued that the assertion of rights can sometimes be politically energizing and illuminating. In an article describing her experiences as a lawyer representing women charged with homicide, Elizabeth Schneider discussed what she calls the "dialectic of rights and politics."[65] Schneider's clients were women who had been attacked by men under circumstances that made them fear for their lives. The cases posed difficult legal issues, however, because judges often viewed the woman's behavior as not satisfying the traditional elements of self-defense, particularly the requirement that the danger must be "imminent" and that the defender use no more than "equal force" to repel the attack.

The feminist legal team charged with defending the women had to come up with arguments to interpret the legal requirements in a way that responded to women's actual experience. They argued, for

[63] Patricia J. Williams, *The Alchemy of Race and Rights: Diary of a Law Professor* 153 (1990).

[64] *Id.* at 163.

[65] Elizabeth M. Schneider, The Dialectic of Rights and Politics: Perspectives from the Women's Movement, 61 N.Y.U. L. Rev. 589 (1986).

example, that even though a man might not threaten a woman with a weapon, given their relative strength and size, the woman might reasonably believe that her only hope of stopping the attack was to shoot the man. Feminist litigators urged a more contextual approach to self-defense, arguing that the concept of "equal force" should not be applied mechanically only to authorize the use of guns versus guns. Over time, the legal team developed theories about the different circumstances under which women and men killed, and described the built-in sex bias in the law of self-defense. Schneider explains that somewhere in the "middle" of the process, the team developed the argument for women's "equal right to trial" as a way of urging judges and juries to assess the reasonableness of their client's response from a woman's perspective. In Schneider's account of this process of rights formulation, the content of the right is not predetermined, but derives from the political strategizing of feminist litigators through interaction with their clients. The articulation of the right, Schneider claims, also advanced the political analysis to a deeper level, as lawyers began to discuss the myriad ways implicit male bias hindered women from defending themselves in the courtroom. In Schneider's dialectic of legal rights and politics, practice generates theory, which is then applied (and changed) in practice. Her more sanguine view of legal rights appreciates the CLS concern for the limitations of rights-based strategy, but insists that "[r]ights can be what we make of them and how we use them."[66]

By the 1990s, the debates over the usefulness of rights-based discourse subsided as scholars began to turn their attention to questions of personal identity and the diversity of viewpoints within minority groups. Critical scholars, however, continued to scrutinize the process of legal categorization, especially the ways in which legal categories tended to hide the clash of political interests. CLS insights also persuaded many feminists that the law was infinitely malleable and always marked by contradiction. The experience of the previous two decades had made it clear to feminists that even progressive legal reform could have unanticipated negative consequences, and that feminists could not control what meanings would attach to legal categories. Despite these complexities, however, legal feminists generally remained committed to using the law as one imperfect strategy for achieving social change.

[66] *Id.* at 652.

G. COMBINING THEORY AND PRACTICE: GENDER BIAS IN THE COURTS

In contrast to the more practical feminist scholarship of the Equality Stage, much feminist legal writing of the 1980s was theoretical in nature, often more preoccupied with uncovering gender differences and patterns of domination than with offering solutions to specific types of discrimination. Feminist legal theory emerged from the 1980s as an intellectual enterprise with its own specialized vocabulary and canon of writings, which at times could seem quite far removed from the practice of law and the daily life of legal institutions. However, at the same time the academic aspects of the field were growing in prominence, there was also a move to put the new theories to use close to home. As the wave of women who had entered law school in the early to mid-1970s became attorneys, they joined women's bar associations and committees on women's concerns within local and state bar associations, and began to express discontent with what they regarded as sexism in the practice of law. The type of practices complained about often consisted of day-to-day minimization and ridicule that undermined women's efforts to be taken seriously within the law: A common example was the practice of referring to female attorneys and clients by their first names, while addressing men by their last names. Starting in 1982, when the New Jersey Supreme Court commissioned the creation of the first gender bias task force, legal feminists became involved in a movement to document, analyze, and remedy institutional bias within the court system. By the end of the decade, more than 30 states had established similar task forces, some focusing on issues of race and ethnicity in addition to gender. In the 1990s, the movement spread to the federal courts.

The gender bias task forces were similar to the commissions on the status of women and similar advisory committees which, beginning in the early 1960s, had been used by state and federal governments to conduct empirical research, determine the existence and extent of discrimination against women in specific contexts, and make recommendations for change. The task forces on gender bias in the courts were unusual, however, because it was the judicial branch of government which sponsored the initiatives and the focus was internal—on bias within the court system itself, where the "perpetrators" were likely to be judges, lawyers, and other actors in legal institutions. Even before such groups issued their final reports and made recommendations, the very establishment of a task force was often viewed as a victory for feminists because it implicitly acknowledged that gender was important enough to merit serious study, and because the supreme court of the state legitimated the enterprise.

The final reports of the task forces show the influence of the various schools of feminist legal thought most prominent in the 1980s. For example, liberal feminist concerns were apparent in the attention given by the task forces to the demographics of the legal profession. Many of the reports documented the underrepresentation of women in the most elite sectors of the profession, highlighting the low percentage of female judges and female partners in large private firms, as well as noting the overrepresentation of women in lower-prestige positions, such as secretaries and clerical court personnel. The theme of many of the state reports, as well as parallel initiatives by the American Bar Association's Commission on Women in the Profession,[67] was that it was naïve to expect that eventually, the near-equal numbers of men and women enrolled in law schools would effortlessly bring about a thorough integration of the profession. Rather, the slow rate of progress suggested that equal access was still an issue of importance for women and that there was a need to identify the barriers that created a glass ceiling for women in legal institutions.

The influence of dominance feminism could be seen in the agenda of the task forces, which often placed a high priority on studying how the court system responded to issues of violence against women. Perhaps the topic subjected to the most sustained analysis was the system's treatment of victims of domestic violence. The final reports painted a picture of judicial insensitivity to women who had been battered by their partners, offering examples of judges blaming women for "provoking" violence against them and displaying irritation at having to spend valuable court time attempting to get to the bottom of family disputes. Citing firsthand experiences of domestic violence victims and their attorneys, the reports conveyed a sense of the difficulty of converting what had long been regarded as a "private" matter into a public trial. The reports stressed that it was not enough

---

[67] The first chair of the ABA Commission was Hillary Rodham Clinton. During her tenure, the commission issued a report in 1988 expressing concern that women lawyers were not advancing at the same rate as their male counterparts.

to rely on formal legal prohibitions against assault and battery or to issue protective orders without also addressing the informal attitudes of everyone in the system, from the judge who ruled on the case to employees in the clerk's office who gave victims information about the process. Often it was the "male" atmosphere of the courtroom itself that proved most intimidating to women, who were required to testify against their spouses and somehow to render their experience of subordination as wives and mothers comprehensible to lawyers and judges who might know little about the dynamics of domestic violence. In an effort to humanize the judicial process, several task forces recommended that courts permit advocates for victims of domestic violence to attend legal proceedings so that they could provide support and act as translators between clients and members of the legal profession. Other structural changes, such as facilitating the process for *pro se* filing by victims of domestic abuse, were often suggested as ways to provide meaningful access to legal remedies for women who could not afford a lawyer or could not easily locate a lawyer willing to take their case.

The imprint of dominance feminism on the task forces' agenda was also evident in their focus on sexual harassment inside and outside the courthouse. After hearing testimony at public hearings about harassment of judicial clerks by judges, harassment of clients by lawyers, and even harassment of female attorneys by clerks of court, several task forces recommended that every institution—law firms, courts, attorneys general offices—should have a policy against sexual harassment and provide a mechanism for filing complaints. In many instances, task forces struggled to devise new procedures that would augment traditional systems for internal policing of the profession, such as judicial and professional disciplinary boards, which had done little to check the prevalence of sexual harassment within their jurisdictions.

Finally, the tracks of cultural feminism were visible in the reports' portrayal of the different "worlds" inhabited by male and female lawyers, male and female judges, male and female litigants, and even male and female witnesses. Gender bias task forces typically conducted surveys, interviews, and focus groups of attorneys, judges, and other actors in the legal system, seeking their views on the quality of daily "interactions" within the court system and eliciting narratives about their experiences of discrimination and bias. To a striking degree, the surveys found that women noticed and were affected by gender bias far more often than men. Women attorneys admitted that because of their sex, they were less likely to obtain favorable results for their clients, and that opposing counsel often treated them with derision and condescension. Women judges reported that their competence was frequently called into question by litigants and lawyers and that they did not receive the respect accorded to male judges. Survey respondents often expressed the view that the interests of women litigants were devalued, particularly in gender-laden sectors of the law such as family law. Finally, there were reports that female witnesses, particularly expert witnesses, suffered from a presumed lack of credibility that often made their opinions and testimony carry less weight than male witnesses. Cumulatively, the survey results generated a picture of legal institutions saturated by gender difference, in the sense that being part of the legal system seemed to have a different meaning for women than for men. The reports made it clear that merely counting the number of women present in the courtroom, in judge's chambers, or in the conference room, while important, missed an important qualitative dimension of gender bias that could only be addressed through changes in the informal legal culture.

When it came to making recommendations, members of the gender bias task forces faced a dilemma that characterizes many feminist undertakings connected to the law. Although their reports often documented widespread and systemic bias in institutions charged with dispensing justice, the task forces were not inclined to issue wholesale indictments of the legal system or call for systemic changes. Most task force members were "insiders" and pragmatists who felt more comfortable advocating incremental changes and trying to enlist support among more mainstream elements in the legal profession. The most sweeping reform frequently recommended was to change the ethical rules of the state bar to add an express prohibition barring lawyers and judges from engaging in sex discrimination in the practice of law. This addition was significant because it filled a gap in antidiscrimination law, which generally protected only employees from discrimination by their employers but did not cover important professional relationships such as attorney-client, judge-lawyer, or lawyer-witness. The changes in the ethical rules also signaled that sex discrimination was on a par with misappropriation of funds, incompetent representation, and other practices that deprived clients and colleagues of the right to be treated fairly by the legal system.

G. Combining Theory and Practice: Gender Bias in the Courts

Judith Resnik, one of the most active law professors in the movement to counter gender bias in the courts, has recently given a mixed
review of the accomplishments of the task forces to date. On the one
hand, she praised the movement for succeeding in moving feminist
complaints about gender bias in the legal system "from allegation to
fact,"[68] and noted concrete progress "measured in terms of appoint-
ments to the bench, integration of court-appointed committees, programs to educate judges and lawyers about their discriminatory
patterns, rule changes, and the like."[69] Perhaps not surprisingly, however, she doubts that the reports will produce fundamental changes in
the legal culture or major structural reform of legal institutions. Not
unlike a familiar pattern found in feminist legal scholarship, the critiques provided by the task forces are often more powerful than the
recommendations for change. In retrospect, the activism represented
by the gender bias task forces was contained by a conservative political
climate in the larger culture which offered little prospect for more
widespread change.

---

[68] Judith Resnik, Asking about Gender in Courts, 21 Signs: J. Women in Culture
& Soc'y 952, 963 (1996).
   [69] Judith Resnik, Ambivalence: The Resiliency of Legal Culture in the United
States, 45 Stan. L. Rev. 1525, 1533 (1993).

CHAPTER 5

The Diversity Stage (1990s)

In the 1990s, diversity among women has been the theme that has most captivated feminist legal scholarship. Prior to this decade, feminist writers tended to be preoccupied with making comparisons between men and women. Even those who vehemently criticized implicit male norms in law and social institutions ultimately were engaged in a comparative analysis, that is, showing how women's lives and needs differed from men's and providing the justification for more inclusive standards. Not surprisingly, this structure of analysis often led scholars, particularly in the 1980s, to overplay the differences between men and women and to underplay the differences among women. Much feminist scholarship in the 1990s has tried to correct for these overgeneralizations about women and to highlight the social and theoretical importance of differences among women, most prominently those differences associated with race, ethnicity, sexual orientation, and social class.

The major political impetus behind the diversification of feminist legal theory came from critiques and divisions within the feminist movement. In women's centers, rape crisis programs, conferences on women's studies, and other sites of feminist politics, women of color argued that the movement was dominated by white women who built their organization's agenda around issues of importance to women like themselves. Thus abortion rights, rather than involuntary sterilization of minority women, tended to be high on the feminist agenda. Feminist organizations tended to be predominately white and to create networks among white women. The pressure put on universities to hire scholars to teach feminist subjects, for example, most often resulted in the hiring of white women. In the 1980s, black feminist scholars organized to challenge not only the white male establishment but the new feminist establishment as well. Their voices opened the way for others dissatisfied with the direction of feminist politics to make their complaints public and to theorize about why feminism had fallen short of its aspiration to connect to the lives of all women. In particular, lesbian feminists who had always been very active in the women's liberation movement and in women's studies insisted that feminist organizations change and take up issues like the legal status of domestic partnerships, artificial insemination for unmarried women, and other issues of greater concern to lesbians than to heterosexual women.

From the outside, it appeared that the feminist movement was breaking apart at the seams and that it was no longer accurate to speak of a single women's movement that could command the allegiance of all left-wing or progressive women. Emblematic of the state of feminist politics, in 1990, the National Women's Studies Association annual meeting dissolved in chaos, splintering into several different caucuses (women of color, lesbians, Jewish women, etc.). Many groups staged walkouts to protest the failure of the organization's leadership to diversify its hiring and programming. Some of the rage that had been directed at male-dominated institutions was now directed inward. The political struggle within the diffuse feminist movement formed the background against which the Diversity Stage of feminist legal theory grew.

A.   CRITIQUES OF GENDER ESSENTIALISM

In broad terms, the cognitive problem diversity critics have addressed is known as "gender essentialism." The term "essentialism" refers to the idea that there is some common, underlying attribute or experience shared by all women, independent of race, class, sexual orientation, or other aspects of their particular situation. Although contemporary feminist legal theorists now rarely discuss the plight of "Woman" in the singular, writers still find it exceedingly difficult to describe and analyze gender subordination without succumbing to the

A. Critiques of Gender Essentialism

essentialist error of overgeneralizing from the situation of only some groups of women.

Katharine Bartlett has theorized that more than one cognitive problem may come under the heading of essentialism and has untangled various strands of gender essentialism.[1] She describes one form of gender essentialism as false universalism, whereby the use of the unstated norm of the most privileged group of women—namely, white, middle-class, heterosexual women—has the effect of eclipsing nonprivileged groups of women, much in the same way mainstream discourse has used implicit male norms to discount women's perspectives. A second form of gender essentialism, which Bartlett calls "gender imperialism"[2] or "gender primacy" makes the mistake of according too much weight to gender oppression, minimizing the impact of oppression based on race, class, or sexual orientation. This brand of essentialism tends to exaggerate the importance of gender and has been called "reductionist," highlighting the tendency to reduce everything to gender. Scholars who are committed to including the perspective of multiple groups of women, particularly those of less privileged women, and who do not regard any one form of oppression as necessarily more important or invidious than any other, describe their approach as "anti-essentialist" or "post-essentialist."

Feminist legal diversity scholarship had its roots in the 1980s, when black feminist scholars first charged that feminist theory was exclusionary.[3] They explained that the exclusion of black women was accomplished, for the most part, not by conscious design, but by habits of thought and unconscious practices that perpetuated white dominance within feminism and marginalized women of color. Feminists, like the male theorists they had criticized, often spoke in universal terms ("women believe," "women are victimized by"), when their descriptions applied to white women only.

---

[1] *See* Katharine T. Bartlett, Gender Law, 1 Duke J. of Gender L. & Pol'y 1 (1994); Katharine T. Bartlett & Angela P. Harris, *Gender and Law: Theory, Doctrine, Commentary* 1007-9 (2d ed. 1998) (discussing seven connotations or meanings of the term "essentialism").

[2] Katharine Bartlett, Gender Law at 16.

[3] Some early influential nonlegal texts were: *All the Women are White, All the Blacks are Men, But Some of Us Are Brave* (Gloria T. Hull et al., eds. 1982); Paula Giddens, *When and Where I Enter: The Impact of Black Women on Race and Sex in America* (1984); bell hooks, *Ain't I a Woman: Black Women and Feminism* (1981); Audre Lorde, *Sister Outsider* (1984).

A prominent example of such "false universality" is the standard feminist analysis of separate spheres ideology. In an early Diversity Stage article,[4] legal theorist Kimberlé Crenshaw noted that feminists often failed to realize that feminine traits of passivity, dependence, and fragility were culturally associated with white women only. In contrast, black women were stereotyped as being too domineering, rather than too weak. Separate spheres thinking thus offered "little insight into the domination of *Black* women."[5] This meant that when liberal feminist theorists identified separate spheres ideology as the theoretical basis for the subordination of women, they implicitly excluded black women from their definition of women. Using feminist insights to criticize feminist theory, black feminist scholars called for a reexamination of the assumptions about women's behavior, experiences, interests, and desires to see if those assumptions were partial and biased toward the experience of only some subgroups of women.

Another exclusionary technique present in feminist as well as mainstream legal discourse is the use of dichotomous, mutually exclusive categories. Diversity theorists explained how dichotomous thinking led to the invisibility of some groups of women. For example, the shorthand term most commonly used to describe subordinated groups in the United States, for example, has been "women and minorities." On a superficial level, there may seem nothing objectionable about the phrase, provided it is understood that minority women occupy both categories. However, Diversity Stage critics argued that the phrase masked a subtle exclusion or erasure of minority women, because the reader tends to assume the unmodified term "women" means "white women," and the term "minorities" means "black men." The impulse toward mutually exclusive categorical thinking, moreover, often forces minority women to articulate their experiences in either/or terms, that is, connected either to their race or to their sex. In an early Diversity Stage article, Regina Austin posed this question to women of color:

> When was the last time someone asked you to choose between being a woman and being a minority person or asked you to assess the hard-

---

[4] Kimberlé Crenshaw, Demarginalizing the Intersection of Race and Sex: A Black Feminist Critique of Antidiscrimination Doctrine, Feminist Theory and Antiracist Politics, 1989 U of Chi. Legal Forum 139.

[5] *Id.* at 155.

A. Critiques of Gender Essentialism

ships and the struggles of your life in terms of your being a woman on top of being black (or whatever color you are) or a black on top of being a woman, as if being a woman or being black were like icing on a cake? As if you and your kind were not an integrated, undifferentiated, complete whole with a consciousness and politics of your own. As if you should be content with being a foot soldier in someone else's army of liberation.[6]

Many women of color maintain that it is impossible to separate the racial and gender aspects of their identity, preferring to describe their sense of self as a "both/and" self. When they are required to split their identity, they are unable to capture the full extent and meaning of their group's experiences.

In her book, *Inessential Woman*,[7] philosopher Elizabeth Spelman explained that these exclusionary techniques were not simply linguistic conventions, but deep-seated habits of thought directing our attention to the most privileged subgroups within subordinated groups. This implicit focus on white women and black men often had the effect of diverting attention away from the distinctive situation of minority women and lead to the mistaken assumption that forms of discrimination facing minority women were additive, that is, simply a combination of the discrimination facing white women and minority men. Transporting Spelman's analysis into legal theory, Kimberlé Crenshaw maintained that racism and sexism intersected in complex ways to affect the lives of women of color, and challenged theorists to place black women at the center of their analyses. She argued for a multiple approach that recognized that

Black women can experience discrimination in ways that are both similar to and different from those experienced by white women and Black men. Black women sometimes experience discrimination in ways similar to white women's experiences; sometimes they share very similar experiences with Black men. Yet often they experience double-discrimination—the combined effects of practices which discriminate on the basis of race, and on the basis of sex. And sometimes, they expe-

---

[6] Regina Austin, Sapphire Bound, 1989 Wis. L. Rev. 539, 540.

[7] Elizabeth V. Spelman, *Inessential Woman: Problems of Exclusion in Feminist Thought* (1988).

rience discrimination as Black women—not the sum of race and sex discrimination, but as Black women.[8]

Crenshaw's theoretical critique had practical implications for anti-discrimination law. Litigation under both the Equal Protection Clause and Title VII has tended to proceed as if sex discrimination and race discrimination were mutually exclusive categories. The result is that women of color are often forced to choose whether to assert a sex discrimination claim *or* a race discrimination claim, with the risk of obscuring important facts that do not fit the chosen framework. Thus, although many of the plaintiffs in the most important sexual harassment and sex discrimination cases were African-American, the racially specific nature of these cases has largely been lost. The problem of imposing a single axis framework onto anti-discrimination litigation has also been exacerbated by recent statutory amendments which treat race and sex discrimination differently by allowing full recovery of damages for victims of race discrimination, but capping recovery for sex discrimination claimants. To correct the anomalies arising from mutually exclusive categories, Crenshaw proposed a theory of "intersectionality," which would explicitly recognize the distinctive harm sometimes experienced by women of color and acknowledge the interlocking nature of the two systems of oppression. Without such emphasis on the intersection between race and gender, the law would fail to appreciate that, for women of color, "experiences of racism are shaped by . . . gender and . . . experiences of sexism are often shaped by . . . race."[9]

During the Diversity Stage, black feminist scholars dissected the work of feminist writers from various camps to pinpoint how their theories took inadequate account of the factor of race and subtly placed white women at the forefront of the discussion. Angela Harris's 1990 critique[10] of gender essentialism in the theories of Catharine MacKinnon and Robin West marked an important juncture in the evolution of feminist legal theory. She charged that MacKinnon's dominance theory literally relegated black women to the footnotes of the

---

[8] Crenshaw, supra note 4, at 149.

[9] Kimberlé Crenshaw, Race, Gender, and Sexual Harassment, 65 S. Cal. L. Rev. 1467, 1468 (1992).

[10] Angela P. Harris, Race and Essentialism in Feminist Legal Theory, 42 Stan. L. Rev. 581 (1990).

A. Critiques of Gender Essentialism

text and erroneously assumed that black women's experience was simply a more intense version of white women's experience. She reads MacKinnon as suggesting that "[i]f things are bad for everybody (meaning white women), then they're even worse for black women."[11] In one section, Harris criticized MacKinnon for underestimating the importance of racism in her analysis of rape and thus mistakenly assuming that black women's experience of rape was comparable to white women's. In Harris's view, black women's experience of rape has been distinctive, "as deeply rooted in color as in gender."[12] For black feminist theoreticians, Harris argued, the paradigm of the rapist was the master or employer who took advantage of the economic vulnerability of his slave or domestic maid. She noted that black women have been stereotyped as naturally promiscuous and have been denied even the skimpy legal protection offered to some white women. Most importantly, because black men have been victimized by false charges of raping white women, Harris viewed rape laws as a form of terrorism of black men and a mechanism through which "white men maintained their control over the bodies of all black people."[13] According to Harris, MacKinnon's neglect of race distorts her account of rape and should be faulted for equating white experience to universal truth.

Harris's critique of Robin West's "connection thesis" focused on West's assumption that the material experiences of pregnancy, childbirth, intercourse, and breast-feeding were somehow the same for all women and paramount in creating a woman's identity. Harris regarded this theoretical position as a kind of gender imperialism because it assumed that these biological experiences were more significant in the lives of women than, for example, race-linked associations, such as relations with members of the extended family or others in the community. West could also be criticized for suggesting that motherhood had the same meaning for all groups of women, despite our society's vastly different treatment of mothers depending on their race, social and marital status, and sexual orientation.

At approximately the same time as Harris's critique, Patricia Cain published her post-essentialist critique of MacKinnon and West,[14] fo-

---

[11] *Id.* at 596.

[12] *Id.* at 598.

[13] *Id.* at 600.

[14] Patricia A. Cain, Feminist Jurisprudence: Grounding the Theories, 4 Berkeley Women's L.J. 191 (1989-90).

cusing on how these scholars had excluded lesbians in building their theory. The structure of Cain's analysis parallels Harris's: MacKinnon is criticized for equating lesbian experience to the experience of heterosexual women (false universalization), while West is charged with ignoring lesbian experience altogether (gender imperialism). Cain cites a passage from MacKinnon analyzing lesbian sexuality as "simply women having sex with women, not with men."[15] MacKinnon's point was that male domination infected even same-sex relationships and that the "definition of women as men's inferiors remains sexual, even if not heterosexual, whether men are present at the time or not."[16] For Cain, however, MacKinnon's insistence on seeing lesbian sexuality as just another kind of male-dominated encounter is essentialist and betrays a failure to listen closely to the accounts of lesbians who describe their relationships as co-equal and who claim to experience "significant periods of nonsubordination, during which we, as women, are free to develop a sense of self that is our own and not a mere construct of the patriarchy."[17]

Cain's critique of West's connection thesis centers on West's failure to consider intimate lesbian relationships as the kind of connection that might be central in constituting a woman's identity. Instead, West's primary connective experiences (notably intercourse, pregnancy, and breast-feeding) are built upon a heterosexual model and seem to limit nurturing to the mother/child relationship, ignoring the possibility of nurturing adult relationships among women. Cain's analysis uncovered the "heterosexist" structure of West's article. The term "heterosexism" is used to describe the "pervasive cultural presumption and prescription of heterosexual relationships"[18] that underlies much legal regulation and commentary. By not considering the possibility that for some women, lesbian intimacy might be central to their identity, West implicitly presumed that all women were heterosexual. In Cain's view, anti-essentialism requires opposition to both sexist and heterosexist cultural practices, so as not to exclude lesbians from any theoretical account of women's viewpoint.

---

[15] *Id.* at 202, *citing* Catharine MacKinnon, *Feminist Theory of State* 141-42 (1989).

[16] *Id.* at 203.

[17] *Id.* at 212.

[18] This definition is drawn from Sylvia A. Law, Homosexuality and the Social Meaning of Gender, 1988 Wis. L. Rev. 187, 195.

A. Critiques of Gender Essentialism

In the latter part of this decade, feminist scholars have looked beyond the borders of the United States and critiqued the essentialism that tends to set Western feminism as the standard for judging women's condition throughout the world. The problem is most acute when law in the United States intersects with laws and cultural practices associated with the Third World. For example, criminal courts in the United States have been asked to rule on whether a Chinese immigrant husband may assert a "cultural defense" to excuse the killing of his wife when he learned she was seeing another man.[19] The term "cultural defense" describes a strategy of defendants, usually recent immigrants to the United States, to ask for leniency based on their assertion that they acted in accordance with the dictates of their "culture."[20] In that case, the defendant produced expert testimony by an anthropologist who asserted that Chinese men are more dishonored by the adultery of their wives than is the average American husband, and would be more likely to react violently to the news of a betrayal. Influenced by this testimony, the trial judge found the defendant guilty of manslaughter (as opposed to murder) and sentenced him to probation.

In another case,[21] a female defendant charged with killing her son and then attempting suicide sought to admit evidence of her cultural background to explain her despair and cultural isolation. She was an immigrant from Macau who was unable to speak English or drive a car and was dominated and manipulated by an abusive husband. The appellate court ruled that the trial court should have admitted the testimony of a transcultural psychologist to put the defendant's actions in perspective and shed light on her state of mind, particularly to show how the defendant might have believed that she had no other choice but to kill herself and take her son with her.

Some commentators have criticized these decisions for permitting foreign cultural values to affect the standards in American trials, particularly if the application of such values seems to conflict with Western feminist ideals of gender equality. Post-essentialist scholars such as Leti Volpp, however, have cautioned against taking such an all-or-nothing position on the cultural defense.[22] Volpp argues that femi-

---

[19] *People v. Chen*, No. 87-7774 (N.Y. Sup. Ct. Dec. 2, 1988).

[20] Leti Volpp, (Mis)Identifying Culture: Asian Women and the "Cultural Defense," 17 Harv. Women's L.J. 57 (1994).

[21] *People v. Wu*, 286 Cal. Rptr. 868 (Ct. App. 1991).

[22] Volpp, supra note 20.

nism should not be pitted against multiculturalism, but should strive to understand women's oppression and their resistance to oppression within their own communities. Volpp approves of admitting evidence of cultural context when the information given to the judge and jury goes beyond stereotypes about the group and gives "insight into an individual's thoughts."[23] Her position is that the evidence of cultural context should "concretely address the individual defendant's location in her community, her location in the diaspora and her history."[24] For example, Volpp would have excluded the anthropologist's generalizations about Chinese men, but admitted evidence of the mother's cultural isolation in the second case.

The major challenge for feminists, according to Volpp, is to avoid the errors often made by essentialists, of regarding non-European cultures as hopelessly sexist and backward with regard to matters of women and gender and of treating feminism as if it were exclusively a Euro-American phenomenon. Volpp maintains that culture is contested even in purportedly traditional societies, and reminds us that Western culture is hardly free of sexism or male domination.[25] From this perspective, understanding the cultural context in which an action is taken is an important aspect of judging, whether the defendant is a recent Asian immigrant or a battered woman who has lived all her life in the same town in the midwest.

B. FEMINIST THEORIES OF MULTIPLE OPPRESSION AND MULTIPLE PERSPECTIVES

In addition to critiquing feminist theorists for excluding the voices and perspectives of nonprivileged women, anti-essentialist theorists in the early 1990s also sought to construct theories about multiple op-

---

[23] *Id.* at 100.

[24] *Id.* In this context, "diaspora" refers to the dispersion of a people away from their original homeland. Volpp believes that it is important to introduce testimony about the experience of people who migrate to the United States, rather than assuming that immigrant culture is the same as that of the country of origin. *Id.* at 89.

[25] Leti Volpp, Talking "Culture": Gender, Race, Nation, and the Politics of Multiculturalism, 96 Colum. L. Rev. 1573, 1592 (1996).

pression that went beyond a focus on gender or any other single factor. This led feminist writers to theorize about "difference" more generally and to deepen their critiques of objectivity and neutrality.

A highly influential theorist of this period is Martha Minow, who developed a relational approach to difference.[26] Minow coined the phrase "dilemma of difference" to describe a phenomenon well known to political activists. The difference dilemma emerges whenever neutral strategies, which ignore difference, and special treatment strategies, which explicitly acknowledge difference, both end up backfiring and reinforcing or recreating the stigma of being different. A familiar example is the treatment of pregnancy in the workplace: If the needs of pregnant workers are not recognized, they may suffer unemployment and/or loss of wages and promotions. But at the same time, affording special maternity leaves may marginalize women workers and cause resentment among co-workers. Rather than simply choosing the strategy which in the particular situation seems to have the least potential to backfire, Minow sought to construct an approach to the difference dilemma that would not end up blaming the victim.

The way out of the difference dilemma for Minow is to discard the conventional view of difference as some intrinsic or objective quality of certain groups, for example, the view that treats pregnant workers as in some natural sense "different" from ordinary workers. Instead, Minow argued for a relational view of difference that recognizes that individuals differ from one another in myriad ways. Minow contended that instead of being natural, difference is actively assigned to others by those with the power to have their perspective or version of events accepted as reality. Through her relational conception of difference, Minow sought to dislodge the oppressive meaning of difference as deviance from the norm by challenging the unstated reference point by which difference is defined. Minow's theory encouraged us to ask, for example: Why are pregnant workers treated as different (i.e., deviant), when so many women become pregnant some time during their working lives? From whom are they different, and why should the lives of those other workers be accepted as the standard?

---

[26] The fullest elaboration of Martha Minow's relational approach to difference can be found in Martha Minow, *Making All the Difference: Inclusion, Exclusion, and American Law* (1990).

The relational approach may be especially useful as a catalyst to developing innovative responses to difference less likely to stigmatize the person labeled as different. To illustrate this potential, Minow discussed a case of a hearing-impaired child whose parents fought a protracted legal battle to force the public school to provide a full-time sign language interpreter for the child in the "regular" classroom. The school was willing only to supplement the regular classes with some separate sign language education for the hearing-impaired child during part of the week. Minow criticized both proposals as failing to find a way around the difference dilemma. Her proposal would be to provide training in sign language for the entire class. Her point was that unless the whole class was taught to communicate in the language of the hearing-impaired child, the norm of the hearing world would remain in place and the deaf child would be stigmatized, either for performing poorly in the "mainstream" classroom or for needing special instruction. In Minow's bilingual classroom, the deaf child's impairment is also an ability. Inclusion is the goal, but it is an inclusion that changes institutional arrangements and takes the onus of difference off the deaf child.

In line with her belief in the social construction of difference, Minow was also one of the chief critics of objectivity who advocated a search for multiple perspectives, rather than an attempt to discover a unitary, universal truth. Minow started from the proposition that everyone sees the world from his or her own perspective, that in some sense, everyone is a biased observer. Rarely, however, do people acknowledge the partiality of their own perspective. Instead it is common, particularly with respect to legal actors, for the observer to regard his or her perceptions as objectively accurate and to ignore the perspectives of others. To counteract this tendency, Minow admonished us to try to understand the perspective of others in the context of their lives, to display a commitment to "the moral relevance of contingent particulars."[27] Minow would have us rethink the Golden Rule and replace the self as the reference point for judging the morality of others' actions. The goal should not be to treat others as you would have them treat you. Minow argued that instead, we should listen to the other person to discover how he or she wants to be treated and determine the justness of that request in the context of the other's

---

[27] *Id.* at 381.

B. Feminist Theories of Multiple Oppression and Multiple Perspectives

situation. In Minow's theory, the discovery of multiple truths, stemming from the multiple perspectives of the various actors, replaces the search for one objective truth.

Perhaps because the law is so deeply committed to discovering objective truth through the adversary process, it is extremely difficult to incorporate a commitment to multiple perspectives into existing legal doctrines. One area in which the influence of post-essentialist scholarship can be glimpsed, however, is in the debate over perspective currently occurring in sexual and racial harassment litigation under Title VII. An element of proof in cases known as "hostile environment" cases is a showing that the harassment suffered by the plaintiff is sufficiently "severe or pervasive" to justify a legal remedy. This requirement means that the plaintiff must convince the jury that her harassment was not isolated or trivial. Recently, several courts have recognized the importance of perspective in determining both what counts as offensive conduct and how much offensive conduct plaintiffs must endure before they are said to have a valid claim. In a few notable cases,[28] courts have cited feminist scholars for the proposition that the harm of discrimination ought to be judged from the perspective of those experiencing the harm. These jurisdictions have adopted the "reasonable woman" standard, an explicitly gendered perspective that focuses on the specific predicament of the female plaintiff.

This move to embrace the reasonable woman perspective is responsive to the feminist insight that men and women often employ different standards in judging the offensiveness of behavior and that women typically define sexual harassment more broadly than men. Barbara Gutek, a social scientist, has explained that the differing responses to sexual harassment by men and women reflects each group's self-interest: "[i]t is in men's self-interest to see relatively little sexual harassment because men are most often the offenders whereas it is in women's self-interest to see relatively more sexual harassment because women tend to be the victims in sexual harassment encounters."[29] Thus the "truth" of the situation may differ depending on the gender of the participant. This "two worlds" phenomenon accounts for the

---

[28] *See especially Ellison v. Brady*, 924 F.2d 872 (9th Cir. 1991), *discussed* infra at pp. 242-43.

[29] Barbara A. Gutek, Understanding Sexual Harassment at Work, 6 Notre Dame J. L. Ethics & Pub. Pol'y 335, 343 (1992).

common situation in which a male employee charged with sexual harassment asserts that he intended no harm and fails to understand why his target is so upset by his conduct. By adopting the reasonable woman standard and refusing to give definitive weight to the prevailing male definition of harm, the courts have edged closer to embracing multiple perspectives.

However, as many feminist writers have pointed out,[30] even the reasonable woman standard poses the risk of essentialism. The danger is that juries and courts might come to regard the viewpoint of the reasonable woman as having a fixed content and simply reconstruct stereotypes about women to fill in the gaps of their understanding of the facts of the case. The search for the viewpoint of the reasonable woman could readily translate into a futile search for a consensus viewpoint among women, with the danger that the values of the dominant members of the group—namely, white, affluent, heterosexual women—are construed as representative of the whole. Some critics have argued that as long as the legal standard includes the modifier reasonable, universalist notions of truth and objectivity will prevail and nondominant perspectives will be viewed as unreasonable. The burning question is whether approaches that accommodate different perspectives are compatible with the law which, of course, ultimately requires that one side be declared the winner and the other, the loser.

C.   POSTMODERN FEMINIST THEORIES

The themes of anti-essentialism and multiple perspectives are often regarded as a part of a larger intellectual trend known as *postmodernism*. In a variety of disciplines, postmodern analyses have not only questioned the existence of universal truth, but have developed a new understanding of the individual. In liberal theory, the individual (often referred to as the "self" or the "subject") is depicted as an autono-

---

[30] The advantages and disadvantages of the reasonable woman standard are discussed in Martha Chamallas, Feminist Constructions of Objectivity: Multiple Perspectives in Sexual and Racial Harassment Litigation, 1 Tex. J. of Women & Law 95 (1992).

C. Postmodern Feminist Theories

mous, rational, self-interested being who exercises free will and makes choices. In contrast, postmodern scholars emphasize that the self is not separate from social, cultural, and ideological forces. In particular, postmodern theorist Mary Jo Frug has stressed the importance of language, including legal discourse, in the construction of both individual identity and power in society.[31] In the postmodern account, cultural representations of women and men are as important as the specifics of legal doctrine.

Katharine Bartlett explains that

> [t]he postmodern view of the individual or the "legal subject" opposes the Enlightenment view of the stable, coherent, and rational self with a more complicated view of the individual as "constituted" from multiple institutional and ideological forces that, in various ways, overlap, intersect and even contradict each other. Although these forces join to produce a reality that the individual subject experiences as real or true, it is in fact a reality or truth that is "constructed."[32]

This postmodern view of the self accords with the view of Diversity Stage theorists, who often describe their sense of identity as multiple. Mari Matsuda, for example, writes about "multiple consciousness,"[33] the ability to approach the world simultaneously from several different vantage points. To explain multiple consciousness, Matsuda takes the example of a woman of color who is a first-year law student studying a case involving the legality of the arrest of a rape suspect. In the class, which is taught by a white male professor, the student adopts the standard legal discourse about Miranda rights and suppresses her racial consciousness. Consequently, she does not focus her attention on the race either of the defendant or of the victim, or look for signs of police brutality. She also knows not to talk about her personal experiences with rape and the fear of rape that she and many of her classmates experience as women. In a class taught by a white female professor, however, the student can articulate issues relating to her consciousness as a woman, such as the prevalence of violence against women. But she still suppresses her "anger at white privilege and her

---

[31] Mary Jo Frug, *Postmodern Legal Feminism* 126 (1992) ("legal discourse should be recognized as a site of political struggle over sex differences").

[32] Katharine T. Bartlett, Gender Law, 1 Duke J. of Gender L. & Pol'y 1, 14 (1994).

[33] Mari J. Matsuda, When the First Quail Calls: Multiple Consciousness as Jurisprudential Method, 11 Women's Rts. L. Rep. 7 (1992).

perception that the dominant white conception of violence excludes the daily violence of ghetto poverty."[34] Only in her support group with other women of color can she be free from the effort of having to shift consciousness to fit the situation, and be reassured of the validity of her multiple views of the world.

Like Minow, Matsuda portrays the self in relational terms. In an important sense, one's awareness of one's self as a woman or as a member of a racial group depends on who else is present. As Angela Harris has observed, a person may be most conscious of her identity as a woman when she is in a male-dominated environment or most aware of her color when "thrown against a sharp white background."[35] This postmodern view of the self as multiple and relational also means that personal identity is not static, but rather is made up of fragments of experience that do not fit into a coherent whole.

One of the most widely read postmodern feminist legal scholars is Patricia Williams, whose eloquent essays address the issue of the fragility of personal identity. Williams's 1991 book, *The Alchemy of Race and Rights: Diary of a Law Professor*, employed personal narrative to examine a wide array of cultural issues and current events, including surrogacy, homelessness, law school politics and pedagogy, hate speech, and affirmative action. Williams's revelations about herself and her sense of identity are interwoven amidst her discussion of social issues. As an African-American female law professor and a commercial lawyer, Williams is often perceived by her students and colleagues as an "inherent contradiction," an "oxymoron." She connects these perceptions to contradictions she experiences internally.

Williams explored the instability of personal identity by reflecting on her own complex personal identity. The book tells about her great-great-grandmother Sophie, a slave who was purchased at age 11 and immediately impregnated by a white lawyer named Austin Miller. Williams wryly observes that it is not a simple matter to claim a child molester as part of one's heritage. The paradox for Williams lies in confronting the part of herself that is "the dispossessor" of another part of herself, an internal conflict that she feels most acutely when

---

[34] *Id.* at 8.

[35] Angela P. Harris, Race and Essentialism in Feminist Legal Theory, 42 Stan. L. Rev. 581, 610 (1990) *citing* Zora Neale Hurston, How It Feels to Be Colored Me, in *I Love Myself When I am Laughing . . . And Then Again When I am Looking Mean and Impressive* 152 (A. Walker, ed., 1979).

C. Postmodern Feminist Theories

she decides to become a lawyer. Just before she enters Harvard Law School, her mother tells her "in a voice full of secretive reassurance, 'The Millers were lawyers, so you have it in your blood.'"[36] Williams's conflicted response to this statement exemplifies the multiple consciousness of oppressed people who see themselves in the denigrating eyes of the dominant society even as they try to create a positive self-image.

Theorists of multiple oppression have had to grapple with the complexity that any one person may simultaneously be privileged and oppressed. White women, for example, derive privileges from their status as white people, but are vulnerable to oppression as women. Williams's writings take this complexity one step further to address the internal conflicts of multiracial persons who struggle against available categories. Williams's postmodern stance suggests she believes that these feelings of splintered identity and dislocation are not limited to particular groups. Through her nonlinear style and open-ended essays, Williams is successful at portraying race and gender as constantly changing social constructions with no fixed context.

Like Minow and Matsuda, Williams also conceives of personal identity in relational terms. Williams, however, concentrates on the danger such interdependency can create. She seeks to forge a new sense of responsibility for "the images of others that are reposited within us" and invents the term "spirit murder," to describe the damage done when we disregard those whose "lives qualitatively depend on our regard."[37] Williams is particularly angered by the resilience of racial stereotypes that systematically erase the accomplishments of people of color. She argues that the negative cultural meaning of blackness as the absence of humanity persists, even though the formal legal apparatus of segregation has been dismantled and antidiscrimination laws have been in place for several decades. Despite her scathing critique of contemporary American culture, however, Williams is not relentlessly pessimistic. As a thoroughly postmodern theorist, Williams regards the dominant culture as just as illusory as the distorted image the majority has constructed about minority life. The chimerical quality of culture means that there is nothing natural or inevitable about even the most firmly entrenched cultural beliefs and

---

[36] Patricia Williams, *The Alchemy of Race and Rights: Diary of a Law Professor,* 216 (1991).

[37] *Id.* at 73.

patterns. For Williams, while the perceptions of the dominant "operate as dictators of the truth, they are after all merely perceptions."[38]

D. BREAKING THE FALSE DICHOTOMY BETWEEN AGENCY AND VICTIMIZATION

The postmodern understanding of the complex nature of personal identity has recently led feminist theorists to revise their accounts of women's subordination and has provoked a new spate of critiques of Catharine MacKinnon's dominance theory. By the 1990s, dominance feminism, particularly its assertion about the prevalence of sexual violence, found acceptance in the popular culture and mass media. However, in its popular form—such as the endless "women in jeopardy" TV dramas—the feminist critique of the structures of male domination was omitted, leaving only a portrayal of women as victims. Helpless, terrified, with no capacity to act in the face of male power, the female subjects in such portrayals typically lack what theorists call "agency." Related to the concept of autonomy in liberal theory, *agency* means the capacity to direct one's own life through individual action and choice. In the newly constructed popular stereotypes, female victims of rape, harassment, and domestic violence are depicted as totally consumed by male domination, the antithesis of autonomous human beings.

For the most part, feminist theorists did not believe that these portrayals were faithful to women's experience of sexual violence. However, in the 1990s, scholars such as Kathryn Abrams, Elizabeth Schneider, and Martha Mahoney began to take the fixation with victimization seriously and to assess the negative impact such cultural images had on both the feminist movement and feminist attempts to use the legal system on behalf of women. By concentrating on women's agency, they hoped to provide a more realistic, dignified account of women's resistance to male domination, without minimizing the harm done by oppression.

[38] Patricia Williams, A Brief Comment with Footnotes, on the Civil Rights Chronicles, Harv. Blackletter J. Spring 1986 at 79, 81 n.3.

D. Breaking the False Dichotomy Between Agency and Victimization

Abrams views the overemphasis on victimization as yet another example of the propensity toward reductive classification and dichotomous thinking. Similar to the insistence that persons be classified on a single dimension of race or gender, Abrams identified the tendency "to dichotomize the agency of perpetrators and victims . . . [whereby] the perpetrator enjoys full agency, and the victim either lacks as a categorical matter, or loses through the experience of discrimination, virtually all capacity for self-direction."[39] There are at least two dangers associated with reducing women to victims. First, the portrayal of the abject victim does not resonate in the experience of most women, even women who have suffered severe forms of sexual exploitation. In the face of battering, harassment, and abuse, women do not always respond passively, but employ a number of strategies to avoid, resist, and reduce their injuries. The stereotype of the passive victim is insulting to many women who have actively struggled to live under oppressive conditions. They may resist the label of victim, even if it means having no legal recourse for their suffering. Second, the flattened image of the victim of sexual abuse can exert such a powerful force that women who fail to conform to the image are seen as having suffered no real harm, as not being real victims. Feminist litigators are then faced with a dilemma: Present a distorted image of their clients as totally lacking in agency in the hope of winning a lawsuit, or risk losing by presenting a fuller picture of the way their clients actually responded to abuse.

Several scholars have criticized MacKinnon's dominance theory for contributing to the tendency to conceptualize victimization in simplistic terms. Mahoney, for example, describes MacKinnon as defining gender exclusively in terms of "what is done to women,"[40] thereby making it difficult to see women as social actors at all. These scholars are not content with the explanation that the emphasis on harm is a necessary strategy to assure that women's suffering will not be discounted. Their concern is that an approach that ignores agency does not take into account the specific actions women have taken to resist male dominance, and also fails to appreciate the role that women have played as oppressive social actors themselves, particularly in the main-

---

[39] Kathryn Abrams, Complex Claimants and Reductive Moral Judgments: New Patterns in the Search for Equality, 57 U. Pitt. L. Rev. 337, 348 (1996).

[40] Martha R. Mahoney, Whiteness and Women, In Practice and Theory: A Reply to Catharine MacKinnon, 5 Yale J. of L. & Feminism 217 (1993).

tenance of white supremacy. The agency theorists thus have forged a connection between agency and race, arguing that dominance theory makes it easier for white women to deny their complicity in racism, because, as victims, they cannot be held responsible for the creation of oppression. A more complex view of personal identity, acknowledging that individuals can be both oppressors and victims, allows for treatment of women as agents who engage in cultural practices that reproduce discrimination, even while living under conditions of male domination.

A focus on the agency of women is also of particular importance to black feminist theorists who want to highlight the history of black women's struggle to survive in a racist and sexist society that has persistently denied their humanity. Angela Harris, for example, believes that black women have found solidarity not through the realization of their shared victimization, but through their "creative action," by which they strive to create a positive personal identity in opposition to dominant forces.[41] Reminiscent of the cultural feminists' desire to change society through revaluing and reaffirming women's culture, Harris's postmodernist approach affirms the goal of transforming society through alliances among groups of women and men who share a liberationist political vision.

Most recently, feminist theorists have attempted to resolve the tension between agency and victimization by refusing to think in dichotomous terms. Abrams has called for a recognition of the "partial agency" of women, to construct a legal subject who is neither as "unencumbered" as the autonomous individual in classical liberal theory nor as "immobilized" as the stereotyped image of the female victim of sexual violence.[42] Schneider, an activist in and scholar of the battered women's movement, has labeled the victimization/agency dichotomy a "false dichotomy" and argued that they represent "not extremes in opposition . . . [but] interrelated dimensions of women's experience."[43] Rejection of the dichotomy in this context requires feminists to analyze the various ways in which women make

[41] Angela Harris, Race and Essentialism in Feminist Legal Theory, 42 Stan. L. Rev. 581, 612 (1990).

[42] Kathryn Abrams, Sex Wars Redux: Agency and Coercion in Feminist Legal Theory, 95 Colum. L. Rev. 304, 352 (1995).

[43] Elizabeth M. Schneider, Feminism and the False Dichotomy of Victimization and Agency, 38 N.Y. L. Sch. L. Rev. 387, 395 (1993).

constrained choices under oppressive conditions, keeping in mind that the choices are real, but not unfettered. This approach also entails a willingness to "learn to accept contradiction, ambiguity, and ambivalence in women's lives."[44]

The theoretical discussion of victimization and agency is grounded in the experience of feminist litigators and activists who have worked with battered women and victims of sexual harassment. Schneider, for example, has represented battered women charged with killing their abusers. Over the years, she has struggled with the delicate task of trying to convince judges and juries that her clients have suffered immense psychological harm, while at the same time refusing to characterize them as insane, irrational, or incapacitated. To this end, feminist defense attorneys have often sought admission of expert testimony on the "battered woman syndrome," including the "learned helplessness" of abuse victims. This expert testimony on victimization helps to explain why women do not leave their abusers, and educates fact finders about the dynamics of domestic violence. The paradox for feminists, however, has been the tendency of some courts and attorneys to interpret this syndrome evidence in a highly conservative fashion, that is, as evidence reinforcing women's incapacitation and passivity in the face of male violence. This nonfeminist interpretation of women's victimization can jeopardize a woman's claim of self-defense, making it harder to persuade the jury that the woman acted reasonably to save her life. It can also backfire in contests over child custody, where the portrayals of battered women as "pathologically weak" can work against mothers in a particularly cruel instance of victim-blaming. The challenge is to find a way to express the agency of a battered woman without blaming her for not extricating herself from the abusive situation.

Martha Mahoney was able to break through the victimization/agency dichotomy by developing the concept of "separation assault" to describe how batterers intensify their violence to prevent women from leaving, retaliate against them for leaving, or forcibly end the separation.[45] By using practice to inform theory, Mahoney offered a feminist interpretation of a woman's decision to stay in an abusive relationship that accords with Abrams's notion of "partial agency." The

[44] *Id.* at 397.

[45] Martha Mahoney, Legal Images of Battered Women: Redefining the Issue of Separation, 90 Mich. L. Rev. 1 (1991).

choice to stay becomes a reasonable response to the constraints produced by oppression, portraying the battered woman as a strategic actor rather than an abject victim.

Sexual harassment litigation also exemplifies the victimization/ agency tension through the legal requirement that plaintiffs prove that their harassment is "severe or pervasive." Employers have argued that harassment is not severe enough to qualify as actionable harm if the woman decides to stay on the job or has not suffered debilitating psychological harm. Women whose agency is apparent, who choose to stay and fight harassment and continue functioning in their job, risk losing their lawsuits because their victim status may be compromised. In the recent case of *Harris v. Forklift Systems, Inc.,*[46] the United States Supreme Court rejected an employer's claim that a showing of severe psychological injury should be a formal prerequisite to recovery. Nevertheless, the difficulty of describing the intangible harms caused by a sexually hostile environment are formidable when the plaintiff does not conform to popular image of the sexualized victim. Again, Mahoney's scholarship has attempted to normalize the sexual harassment victim who does not take the drastic step of quitting her job in the face of severe harassment. She makes a strong case for the proposition that few workers actually have the luxury to quit, arguing that "[w]hen women face particularly agonizing choices in relation to work, they often internalize the pain and keep the job."[47]

Not surprisingly, the partial agency of women workers confronting harassment manifests itself in a wide variety of responses and coping mechanisms, from blocking out the event, to avoiding the workplace or the harasser, to trying to defuse the situation by joking, to telling the harasser to stop, to filing a complaint. Feminist litigators in harassment suits, like those in domestic violence litigation, face the difficulty of breaking through the dichotomy and persuading judges and juries that coping behavior is not inconsistent with victimization. When they succeed, protection from sexual harassment becomes available to a more diverse group of women with different styles, personalities, and cultural backgrounds.

[46] 114 S. Ct. 367 (1993).

[47] Martha R. Mahoney, Exit: Power and the Idea of Leaving in Love, Work and the Confirmation Hearings, 65 S. Cal. L. Rev. 1283, 1289 (1992).

E.   INVESTIGATING WHITE PRIVILEGE

The newest outgrowth of anti-essentialist feminist thought is a body of scholarship focusing on *white privilege*. "White privilege" in this context means the social advantages that whites enjoy in our society, often without recognizing them as privileges. Inspired by a manuscript by Peggy McIntosh detailing more than forty concrete examples of white privilege in everyday American life,[48] legal scholars have begun to analyze the flip side of oppression—investigating how even well-meaning whites perpetuate racism by failing to understand their own advantages. Some of these everyday privileges—for instance, the ability to shop in a department store without being followed by security personnel—are justified and should be accorded to everyone. Others—like the ability to ignore people of lesser status—are unjustified and constitute what Martha Mahoney describes as "unearned power that is systematically conferred."[49] Particularly for whites, white privilege is most often invisible. It is naturalized and normalized: Whites can exercise their privileges, believing it is simply the way things are.

The nature of white privilege scholarship is decidedly intersectional. It fits comfortably within both feminist legal theory and critical race theory. The investigation of white privilege responds directly to the black feminist and agency critiques of dominance theory, focusing attention on the ways white women (and white men) act upon their privileges and unwittingly contribute to white supremacy. The white privilege scholarship also expands on the feminist anti-essentialist critique of "false universalism," this time concentrating on the failure to recognize the exclusionary and race-specific nature of white norms. Some of the white privilege literature also incorporates a feminist respect for consciousness-raising and places a high value on listening closely to the stories and experiences of people different from oneself.

The obvious link to critical race theory in the white privilege literature is the central importance it places on race. Writers such as Bar-

---

[48] Peggy McIntosh, White Privilege and Male Privilege: A Personal Account of Coming to See Correspondences Through Work in Women's Studies (Wellesley College Center for Research on Women Working Paper No. 189, 1988).

[49] Mahoney, supra note 40, at 235.

bara Flagg, Stephanie Wildman, and Trina Grillo start from the proposition that "race matters" (a central tenet of critical race theory) even when the actors are white. This new genre of scholarship is sometimes referred to as "critical white studies," locating it squarely within critical race theory and highlighting that white privilege and the construction of an anti-racist white racial identity are among its chief topics of interest.

The McIntosh manuscript that has been so influential to this body of scholarship is a reflection piece that starts off describing how, as a teacher of women's studies, she has noticed that individual men often deny they are personally advantaged vis-à-vis women, even when they accept that society is sexist. McIntosh hypothesizes that male privilege is often invisible and that men have been carefully taught not to recognize their own privilege. This is coupled with a greater willingness to support women when it comes to improving women's status, but not when it amounts to lessening male privilege.

McIntosh decided to apply these insights to her own situation as a white woman. The most cited portion of her manuscript is her list of some of the "daily effects of white privilege" on her life.[50] The list is surprising in that it does not consist of the usual catalogue of economic advantages, such as better jobs or more family wealth. Instead, McIntosh takes the daily discriminations felt by people of color and translates them into examples of white privilege, with the effect of making white readers realize that much of what they accept as normal is normal only for them. Thus, for example, McIntosh lists "Whether I use checks, credit cards, or cash, I can count on my skin color not to work against my appearance of financial reliability,"[51] and "I can be late to a meeting without having the lateness reflect on my race."[52] Her examples also dramatize the psychological energy it takes for minorities to confront and negotiate racism in their daily lives. Thus, being white means that "I can be pretty sure that my children's teachers and employers will tolerate them if they fit school and workplace norms; my chief worries about them do not concern others' attitudes toward their race,"[53] and "I can take a job with an affirmative action employer without having my co-workers on the job suspect that I got it

---

[50] McIntosh, supra note 48, at 5.
[51] Id. at 6.
[52] Id. at 8.
[53] Id. at 6.

E. Investigating White Privilege

because of my race."[54] McIntosh's approach is a clever way of "de-centering" whiteness because the examples she uses of white privilege are implicitly premised on the oppressive experiences of minorities. The list reads as if a person of color were telling a white person to count her blessings by detailing the concrete ways in which their lives differed.

McIntosh's examples bring home the point that whites have the luxury of not having to think about race in most of their daily interactions. Stephanie Wildman and Trina Grillo have theorized that the "privilege to ignore their race gives whites a societal advantage distinct from the advantage received from the existence of discriminatory racism."[55] Because our society is structured around white norms and whites are usually oblivious to white privilege, whites approach the world without being conscious of race and its complexities. Wildman and Grillo provide a poignant illustration of a similar phenomenon in their description of how Trina Grillo had to learn to live with cancer. As a cancer patient, Grillo saw the world through the "filter" of cancer. She could not even watch the World Series "without wondering which players have had cancer or who in the players' families might have cancer."[56] This acute awareness of cancer, of course, stemmed from the fact that cancer posed an imminent threat to her well-being. People without cancer have the luxury of being ignorant of the risks of cancer and might well regard Grillo's response to the World Series as hypersensitive or bizarre. The example suggests, however, that Grillo's cancer-aware perspective was not less valid than the majority's cancer-blind perspective. Instead, the objective of the essay is to encourage whites to notice their privilege and to begin to understand why race often seems more salient to people of color.

The invisibility of privilege permits whites, or other privileged groups, such as men or heterosexuals, to take a narrow view of what counts as discrimination. The contemporary constitutional law doctrine, for example, requires a showing of intent to discriminate before the action will be held to violate the Equal Protection Clause. This ap-

---

[54] *Id.* at 8.

[55] Trina Grillo & Stephanie M. Wildman, Obscuring the Importance of Race: The Implication of Making Comparisons Between Racism and Sexism (or other Isms) in Stephanie M. Wildman, *Privilege Revealed: How Invisible Preference Undermines America* 87 (1996).

[56] *Id.* at 86.

proach fails to capture the systematic inequity produced by a system of white privilege because there is no attempt to use the law to take away the unjustified advantages of whites. Under the current approach, discrimination is reduced to mean-spirited behavior that seeks to inflict harm for its own sake. The white privilege literature advances a broader conception of discrimination which includes not only deliberate discrimination and stereotyping but also the failure to extend justified privileges to everyone, and advocates putting an end to the exercise of unjustified white privilege.

Another major theme of this genre of scholarship is the "normalization of privilege."[57] The vast majority of our institutional practices, legal norms, and legal categories were developed without the participation of people of color. Yet, in dominant legal discourse, the racial specificity of these norms is rarely noticed—they are regarded simply as established practices, rather than "white norms." Barbara Flagg has used the term "transparency phenomenon" to describe the "tendency of whites not to think about whiteness, or about the norms, behavior, experiences, or perspectives that are white-specific."[58] This obliviousness to the operation of race has generally meant that the law requires only equal application of the rules, with no examination of the inclusiveness of the rules themselves. Noticing the cultural specificity or white-specific origin of prevailing policies and practices could significantly affect how courts and lawyers interpret anti-discrimination laws governing the interactions of people in multicultural settings, such as the workplace. Once a practice is judged to be race-specific, it immediately raises the question of whether requiring assimilation is fair or serves merely as a reinforcement of privilege. Current controversies, such as employers' right to have their employees speak English on the job or to prohibit the wearing of cornrows, might be recast as instances of cultural domination rather than assertions of employer prerogative. On a broader level, noticing the whiteness of cultural norms makes the concept of merit more problematic. Decisions that appear to be merit-based may instead represent preferences for credentials that

[57] Stephanie M. Wildman & Adrienne D. Davis, Language and Silence: Making Systems of Privilege Visible, 35 Santa Clara L. Rev. 881, 890 (1995).
[58] Barbara J. Flagg, "Was Blind, But Now I See": White Race Consciousness and the Requirement of Discriminatory Intent, 91 Mich. L. Rev. 953, 956 (1993).

are easier to come by for whites. As McIntosh observed, "many doors open for certain people through no virtues of their own."[59]

The investigations into the nature of white privilege has led Martha Mahoney to theorize about what it might mean to look at race, particularly whiteness, as a social construction.[60] Similar to the way white privilege has been normalized, whiteness has also been naturalized. For their inhabitants, predominantly white neighborhoods, schools, and other institutions appear to be a natural part of the landscape, simply an outgrowth of the places where individuals live and the choices they make. The high degree of racial segregation in our society also means that many whites rarely encounter people of color and that life in a white world comes to seem natural. Mahoney argues that residential segregation is the product not primarily of individual choice, but of systematic practices over a long period of time by the federal government, along with lending agencies and other private forces, designed to exclude blacks from predominantly white areas. When companies began relocating to the white suburbs, making manufacturing jobs scarce in the city, the material consequences of residential segregation increased.

Mahoney's thesis is that the creation of white suburbs and the isolation of minorities in the inner cities has also produced the social meaning of race. Through this process, whiteness became associated with "good neighborhoods," employment, stability, and self-sufficiency, while blackness was linked to "bad neighborhoods," unemployment, crime, gangs, and instability. Her main point is that segregation, and the meanings of "race" produced by segregation encouraged whites to prefer living and interacting with other whites. Thus, whites who do not consider themselves prejudiced may nevertheless avoid and fear blacks. This has little to do with skin color or natural affinities for one's own group. Mahoney explains that in many instances the "preference for whiteness reflects a preference for the qualities that have been attached to whiteness."[61] By retrieving the history of residential segregation and the coercion underlying current patterns, Mahoney aims to denaturalize individual preferences and to locate them with larger systems of privilege and oppression. Reminiscent of Patricia Williams's

---

[59] McIntosh, supra note 48, at 9.

[60] Martha R. Mahoney, Segregation, Whiteness and Transformation, 143 U. Pa. L. Rev. 1659 (1995).

[61] Id. at 1676.

liberationist postmodern vision, Mahoney's theory retains hope that there could be a reconstruction of the social meaning of race, if privilege is revealed and the shared interests of blacks and whites are not always blocked by thinking that regards whiteness as the opposite of blackness.

The scholarship investigating privilege is in its early phase and could take several directions. So far, the work has concentrated mainly on white privilege, although scholars such as Stephanie Wildman and Peggy McIntosh have also analyzed heterosexual privilege. White heterosexual male legal scholars have not yet developed a body of work exploring the social construction of masculinity with a goal of redefining masculinity along pro-feminist lines.

A new kind of intersectionality has emerged, however, focusing not only on multiple forms of oppression but on multiple forms of privilege. This opens the way for scholars in addition to women of color to describe their own experiences of multiple consciousness. Perhaps the greatest potential of the new move to examine privilege is its capacity to reopen the discussion about the legal definition of equality. The focus on privilege offers a new vocabulary to debate the fairness of such pivotal issues as de facto segregation and meritocracy. The narrow definition of discrimination given by the courts and legislatures in the 1990s can be challenged by a vision of equality that includes the dismantling of unjustified privilege. Looking at the flip side of oppression and arguing that equality means "equally privileged" gives postmodern feminist theory a chance of exerting a greater impact on law.

F. BACKLASH: PROLIFERATION OF CRITICS OF FEMINIST LEGAL THEORY

The developments in feminist legal theory in the 1990s, like the trends in the 1980s, have taken place in a social context fraught with complexity and contradiction. In the crosscurrents of the 1980s, feminist legal theory emerged as a serious academic topic, despite the resurgence of conservative politics in the larger society. The parallel in the 1990s is that while feminist legal theory has become established in the legal academy, critics of legal feminism have also proliferated, becoming more visible and more organized. Much of the criticism is constructive and directed toward finding genuine points of agreement and disagreement. Some of it, however, displays an unmistakable contempt for feminist scholars and their projects. This decade has thus been characterized both by a growing respect for feminist legal theory in some quarters and by a persistent backlash that continues to mark the field as controversial and risky for many students and writers.

Perhaps the most telling evidence of the rise of feminist legal theory has been the growth in the number and diversity of casebooks in the field. In law schools, the casebook has an unusual place in the curriculum because it is often the only text assigned for a course. Typically, as fields in the law begin to emerge, professors will assemble unpublished packets of materials for new courses or seminars before they attempt to define the area through means of a published casebook. The appearance of a casebook often signals that the subject has "arrived," in the sense that publishers have confidence that there will be a market for the book in coming years. As mentioned earlier,[62] the first two casebooks on the law of sex discrimination were published in the mid-1970s, with a heavy emphasis on case analysis of constitutional law, family law, and employment discrimination law. As of this writing, there are seven casebooks published or forthcoming, with titles such as *Gender and Law, Feminist Jurisprudence,* and *Law and Violence Against Women.*[63] One of the most prominent features of the new and revised casebooks is that they each contain extensive treatment of feminist legal theory, although several retain an emphasis on case analysis and historical context.

The burgeoning interest in feminist legal theory is also in evidence among law students, the group responsible for editing and run-

---

[62] *See* supra at p. 43.

[63] The six casebooks published so far are: Herma Hill Kay & Martha S. West, *Sex-Based Discrimination* (4th ed. 1996) (West Publishing Co.); Barbara Allen Babcock, Ann E. Freedman, Susan Deller Ross, Wendy Webster Williams, Rhonda Copelon, Deborah L. Rhode & Nadine Taub, *Sex Discrimination and the Law* (2d ed. 1996) (Little, Brown & Co.); Mary Becker, Cynthia Grant Bowman & Morrison Torrey, *Feminist Jurisprudence* (1994) (West Publishing Co.); Katharine T. Bartlett & Angela P. Harris, *Gender and Law* (2d ed. 1998) (Aspen Law & Business); Mary Jo Frug, *Women and the Law* (1992) (Foundation Press); and Beverly Balos & Mary Louise Fellows, *Law and Violence Against Women* (1994) (Carolina Academic Press). The seventh, Catharine MacKinnon's casebook, is scheduled for publication by Foundation Press in 1998.

ning most law reviews and law journals. By the end of the decade, there were sixteen legal journals specifically devoted to gender issues and several more concentrating on the intersection of race, sexuality, and gender.[64] Among the "mainstream" law journals, moreover, citation counters noticed that feminist articles and articles written from a critical race perspective were increasingly making it onto the "most cited" lists, indicating an interest in, if not wholehearted acceptance of, these new scholarly movements.[65]

The creation of these new outlets for feminist-oriented articles and books has had a material impact beyond the circulation of feminist ideas and theories to a wider audience. Some feminist law teachers—the vast majority of whom are women—found it possible to secure tenure, promotions, and even chaired professorships on the basis of "outsider" scholarship that might not have qualified as "legal" scholarship a decade ago. Law students with feminist inclinations discovered that there was at least a corner of the curriculum receptive to their interests and that they did not necessarily have to abandon their interest in feminist topics when they made law review.

Perhaps because of the rapidity of some of these feminist incursions into legal education and legal scholarship, it is easy to overstate the degree of change that has taken place. Neither the presence of women in the profession nor the existence of feminist legal theory has gone unchallenged. Several studies of the experience of women law students in the late 1980s and early 1990s indicate that large numbers of women continue to regard the law school environment as hostile, male-dominated, and alienating. The most publicized study,[66] which Lani Guinier and others conducted at the University of Pennsylvania Law School, found that, despite equal entry-level credentials, male law students were three times more likely than women to end up in the top 10 percent of the class and were disproportionately represented in prestigious positions and extracurricular activities. The researchers hypothesized that a hostile learning environment existed at Penn, which, to a significant degree, accounted for women's disparate perfor-

---

[64] *Anderson's 1997 Directory of Law Reviews and Scholarly Legal Periodicals* 24-25, 27-28 (1997).

[65] Fred R. Shapiro, The Most-Cited Law Review Articles Revisited, 71 Chi.-Kent L. Rev. 751 (1996).

[66] *See* Lani Guinier, Michelle Fine, & Jane Balin, Becoming Gentlemen: Women's Experiences at One Ivy League Law School, 143 U. Pa. L. Rev. 1 (1994).

F. Backlash: Proliferation of Critics of Feminist Legal Theory

mance.[67] The qualitative portion of the study indicated that women were often silenced in class by the taunts and ridicule of their classmates or intimidated by belittling comments from professors.[68] Over the course of three years, women reported lower levels of class participation than their male peers and a disaffection with the Socratic method, which many perceived as humiliating, overly aggressive, and intolerant of different perspectives.[69] Although studies from other schools did not always replicate the Penn findings on disparate performance between men and women, they did tend to confirm that equality remained elusive for large numbers of women law students, despite the fact that nationally women make up 43 percent of the law school enrollment.

Moreover, as feminism has become established in the legal academic world, a vigorous critique has emerged along with it, focusing on some of feminism's basic premises and accompanied by resistance to what some perceive to be the feminization of legal studies, whether represented by increasing numbers of women students and women faculty or the influence of feminist thought. One particularly caustic op-ed essay in the National Law Journal,[70] for example, recently complained that the feminization of law schools had produced lawyers ill-suited to the practice of law and lambasted progressive law faculty for embracing ideals of "feel-goodism and empathy." In terms that echoed Nineteenth-Century tracts against the higher education of women, the author warned that enrolling yet more women in law school would not ease the problems of the profession because "a lawyer's success depends on skill, not ideology."

As was characteristic of many backlashes in the past, this latest backlash against feminist legal theory has occurred well before the establishment of gender equality in law schools or in the legal profession. The point made by Susan Faludi in her popular book *Backlash*, published in 1981, seems appropriate to describe a quality of the response to feminist legal theory in the 1990s. As Faludi sees it, "the antifeminist backlash has been set off not by women's achievement of full equality but by the increased possibility that they might win it. It is

---

[67] *Id.* at 59.

[68] *Id.* at 43, 51-52.

[69] *Id.* at 46-47.

[70] Arthur Austin, Womanly Approach Harms Future Lawyers, Nat'l L.J., May 18, 1998.

a preemptive strike that stops women long before they reach the finish line."[71]

It has probably always been the case that the critics of legal feminism have been as plentiful and diverse as the field of feminist legal theory itself. In the 1970s and 1980s, the most prevalent negative response to feminist legal theory was simply to ignore it and proceed to analyze an area of law as if feminist approaches to the subject were nonexistent or unimportant. Such marginalization of the field persists, as evidenced by the fact that feminist legal scholars still tend to be classified separately from their colleagues in the mainstream of legal philosophy and jurisprudence. However, as feminist legal theory has become more established in the 1990s, the critiques have also become more explicit and elaborate. There is now a fairly large number of articles and books devoted principally to attacking feminist legal theories, tracking a growing criticism of women's studies and feminism more generally.

The criticism has come from so many quarters that it is impossible to capture it fully in a short summary such as this one. Some of the critics would not hesitate to label themselves anti-feminists. Others, however, regard themselves as feminists, even though they disagree with much of what conventionally comes under the heading of feminist legal thought. To give you a flavor of the types of arguments directed against feminist legal theory, I mention here three distinct genres of criticism that have proliferated in the 1990s. This sample by no means exhausts the varieties of critiques leveled at feminist legal theory, but it will suggest some of the different attitudes, tones, and intellectual stances of the critics.

The first genre of criticism employs the perspective of evolutionary biology (sometimes referred to as sociobiology) to explain and justify women's unequal status. Evolutionary biology is an active field of study outside the law that has begun to attract law professors to its ranks. Some in this group of predominantly male scholars have challenged feminist assertions that phenomena such as the wage gap, occupational segregation, the glass ceiling, and the prevalence of sexual harassment should be regarded as systemic forms of sex discrimination and made subject to legal sanctions. In a modern version of "biology is destiny," they argue that different biological predispositions

---

[71] Susan Faludi, *Backlash: The Undeclared War Against American Women* xx (1981).

of men and women are responsible for the gendered patterns and practices in our society, and propose repeal of many of the civil rights laws prohibiting sex discrimination.

The second genre has focused its attack largely on what it regards as feminism's excessive focus on the victimization of women. Many in this group are younger women who write primarily for a popular audience. Their particular targets have been laws and institutional policies related to date rape, pornography, and sexual harassment, which they believe have inaccurately portrayed women as passive and powerless. Critics in this second group are more likely to identify themselves as feminists, although their work is largely directed toward exposing the flaws of feminist theory and activism, and proceeds from a premise that a primary cause of women's inequality is the feminist movement itself.

The third genre, represented most recently by the Independent Women's Forum, is a familiar brand of social conservatism that espouses traditional family values and promotes sex segregation in education and military training. Critics in this group believe that women have already achieved equality, embracing a contemporary version of "separate but equal." They have set as their goal the defeat of the "feminist establishment," particularly through initiation of law-related battles in the media, legislatures, and courts.

1.   Evolutionary Biology

Criticism based on the perspective of evolutionary biology resonates strongly with familiar narratives of gender difference in popular culture. Within academia, scholarship emphasizing the socially constructed nature of gender difference is on the rise in a variety of disciplines, particularly in feminist and postmodern writings. Outside the ivory tower, however, gender difference is most often discussed as if it were largely a "given," with its source in biological or natural differences between men and women and between boys and girls. The discomfort popular writers often display when addressing racial differences has no parallel in discussions of sex differences. Resorting to code words to signal race, such as "inner city" or "gang," is often unnecessary in media discussions about gender because it remains acceptable journalism to draw sharp contrasts between men and women and to assume that women and men have fundamentally different human natures.

Academic versions of the biological approach to gender differences generally pay more attention to the origin of such differences than do their popular counterparts. For Kingsley Browne, for example, the key to the evolutionary approach is accepting the notion of "reproductive success" in the development of human psychology.[72] He starts from the premise that there is a biological imperative for each sex to maximize the chances that they will produce offspring who will survive, and the more offspring, the better. Evolutionary theorists propose that the strategy for reproductive success differs greatly for males and females. As Richard Posner asserts, supposedly females have to "make every pregnancy count,"[73] and to this end they are "choosier" when selecting a mate. Browne posits that females have little interest in casual sex that is unlikely to result in another successful pregnancy.[74] The successful strategy for males, on the other hand, is said to entail far less "parental investment"—the theory is that males are better off pursuing many females and thereby multiplying the chances that some of their conquests will result in biological offspring. Part of this evolutionary story is also that males put considerable energy into competing with other males for the most "desirable" (i.e., young, beautiful, sexy) females.

Evolutionary theorists do not contend that, under current social arrangements, reproductive success is the most important value for men and women to pursue. Indeed, in an age where many persons choose not to have children, decide to abort fetuses, or decide to have only one child, it seems strange to insist that what matters most is having genetic offspring, particularly in those cases where parents have no day-to-day relationship with their children. Instead, what often distinguishes contemporary evolutionary theorists from many popular commentators is the theorists' understanding that the biological predispositions may not be functional under modern conditions. They contend that men and women are the way they are in part because such biological predispositions somehow become "embedded in the

---

[72] Kingsley R. Browne, An Evolutionary Perspective on Sexual Harassment: Seeking Roots in Biology Rather than Ideology, 8 J. Contemp. Legal Issues 5, 12-15 (1997).

[73] Richard A. Posner, *Sex and Reason* 91 (1992).

[74] Browne, supra note 72, at 17.

F. Backlash: Proliferation of Critics of Feminist Legal Theory

brain"[75] or "hard-wired" into human beings, persisting long past the time of their usefulness.

The gender differences most often highlighted by legal scholars from the evolutionary camp echo familiar scripts about "male" and "female" traits. They are often synonymous with masculine and feminine behaviors commonly regarded as stereotypes. Thus, evolutionary scholars claim that men are risk-takers, more driven to competition than women, and more focused on acquiring resources—that is, more interested in money. Women are said to be nurturers, interested in children and oriented towards others. With respect to sexuality, these authors assert that men are most interested in the physical aspects of sex, while women are more concerned with love and intimacy. Finally, evolutionary scholars contend that men are better at spatial relationships, while women tend to excel in language skills.[76]

The interesting twist that evolutionary writers give the old repertoire of gendered traits, however, is their insistence that they are predispositions inherited from an ancient time which live on into the present. For many of these scholars, the fact that many individuals do not follow the gendered script does not undercut their hypotheses. In this genre of legal scholarship, the method is to link perceived patterns of behavior to general predispositions, most often followed by a defense of the status quo.

Writers from an evolutionary perspective have focused on two topics of particular interest to feminists: motherhood and sexuality. In an early example of the sociobiological approach, for example, Richard Epstein attempted to explain and justify the gender division of labor in the workforce by linking it to gender differences in spatial perception and women's distinctive capacity to breast-feed. After listing the benefits to be gained from specialization, Epstein hypothesized that women were naturally suited to child-raising, while men were predisposed to do everything else.

> The mere fact that the mother carries with her a supply of milk makes it clear that she is the better candidate for staying with the child, consequently leaving the male of the species to engage in a broad class of explorative activities. The nurturing instincts usually attributable to

[75] Richard A. Epstein, Gender is for Nouns, 41 DePaul L. Rev. 981, 990 (1992).
[76] *See* Kingsley R. Browne, Sex and Temperament in Modern Society: A Darwinian View of the Glass Ceiling and the Gender Gap, 37 Ariz. L. Rev. 971 (1995).

women are a set of attitudinal adaptations that reduce the cost of doing activities that help promote the survival of both her and her offspring. Although modern women operate in settings far different from those of their ancient mothers, the initial tendency remains: If nurturing brings greater pleasure or requires lower cost for women than for men, then we should expect to see women devote a greater percentage of their resources to it than men. This specialization will endure in the aggregate and should be accepted for what it is: a healthy adaptation that works for the benefit of all concerned . . .[77]

As could be expected, feminists have disputed Epstein's sociobiological account of the gender division of labor at the various critical points of his analysis. In particular, Kathryn Abrams has sought to advance feminist theory by engaging some of its fiercest critics. In response to Epstein, Abrams first sought to "interrogate the assertions of biological influence"[78] on women's supposed preference for nurturing. She noted that there was no convincing scientific evidence locating a predisposition to nurture in a particular portion of the brain. Without totally rejecting the possibility of biological influence, Abrams offered a cultural account of women's propensity to nurture. Rather than being inherited, Abrams argued that the special capacity to nurture could just as easily be viewed as an adaptation to specific situations, as behavior learned by "women watching and mothering each other."[79] Abrams also doubted the rationality of singling out breast-feeding as the difference that produced the gender division of labor, particularly since for quite some time there have been adequate substitutes for nourishing infants. Rather than accept women's "instinct" to nurture as biologically driven, Abrams deconstructed women's "choice" to nurture by spelling out the powerful cultural reinforcements behind such choices, including husbands' disapproval of their wives working outside the home, the social labeling of child care as "women's work," and the entire history of exclusion, discrimination, and lack of accommodation of women in the workplace, particularly with regard to pregnant employees and new mothers.

[77] Richard A. Epstein, supra note 75, at 990.
[78] Kathryn Abrams, Social Construction, Roving Biologism, and Reasonable Women: A Response to Professor Epstein, 41 DePaul L. Rev. 1021, 1023 (1992).
[79] *Id.* at 1026.

F. Backlash: Proliferation of Critics of Feminist Legal Theory

Perhaps the most well-known book embracing an evolutionary perspective on the law is Richard Posner's *Sex and Reason*. In it, Posner develops an economic or rational-choice theory of sex. His approach is also informed by evolutionary biology, which he regards as "a parallel mode of inquiry to economic analysis."[80] His analysis of rape, sexual harassment, and a host of other sexually oriented topics proceeds from the assumption that "men and women have traditionally pursued different sexual strategies, that these are related to the different reproductive capacities of the two sexes, and that sexual attractiveness is related to reproductive fitness . . ."[81] Similar to Epstein's analysis, Posner's theory incorporates a belief that men strive to have intercourse with as many women as possible, while women are interested in a stable relationship with a man who can provide for their children.[82]

Despite the use of some economic vocabulary, the narrative of men's and women's different sexual strategies in *Sex and Reason* is reminiscent of conventional 1950s attitudes toward marriage, sex, and dating. This feature is perhaps most pronounced in the chapter on coercive sex. In marked contrast to feminist accounts such as MacKinnon's, for example, Posner's analysis of rape downplays power and accentuates sexual desire. He regards rape as "primarily a substitute for consensual sexual intercourse rather than a manifestation of male hostility toward women or a method of establishing or maintaining male domination."[83] In his sexual version of rape, it is because men's sex drive is stronger than women's that women are given the assignment of controlling natural male "promiscuity" and must do their best to "screen out potential rapists."[84] Rape is described as if it were a market transaction in which women try to protect their sexual goods from men bent on stealing them, if they cannot arrive at a satisfactory price. For Posner, date rape inevitably occurs when men who are single-mindedly searching for sex find it hard to distinguish among "coy women" who pretend to resist (but "no" really means "yes"), from women who mean it when they say no.[85] The downside to prosecuting

---

[80] Posner, supra note 73, at 108.
[81] *Id.* at 110.
[82] *Id.* at 90-94.
[83] *Id.* at 384.
[84] *Id.* at 391.
[85] *Id.*

date rape in Posner's view is that it might discourage some men from dating, which he worries might harm heterosexual women who use dating as a means of finding the right man.[86]

Throughout his analysis, Posner treats injury to women's reproductive autonomy as the central injury of rape, in line with the evolutionary emphasis on reproductive fitness. He notes that marital rape is of concern because it can cause an unwanted pregnancy,[87] suggesting that the injury might be less if there were no chance that the woman would become pregnant. By linking sexual autonomy so closely to reproductive choice, Posner's commodified view of sex eclipses women's interest in personal autonomy apart from concerns about pregnancy.

Carol Sanger's feminist review of Posner's book took issue with two of its underlying assumptions: that the male need to have sex should be treated as a "given" or a "prior preference,"[88] and that sex is an undifferentiated commodity, equally encompassing consensual intercourse and rape. In He's Gotta Have It, Sanger charged that Posner's evolutionary/economic perspective was fundamentally male-oriented, reflecting "sex and reason from a boy's point of view."[89] For Sanger, Posner's very concept of "sex" reflected male experience: She protested that by the book's definition, "sex begins, and to a large extent quickly ends, with male ejaculation."[90] She pointed out that with this singular focus on intercourse, many relational and emotional aspects of sexuality are likely to be lost, with the result that women's experiences of sex are largely unrepresented in the book. Echoing a dominant theme in radical feminist accounts of rape,[91] Sanger disputed the view that rape was primarily about sex. She insisted that "rape is not a sex substitute,"[92] citing empirical studies of men who are sexually active with consenting wives and partners at the time they rape other women. In Sanger's world, many men as well as women "simply define sexual intercourse to exclude

---

[86] *Id.* at 395.

[87] *Id.* at 390.

[88] Carol Sanger, He's Gotta Have It, 66 S. Cal. L. Rev. 1221, 1224-25 (1993) (review of Richard Posner, *Sex and Reason*).

[89] *Id.* at 1223.

[90] *Id.*

[91] *See* supra at p. 56.

[92] Sanger, supra note 88, at 1232.

rape."[93] In a Gilliganesque approach to moral reasoning, Sanger argued that it was not irrational for an individual to act out of respect or sympathy towards another and yet to regard such action as within one's *self*-interest. Her scathing review of *Sex and Reason* demonstrates how some of the basic premises of the evolutionary approach conflict with feminist theories, from both radical and cultural feminist viewpoints.

Up to this point, the legal writers espousing an evolutionary perspective have tended to be anti-feminist, or at least not sympathetic with the desire for thoroughgoing social change that characterizes most feminist writings. One reviewer has suggested that evolutionary psychology may be fundamentally aligned with social conservatism because the evolutionary approach "identifies the main obstacles to radical social change as lying within the individual rather than outside of him."[94] Particularly when it comes to analyzing women's choices with respect to work and family, evolutionary writers often seem happy to have a crisp answer ("it's in the genes") to explain why women would voluntarily choose paths that produce poverty, expose them to violence, and accord them low social status and esteem.[95]

However, as several scholars have pointed out, acceptance of an evolutionary perspective need not necessarily be anti-feminist. Few assert these days that biologically influenced preferences can never be altered. Indeed, some cultural conventions may be more resistant to change than biological conditions. Thus, the nature/nurture debate over origins should not be confused with the very different question of whether patterns can be changed, and whether it is worthwhile to do so.[96] Nevertheless, perhaps because of the long history of subordinating women in the name of nature, the rhetoric and reasoning of the work inspired by evolutionary biology most often reads like an apology for sex discrimination and an attack on feminism. For this reason, it is difficult to envision this genre of criticism taking a feminist turn.

---

[93] *Id.* at 1231.

[94] Amy L. Wax, Against Nature—On Robert Wright's *The Moral Animal*, 63 U. Chi. L. Rev. 307, 336 (1996).

[95] *See especially* Kingsley Browne, supra note 76, at 1083-92.

[96] For elaboration on this point, *see* David A. Strauss, Biology, Difference, and Gender Discrimination, 41 DePaul L. Rev. 1007 (1992).

2.   *Victim Feminism*

The portrait of women most often projected by evolutionary theorists is maternal and oddly reminiscent of Victorian stereotypes: The woman maximizes her chances for reproductive success by being modest, uninterested in casual sex, and nurturing toward children. Critics such as Epstein chastise feminists for denying gender differences and for embracing an equality of "equal outcomes" that seeks elimination of gender disparities in wealth, occupations, and material aspects of life. In the evolutionary critique, feminism is often equated with a wooden type of liberal feminism and the most immediate targets of these critics are anti-discrimination laws characteristic of the equality stage of feminist activism.

The next group of critics—those decrying what they call "victim feminism"—have little quarrel with liberal feminism. Like feminists of the late 1960s and 1970s (their mothers' generation), they employ a rhetoric that deplores protectionism and cherishes freedom and equality. This younger group of writers is most troubled by what they perceive as the wrong turn feminism took in the 1980s, when scholars such as MacKinnon began to focus on issues of coercive sexuality, particularly rape, sexual harassment, and pornography. Interestingly, the image of women that this second group of critics finds so objectionable is also a Victorian portrait of femininity—namely, the image of the innocent, fragile, vulnerable, sexless woman. What is most striking about their critique, however, is that they connect this image to dominance feminism and largely hold feminists, rather than more traditional groups, responsible for constricting young women's freedom and opportunities.

One widely read book that captures the flavor of the victim feminism critique is Katie Roiphe's *The Morning After: Sex, Fear and Feminism* (1993). The title evokes a prominent theme in the book, questioning the crisis surrounding date rape. As a Harvard undergrad in the late 1980s and Princeton graduate student in the early 1990s, Roiphe encountered a feminism that she felt was obsessed with sexual danger and robbed her and her classmates of the excitement and freedom that comes with sexual experimentation. She describes how organized efforts on college campuses, from Take Back the Night marches to safe-sex workshops, managed to instill a fear of AIDS and rape in young women, but did little to help women deal with the ambiguity and complexity of real sexual relationships. She claims that although there is no longer talk about affronts to women's honor or virtue, the contemporary discussion about "post-traumatic stress syndrome" and "trauma" continues to construct women as passive victims of male sexual aggression. According to Roiphe, feminists are now in the strange position of warning women against the dangerous ways of men and in the process, they treat women as if they lacked the intelligence and courage to take care of themselves.

> The image that emerges from feminist preoccupations with rape and sexual harassment is that of women as victims, offended by a professor's dirty joke, verbally pressured into sex by peers. This image of a delicate woman bears a striking resemblance to that fifties ideal my mother and the other women of her generation fought so hard to get away from . . . But here she is again, with her pure intentions and her wide eyes. Only this time it is the feminists themselves who are breathing new life into her.[97]

Roiphe equates feminism with a rigid and caricatured version of dominance feminism (which she calls "rape-crisis feminism") that revels in tales of women's victimization and has the effect of duping college-age women into believing that they have been sexually exploited by men, sometimes after the fact—as the title puts it, the morning after. She is skeptical of accounts of professed rape victims at public rallies because, for Roiphe, their stories all sound the same and their credibility is undermined by a self-congratulatory rhetoric that belies genuine trauma. Rather than being transgressive or unconventional, Roiphe regards feminism as the new orthodoxy, with pages taken from the recovery movement (such as the Twelve-Step Program) and social conservatism. Her critique trades on the backlash against "political correctness" by claiming that it is the feminists themselves who are most adept at silencing dissent, as they "vie for the position of being silenced."[98]

Roiphe's critique of feminism blends in with more traditionalist views about dating and sex when she approaches the topic of individual responsibility. She has little patience for women who complain that they were induced by men to drink too much at a party, remember little about the circumstances under which they had intercourse,

---

[97] Katie Roiphe, *The Morning After: Sex, Fear and Feminism* at 6.
[98] *Id.* at 34.

and wake up to find themselves alone in a strange room. In such circumstances, Roiphe would hold the woman responsible for "[her] choice to drink or take drugs,"[99] even if her judgment was impaired at the time she had sex. For Roiphe, to do otherwise would be to assume that women are "helpless and naïve" and to buy into Victorian stereotypes of women as devoid of passion and sexual desire.

There is a strong strain of individualism in critiques such as Roiphe's. Rather than enforce rules against sexual harassment, Roiphe commends the "sticks and stones" approach to verbal harassment, urging women to "put offenders in their place" by sharp retorts or even physical retaliation. She recounts with approval one incident in which a college woman was playing pinball at the local lunch place when a teenage boy came up and grabbed her breast. Roiphe was impressed by the way the woman responded: "She calmly went to the counter and ordered a glass of milk and then walked over and poured it over his head."[100] More recently, another critic has made a similar plea for "female Rambo-ism" in an essay about Paula Jones's lawsuit against President Clinton. Her view is that even though Jones justifiably might have been offended by Clinton's alleged exposure of his penis, she should not have resorted to the courts. She felt that Jones should have responded by "suitable speech (the phrase 'Put that shrivelly stump back in your pants' comes to mind), or by ignoring the conduct, or by storming out of the room . . ."[101] For such critics of victim feminism, these individualistic responses have the advantage of showing women to be strong and capable of "taking it" because "[a] woman who disses the phallus, whether by disrespect or disregard, denies its power."[102] The disadvantage, of course, is that few people, men *or* women, have the presence to respond at the moment with style or confidence. Particularly for women, many attempts at retaliation simply come off as being silly, or overreactions, or incoherent.

In its more extreme form, individualism translates into libertarianism and an argument for deregulation. For example, journalist

---

[99] *Id.* at 53-54.

[100] *Id.* at 101.

[101] Terry Diggs, Reach Out and Slap Someone: The Real Reason Why Working Women Have Snubbed Paula Jones, Legal Times, April 13, 1998 at 24.

[102] *Id.*

F. Backlash: Proliferation of Critics of Feminist Legal Theory

Cathy Young[103] takes the victim feminism critique so far as to regard advocacy of the "reasonable woman" standard in sexual harassment litigation as "protective feminism," and virtually indistinguishable from social conservatives' call for decency and a return to traditional sex roles. Young believes that legal regulation of sexual conduct in the workplace is invariably a form of legal paternalism, and she is even wary of equality feminists such as Justice Ruth Bader Ginsburg who support using the law to eliminate all forms of disparate treatment of men and women.[104] Like Roiphe, Young seems to believe that women as individuals possess a preexisting power that can liberate them from second-class citizenship, if only feminists, institutions, and the state will get out of the way.

As part of her more extensive analysis of the relationship between victimization and agency,[105] Kathryn Abrams has responded to the victim feminism critics by articulating the ways in which their critique misunderstands the arguments of MacKinnon and other dominance theorists. In a review of Roiphe's book, Abrams argues that Roiphe confuses advocacy of legal intervention with a concession that women are inherently too weak to protect themselves. Abrams's position is that establishing a legal cause of action against sexual harassment or acquaintance rape says nothing specific about the actions or the character of the victims, drawing the analogy that "[l]aws that make theft or assault a crime make no statement about the capacity of victims, and require nothing more than that victims give evidence."[106] Abrams denies that affording women a legal right to sue for sexually offensive conduct necessarily discourages women from developing assertive individual responses to harassment or somehow implies that such individual responses are inappropriate. In defense of dominance feminism, Abrams underscores the difference between spelling out how women have been victimized, that is, exposing mechanisms of subordination, and claiming that women are the "walking wounded" who have been personally immobilized by male aggression.

---

[103] Cathy Young, The New Madonna/Whore Syndrome: Feminism, Sexuality, and Sexual Harassment, 38 N.Y.L. Sch. L. Rev. 257 (1993).

[104] *Id.* at 268-69.

[105] *See* supra pp. 102-106.

[106] Kathryn Abrams, Songs of Innocence and Experience: Dominance Feminism in the University, 103 Yale L.J. 1533, 1553 (1994).

The most important question for Abrams is how feminist accounts of victimization can so easily be misread and taken as "insults," even by writers such as Roiphe who identify themselves as feminists. Abrams theorizes that critics such as Roiphe have thoroughly embraced the liberal view of the individual as autonomous and self-directing. For them to acknowledge that women are constrained in their choices by a sexist society becomes tantamount to saying that women "suffer a kind of compromised personhood"[107] or are less than full-fledged individuals. Abrams thus has a response to Roiphe's complaint that contemporary feminism has catapulted women back into the 1950s, forgetting the lessons of liberal feminism. As I read Abrams, she is claiming that it is Roiphe who missed out on the teachings of the 1980s difference theorists, particularly their powerful critique of liberalism. While presumably both writers would agree that feminism, of whatever variety, has not yet succeeded in freeing women, Abrams does not take feminism's lack of success to mean that the movement itself is a principal cause of women's subordination. Instead, she seeks to understand women simultaneously as agents and victims, placing feminism also on the side of agency.

3.   The New Right-Wing Attack

The charge of victim feminism is just one of many charges leveled at legal feminism by right-wing critics such as the leadership of the Independent Women's Forum, who exemplify a third genre of criticism. Unlike evolutionary theorists or liberal individualists like Roiphe, critics in this third group do not endorse a theoretically unified set of beliefs about gender, sexuality, or equality. Their positions are more reactive, taking aim at what they regard as the priorities in the agenda of the feminist "establishment." Thus, they sometimes advocate formal equality and sex blindness, as in their campaigns against affirmative action and in opposition to the Violence Against Women Act.[108] With respect to other controversies, however, they defend sex segrega-

---

[107] *Id.* at 1554.

[108] *See* Testimony of Anita Blair on Behalf of the Independent Women's Forum Before the House Appropriations Committee, Subcommittee on Commerce, Justice, State and Judiciary and Related Agencies, May 11, 1995 (urging Congress not to fund Violence Against Women Act).

F. Backlash: Proliferation of Critics of Feminist Legal Theory

tion and the use of explicit classifications based on gender. The politics of this third group of critics are very close to that of older, ultra-conservative groups such as Phyllis Schlafly's Eagle Forum, which was most famous for its opposition to equality feminism, particularly the proposed Equal Rights Amendment. The new rhetoric associated with the Independent Women's Forum, however, eschews labels like liberal or conservative, claiming instead to be "the voice of reasonable women," who make arguments from "common sense" and "logic," rather than "divisive ideology."

What is most striking about the publicity of the Independent Women's Forum, however, is their intemperate tone with respect to people and ideas allied with feminism. The executive director of the group, lawyer Anita Blair, regards feminism as on a par with racism, and has stated that "a feminist is a person who irrationally puts women ahead of men and frequently ahead of children," which echoes her definition of a racist as "somebody who irrationally puts his own race ahead of others."[109] In her view, feminism is a cynical enterprise that elitist women use to gain advantages over less elite women.[110] In this critique, feminists have no genuine interest in solving real problems facing women, such as domestic violence, but want only to assure that there is "a constant stream of victims"[111] to justify their requests for government funding. The Independent Women's Forum has tried to position itself as the voice of reason, offering "an intelligent refutation of the leading feminist nonsense that is swallowed so uncritically by the mainstream press."[112]

As the preceding paragraph suggests, this third genre of criticism is full of ironies and internal contradictions. In my view, Anita Blair embraces an upside-down worldview that distorts and lumps together the varieties of feminist approaches in a pugnacious style not likely to produce thoughtful responses and rejoinders. By labeling feminist positions as irrational and nonsensical, her call to "reason" and "common sense," for example, has the opposite effect, that of cutting off debate before the merits of a position are addressed. Feminist concerns about diversity and feminist opposition to hierarchy are dis-

---

[109] Stephen Goode, Armed with Common Sense, Anita Blair Attacks Feminism, Insight on the News, Nov. 24, 1997 at 31.

[110] *Id.*

[111] *Id.*

[112] Web page: <http://www.iwf.org/about.cfm>.

missed out of hand as disingenuous, simply by claiming that it is feminists, not anti-feminists, who are the elitists. Perhaps most importantly, feminists' struggle for equality for women is recast as a plea for special rights, playing into the stereotype of feminists as man-haters and abortion supporters who have little regard for children.

The Independent Women's Forum's critique of feminism resembles what Carolyn Heilbrun has called "The Smear." In Heilbrun's analysis, the right-wing backlash against feminism and multiculturalism in the 1980s and 1990s has often taken the form of name-calling and accusations, and employs a political version of projection: accusing your opponent of what you yourself are doing.[113] One response to Blair's critique, for example, would be to point out how the campaign of the Independent Women's Forum relies heavily on divisive ideology and is often short on reasoned analysis. For this reason, it is difficult to summarize this genre of criticism by teasing out recurrent themes or positions. The following three lines of opposition to feminism, however, can be seen in recent publicity from the group.

First, particularly with respect to issues relating to segregation, critics in this third group believe that it is inappropriate to analogize sex and race discrimination. In marked contrast to many feminist writers who see racism and sexism as interrelated forms of oppression, many of today's conservative critics argue for different legal treatment of explicit race and sex classifications. Thus, in a brief in support of Virginia Military Institute's policy of excluding women, the Independent Women's Forum argued that while "racial differences are purely superficial," differences between men and women are "real and substantial."[114] Implicit in their argument is the belief that gender differences are biologically based and that segregating the sexes is an appropriate way of marking and responding to such differences. The group has also opposed gender integration during basic training in the military, on the grounds that integration reduces standards and compromises the military's effectiveness. Unlike some feminists who support women-only institutions as a way of helping women overcome sexism in society, the concern of critics such as the Independent Women's Forum is with protecting male institutions from women and their values.

---

[113] Carolyn G. Heilbrun, The Thomas Confirmation Hearings or How Being a Humanist Prepares You for Right-Wing Politics, 65 S. Cal. L. Rev. 1569, 1571 (1992).

[114] *Supreme Court v. VMI* Amicus Brief by IWF, <http://www.iwf.org/newsitem.cfm>, May 11, 1998.

F. Backlash: Proliferation of Critics of Feminist Legal Theory

A second, somewhat contradictory theme of this genre of criticism is antipathy to gender consciousness and the corresponding belief that gender has no proper place in the framing of public policy. This theme has been most evident in the group's opposition to the work of the task force on gender and race bias in the D.C. Circuit.[115] In a statement criticizing the task force's report, Blair took the position that it was objectionable for the task force even to count the number of women and minority judges in the D.C. Circuit, claiming that any evaluation of the demographics of the judiciary infringed on the President's right to nominate judges and the Senate's right to confirm judicial nominations.[116] Such extreme hostility to gender and race consciousness echoes conservative complaints against affirmative action, which proceed from the assumption that any use of race or gender is discriminatory, even when the objective is to eliminate or prevent race or gender discrimination. From this perspective, merely searching for possible bias undermines judges' impartiality and threatens to erode public confidence in the courts. This position also makes changing the status quo nearly impossible. Judith Resnik sees such opposition to the usually uncontroversial work of the gender and race bias task forces as part of a larger right-wing backlash that generally disputes the existence of systemic discrimination in legal institutions and regards feminism as the evil to be guarded against:

> Task forces, the critics claim, violate "our" traditions by creating "faction in civil society." Under this plot, we (that is literally all of us) are equal before the law. Courts are blind to distinctions based on race, color, gender, and/or ethnicity. Objectors accuse task forces that mark differences of *making* differences by seeking special favor and undermining the impartiality of law [and contend] that naming differences between women and men creates differences, that affirmative action creates prejudice rather than responds to it.[117]

The third and perhaps most prominent theme in this genre of criticism is that women have already achieved equality. The critics part

[115] *See* supra pp. 79-83 for discussion of the work of task forces on bias in the courts.

[116] Anita Blair, Proceedings of the 55th Judicial Conference of the District of Columbia Circuit, 160 F.R.D. 169, 194 (1994).

[117] Judith Resnik, Changing the Topic, 8 Cardozo Stud. L. & Literature 339, 347-48 (1996).

company with feminists most sharply in their denial of systematic bias against women in society. For example, representatives of the Independent Women's Forum claim that there is no widespread gender discrimination in compensation, despite acknowledging the fact that full-time women workers in 1992 earned only 72 percent of wages of men working full-time. In support of their claim that there is no inequity, they rely on a study finding that among people age 27 to 33 who have never had a child, women earn almost 98 percent of men's wages.[118] The selection of that statistic is revealing because it suggests that the disparity in compensation is correlated to motherhood and does not affect the relatively small number of younger women workers in this cohort with no children. It also underscores an important point of disagreement in the interpretation of workplace statistics between feminists and conservative critics. Feminists tend to infer discrimination from data showing that males on average earn more than females, controlling for type of work and number of hours of work. In contrast, conservative critics more often assume that mothers earn less than similarly situated fathers because they have voluntarily chosen to subordinate their work to family concerns. What feminists suspect is discrimination, conservative critics ascribe to women's choice. Underneath the conservative contention that gender equality already exists lies a conception of motherhood as being fundamentally different from fatherhood, and a belief that women who also care for children cannot expect to achieve parity in the workplace. The "equality" heralded by the Independent Women's Forum is a vastly different concept of equality than the vision embraced by legal feminists, and, to my mind, it marks the boundary between feminism and the backlash against feminism.

Much of the criticism of feminism and feminist legal theory described above assumes that feminism has become the dominant ideology and positions its critics as dissenters who wage an uphill battle against the establishment. Feminists find this claim amusing because, from their vantage point, the forces undermining feminism have always been strong and have only gained considerable strength during the "culture wars" of the 1990s. There is fundamental disagreement about what constitutes the "mainstream." The degree of recognition recently accorded to feminist legal theory hardly seems enough to

---

[118] *See* supra note 112.

F. Backlash: Proliferation of Critics of Feminist Legal Theory

transport the field from the margin to the center of legal discourse. Instead, as a teacher of feminist law courses, I find that the backlash has had a concrete and cumulative effect. Each year, students shy away from courses with "feminism" in their title because they sense that their careers might suffer if they are linked to the feminist movement, however tangentially. They admit that they worry about having the "f" word appear on their transcript of courses or on their résumé, in case a prospective employer might get the wrong impression. The day has not yet arrived when students can satisfy their curiosity and interest, sign up for courses in feminism, and not hesitate even for a moment. Until the stigma of feminism has been erased, it seems premature to speak of the "feminist establishment" or to locate feminist legal theory within the mainstream of legal thought.

CHAPTER 6

Allied Intellectual Movements

Two intellectual movements—critical race theory and gay and lesbian legal studies—are currently so closely allied with post-essentialist feminist writings that it is difficult to tell whether all three will eventually merge into a more unified approach (such as anti-subordination theory) or will continue to develop along more distinctive lines. Not surprisingly, each movement has been particularly interested in documenting its own historical roots. Critical race scholars have paid close attention to the black civil rights era (sometimes referred to as the Second Reconstruction) and the struggles that preceded it. Gay and lesbian writers have examined the causes of the heightened degree of activism and openness in their communities since the Stonewall Riots in 1969, the event that marked the beginning of the contemporary gay rights movement. Feminists have built upon the experience of consciousness-raising groups in the early 1970s to develop a feminist method of political analysis.

The predominant theoretical approach in the three fields is strikingly similar. Most of the contemporary scholars in these fields are social constructionists. Their writings start from the premise that race, gender, and sexual orientation are shaped by historical, cultural, and ideological forces. Although individual scholars differ as to the role they assign to biology in this process, they tend to reject popular beliefs that the sexes or races possess innate traits or that homosexuality is unnatural. A major theme is that the "essential" qualities often associated with gender, race, and sexual minorities are distortions that tell us more about the majority's perceptions and preoccupations than they do about the groups themselves.

The three schools of intellectual thought are also allied in the sense that each is highly critical of the status quo. Transformation of the current political and social order appears to be an objective of even the most highly theoretical work. In this respect, the three allied fields of inquiry differ from other intellectual trends, such as neopragmatism, law and literature, or civic republicanism. The difference is that feminism, critical race theory, and gay and lesbian studies are tied, respectively, to the plight of women, people of color, and gay men and lesbians in the larger society. Unlike the more exclusively academic trends, these intellectual movements can be said to have a constituency. To some degree at least, their success is measured by their ability to inspire changes in the treatment, status, and self-understanding of the constituent groups.

A.   CRITICAL RACE THEORY

The school of inquiry known as "critical race theory" is about ten years old, dating from the formation in the mid-1980s of a movement of law professors of color whose scholarship addresses the importance of race in American law and legal culture. To some degree, the critical race theorists continued the work of more traditional civil rights scholars of the 1960s and 1970s who advocated legal reforms to redress past and present discrimination against African-Americans. Thus, topics such as affirmative action, equal protection, and school desegregation have been revisited by this new generation of legal academics whose ranks no longer are dominated by white men.

The scholarship of the critical race theorists, however, tends to differ in both style and substance from the earlier, liberal civil rights research. The use of narrative figures prominently in critical race writing, reflecting a desire to tell the "outsider's" story and to draw upon an African-American tradition that values passionate and inspirational speech.[1] The new critical race theorists also regard racism, and the ideology of white supremacy, as a pervasive and perhaps permanent fea-

---

[1] Charles R. Lawrence III, The Word and the River: Pedagogy as Scholarship as Struggle, 65 S. Cal. L. Rev. 2231 (1992).

ture of American law. In contrast to liberal scholars who urge color-blindness in the law, critical race theorists advocate color-consciousness and a greater understanding of unconscious cognitive mechanisms that operate to perpetuate race bias. Much like the 1980s feminist critics of liberalism who emphasized difference and domination, critical race scholars of the same era started from the premise that race matters in almost every facet of life and that formal racial equality in the law has done little to eliminate race-based injustice. To explain the resilience of racial hierarchy, despite the victories of the civil rights movement, many critical race scholars have focused on the theme of cultural domination. Cultural domination theorists emphasize the importance of what might be called "cognitive bias"—racial stereotyping and other habitual ways of thinking about race that inhibit understanding and compassion for difference. In particular, cultural domination theories contrast the positive values attached to whiteness in our society with the negative cultural associations most often linked to blackness.

In the 1990s, critical race scholarship has also been marked by attention to diversity among racial minority groups. Breaking out of a white/black discourse, Latino, Asian-American, and Native American scholars have begun to articulate how the effect of white supremacy differs with respect to particular ethnic groups and to observe the lack of visibility of minority groups other than African-Americans. Scholars are also exploring what it means to be biracial, multiracial, or a person who defies conventional racial categories. Finally, a postmodernist strain in the most recent critical race writing regards the concept of "race" itself as a social construction and has set a goal of destabilizing racial categorizations.

1. The Theme of Cultural Domination

The individual most often cited as a founder of critical race theory is Derrick Bell, an African-American law professor whose career has been marked by protest, activism, and innovation in scholarship. His most publicized protest occurred in 1990 when he was a faculty member at the Harvard Law School.[2] The impetus for the protest was Har-

---

[2] Bell's autobiographical work *Confronting Authority: Reflections of an Ardent Protestor* (1994) gives a full account of the Harvard protest.

vard's failure to make an offer of permanent employment to an African-American woman who was on a visiting faculty appointment. Bell contended that Harvard discriminated by keeping the number of women and minority faculty members artificially low. At that time, of the 62 tenured faculty, there were only five white women and three African-American men, with no representation of any other racial minority nor any women of color. Bell initially took a leave of absence without pay to dramatize his dissatisfaction with the hiring policy, which he saw as fundamentally inconsistent with the sizable representation of minority students at Harvard and the growing importance of black feminist scholarship. He vowed not to return until Harvard hired a woman of color in a tenured position. Two years later, when the university refused to extend his leave, Bell's employment was terminated.

Bell's real-life protest enacted a prominent theme in critical race scholarship: the belief that dominant institutions are governed by policies that reflect a deep-seated, if unconscious, desire for white domination. In his writings, Bell has developed the theme that even institutions that profess to be affirmative action-minded can be expected to resist racial integration, particularly when a "tipping point" is reached that threatens to change the culture and image of the institution. In his "Chronicle of the DeVine Gift," subtitled "the unspoken limit on affirmative action," Bell uses a fictional character, Geneva Crenshaw, to explain the resilience of racism in contemporary life.[3] In the tale, Crenshaw was the only black professor at a major law school. She explained that she had become increasingly overloaded with doing the extra work that comes with being a "token"—counseling students, serving on endless committees, being called on to help when there is a racial crisis. She had watched as the faculty rejected other minority candidates as unqualified, even some with credentials better than her own. In the chronicle, the DeVine gift came in the form of superqualified minority candidates who magically became available to fill the curricular and other needs of the school.

---

[3] The chronicle was first published in Derrick Bell, The Supreme Court, 1984 Term—Forward: The Civil Rights Chronicles, 99 Harv. L. Rev. 4, 39-57 (1985) under the title "The Chronicle of the DeVine Gift." The chronicle is included in Derrick Bell, *And We Are Not Saved: The Elusive Quest for Racial Justice* 140-61 (1987).

A. Critical Race Theory

By the time there were six minority faculty, diverse in ethnicity and gender, the law school seemed poised to go beyond tokenism. The moment of insight occurred, however, when the faculty refused to hire the exceptionally talented seventh candidate. The dean explained that just as Howard University wished to stay a black institution, the law school wished to maintain its image as a white school and could not afford to go higher than 25 percent in representation of racial minorities.

As I read the moral of Bell's chronicle, the unspoken limit on affirmative action and the source of the resistance to diversity lies in the faculty's and the dean's unconscious desire to preserve the white racial identity of the school. The somber message implicit in this cultural domination account of racism is that institutions will resist change simply because they cannot believe that high quality is consistent with diversity, even when there is no shortage of highly qualified minority candidates. For critical race theorists such as Bell, it is the cultural association of whiteness with merit and value, and the corresponding myth of black inferiority, that leads people to believe that exclusionary sites are the most prestigious.

Cultural domination theorists tend to regard "merit" as a moving target. For example, when there is integration in one sector, such as law school admissions, it is likely that being a law school graduate will no longer suffice as a credential for persons seeking to become law professors. Instead, an additional credential that far fewer minority or female candidates for faculty positions possess—for example, having a Ph.D. in economics or being a Rhodes Scholar—will tend to emerge as the new indicator of excellence. In much the same way that feminists are alert to implicit male bias in purportedly neutral standards, critical race theorists look for implicit white norms embedded within commonly used but ever-changing measures of merit.

Another prominent theme in Bell's scholarship is that cultural patterns of racial hierarchy are reproduced in different or updated forms over the course of time. Many critical race scholars believe that oppression can be reproduced and that progress is not inevitable. They strongly contest the popular view that racism is a thing of the past, and instead assert that despite the 1960s civil rights movement, the social status of the majority of blacks has not substantially improved. For example, in his latest book, *Gospel Choirs*, Bell wonders whether black civil rights lawyers such as himself, who fought for integration in schools and other institutions in the 1960s, made any lasting dent in the racist structures of our society. Similar to the arguments of 1980s feminists who exposed the inadequacy of formal legal equality, Bell contends that, compared to its predecessor, the current "colorblind" legal system is not much of an improvement, if we measure progress by the material reality of the lives of most black people. He cautions that, in the long run, even major civil rights victories can prove to be irrelevant and ultimately can be subverted to serve the interests of whites. Bell's view of the impact of the legal reforms of the Second Reconstruction is pessimistic:

> In challenging the white world on behalf of black people, we civil rights lawyers succeeded in assisting the society to rid itself of a policy of racial subordination—*segregation*—that had outlived its usefulness. At the same time, we urged the adoption of a racial reform—*equal opportunity*—that has, in this determinedly racist society, become a more subtle but no less effective means of maintaining the status quo of white dominance.[4]

Although not all critical race scholars share Bell's view that racism is permanent, there seems to be a consensus that the roots of racism are so deep that it should be regarded as a fundamental feature of American law and culture, not simply an aberration in an otherwise just and impartial system. The pervasiveness of racism suggests that it often takes something more than reasoned argument and exposure of double standards to bring about social change. Bell, for example, theorizes that change comes about only at those moments in history when the interests of whites converge with those of blacks and it becomes in the self-interest of policymakers to endorse progressive measures. As Bell analyzes it, *Brown v. Board of Education*[5] was more of a product of Cold War international politics and domestic economic pressures than of moral enlightenment. Bell's "interest-convergence" theory of *Brown* viewed the dismantling of segregation as a way to enhance America's credibility in the struggle against Communism and to aid the South in making the transition to a modernized Sunbelt economy.[6]

---

[4] Derrick Bell, *Gospel Choirs: Psalms of Survival in an Alien Land Called Home* 54 (1996).

[5] 347 U.S. 483 (1954).

[6] Derrick Bell, *Race, Racism and American Law* 640-41 (3d ed. 1992).

140

A. Critical Race Theory

Bell's version of cultural domination theory emphasizes differences in power and the difficulty of convincing whites to relinquish their privilege. In this respect, his body of work resembles MacKinnon's, particularly insofar as each scholar searches for the deep cultural roots of oppression and exposes the hazards of liberal reforms. However, MacKinnon locates the source of women's subordination in the cultural meaning of sexuality, specifically the eroticization of dominance. Bell's explanations for racial subordination are more materialist in nature. He stresses the economic self-interest of whites and the use of blacks as scapegoats for the ills of society, as a way to deflect attention of working-class people away from the increasingly unequal distribution of wealth in America.

2. Unconscious Racism and the Critique of Color-Blindness

Not unlike the paradox facing feminists since the 1980s, critical race scholars constantly confront the need to explain why they believe that racism is so pervasive when much of the American public has concluded that the civil rights campaign of the 1960s succeeded in ending race discrimination against minorities. In contrast to the public debate about race which has centered on whether to eliminate affirmative action, critical race scholarship has taken an oppositional stance and has sought to challenge the terms of the debate. Mainstream discourse seems to assume that racism has largely disappeared, while critical race theory assumes that racial hierarchies have remained largely intact.

The difference in the mainstream and critical race positions starts with the definition of race discrimination and racism. Reflecting the mainstream view, the legal definition of race discrimination is narrow in scope, generally encompassing only actions or policies that are the product of deliberate or intentional bias or animus toward an individual or group. Current anti-discrimination law outlaws openly prejudiced practices and punishes the bigot who acts out of hatred or animosity. For critical race scholars, the problem with this definition is that it fails to capture the vast majority of racist practices that stem from unconscious, rather than deliberate, processes.

Charles Lawrence has written extensively about the phenomenon of unconscious racism, comparing it to a disease that is widespread, hard to control, and insidious. He argues that racism affects not only bigots but well-intentioned whites who may sincerely believe that they are antiracist. In its unconscious form, moreover, racism infects the psyches of blacks who internalize racist attitudes and stereotypes. In this famous passage from a 1987 article, Lawrence describes the breadth and scope of unconscious racism:

> Americans share a common historical and cultural heritage in which racism has played and still plays a dominant role. Because of this shared experience, we also inevitably share many ideas, attitudes, and beliefs that attach significance to an individual's race and induce negative feelings and opinions about nonwhites. To the extent that this cultural belief system has influenced all of us, we are all racists. At the same time, most of us are unaware of our racism. We do not recognize the ways in which our cultural experience has influenced our beliefs about race or the occasions on which the beliefs affect our actions. In other words, a large part of the behavior that produces racial discrimination is influenced by unconscious racial motivation.[7]

Lawrence's account of the dynamics of unconscious racism means that it is not enough to root out only deliberately biased conduct and that a legal system so designed will barely scratch the surface of the problem. The techniques needed to recognize and correct for unconscious racism bear little resemblance to the search for invidious motivation that characterize legal standards of proof under the Constitution's Equal Protection mandate or Title VII's disparate treatment theory of liability. The law currently insists only on a neutral process, requiring that individuals make decisions without regard to race. Critical race theorists advocate a more substantive, race-conscious stance that seeks to eliminate systematic racial disadvantage and racial privilege.

Most critical race scholars regard the legal commitment to color-blindness as perpetuating rather than decreasing racial subordination. In the past, explicit legal classifications may have been highly effective in maintaining white supremacy. Now that racial hierarchies are primarily maintained through other means, however, the legal mandate of color-blindness has the negative effect of creating the illusion of equality and encouraging the denial of the prevalence of racism. This cri-

---

[7] Charles R. Lawrence III, The Id, the Ego, and Equal Protection: Reckoning with Unconscious Racism, 39 Stan. L. Rev. 317, 322 (1987) (citations omitted).

A. Critical Race Theory

tique of color-blindness fits into the larger postmodern critique of neutrality and objectivity, making the point that what passes for color-blindness is neither neutral nor objective, but a new mechanism for reproducing racism. Charles Lawrence argues that the rhetoric of color-blindness has been appropriated by reactionary forces:

> "Affirmative action" and "colorblindness" themselves become race-coded words used by politicians who rely on the social construction of race to convey racist meanings. The anti-affirmative action provision recently proposed as a California ballot initiative is the latest example of a political campaign that relies on the intersecting ideologies of formal equality and white supremacy to send the racist message, "It's time to put them back in their place," while trumpeting the rhetoric of equal rights.[8]

The prevalence of unconscious racism and the inadequacy of color-blindness as a legal standard to capture contemporary manifestations of racial bias has led critical race theorists to suggest new legal approaches grounded on anti-subordination, rather than liberal, premises. Particularly because unconscious racism is so hard to prove and observe, the challenge is to devise legal standards that are workable and create meaningful boundaries between lawful and unlawful behavior, without minimizing the injuries of unconscious race-biased thinking. Lawrence, for example, has advocated that the constitutionality of a practice be judged by its "cultural meaning." Rather than search for hostile intent or racial animus, the cultural meaning test focuses on how a practice is understood, asking whether people affected by the law or governmental action believe that it has racial significance.

By fastening on cultural meaning rather than intent, the test is concerned less with assessing blame than it is with assessing harm. Critical race theory proceeds from the assumption that actions which convey racist meanings are apt to do as much harm as deliberately prejudiced behavior. Critical race theorists seek to have the courts engage in a contextual and historical analysis of the law and urge adoption of standards, such as the cultural meaning test, that emphasize group experience rather than individual state of mind. They share with contemporary feminists the belief that when practices are abstracted

---

[8] Charles R. Lawrence III, Race, Multiculturalism, and the Jurisprudence of Transformation, 47 Stan. L. Rev. 819, 838 (1995).

and taken out of historical context, it is easier to mistake bias for equal opportunity.

3.   Perspectivity and Hate Speech

Other hallmarks of much of the critical race literature are its distrust of claims of objectivity, and its commitment to identifying and articulating legal issues and legal harm from the perspectives of people of color. For critical race scholars, this attraction to a perspectival approach often starts with a personal awareness of seeing the world through different eyes. The theory of "double-consciousness," and probably the most famous statement on multiple perspectives, comes from W.E.B. DuBois, a black scholar and activist who published *The Souls of Black Folk* in 1953. At a time when racism in America was frequently described as "The Negro problem," DuBois posed to himself the question "How does it feel to be a problem?" He replied, "I answer seldom a word," and yet, "being a problem is a strange experience." To illuminate how his experience of himself and the world was different from others, DuBois spoke of the "second-sight" of African-Americans:

> [T]he Negro is a sort of seventh son, born with a veil, and gifted with second-sight in this American world—a world which yields him no true self-consciousness, but only lets him see himself through the revelation of the other world. It is a peculiar sensation, this double consciousness, this sense of always looking at one's self through the eyes of others, of measuring one's soul by the tape of a world that looks on in amused contempt and pity. One ever feels his twoness—an American, a Negro; two souls, two thoughts, two unreconciled strivings; two warring ideals in one dark body, whose dogged strength alone keeps it from being torn asunder.[9]

Being cast as the "other" in a hostile or indifferent world carries pain and injury that is often invisible to the majority who do not appreciate that their social position insulates them from certain harms. Analogous to the feminist move to have sexual harassment defined from the point of view of women who experience the abuse, some criti-

[9] W.E.B. DuBois, *The Souls of Black Folk* 16-17 (1953).

A. Critical Race Theory

cal race scholars—notably Richard Delgado,[10] Mari Matsuda,[11] and Charles Lawrence[12]—have argued in favor of considering the victim's perspective when determining what constitutes legal harm, particularly in the regulation of hate speech. They charge that the controversy about racist speech on campus has often become enmeshed in abstract discussion of First Amendment values without a full understanding of the interests at stake from the victim's point of view.

The perspectival approach to hate speech starts with a textured account of the effects of hate speech on its targets. Contrary to the "sticks and stones" version of the harms of verbal abuse, these scholars contend that words alone can inflict wounds that might be more severe than some forms of physical injury. Racist epithets and slurs are not only insulting and offensive. Because they constitute part of a long history of racial violence, segregation, and oppression, they are also effective in conveying an implicit, but clear, threat to the health, safety, and dignity of the targeted person. The injurious power of racist speech blurs the line between physical and mental injury. Charles Lawrence likens racist hate speech to a slap in the face and argues that its effect is experienced in ways resembling a racially motivated physical attack:

> When racial insults are hurled at minorities, the response may be silence or flight rather than a fight, but the preemptive effect on further speech is just as complete . . . Women and minorities often report that they find themselves speechless in the face of discriminatory verbal attacks. This inability to respond is not the result of oversensitivity among these groups . . . Rather, it is the product of several factors, all of which reveal the non-speech character of the initial preemptive verbal assault . . . [T]he visceral emotional response to personal attack precludes speech . . . Fear, rage, shock, and flight all interfere with any reasoned response. Words like "nigger," "kike," and "faggot" produce physical symptoms that temporarily disable the victim . . . When one is personally attacked with words that denote one's subhuman status and un-

---

[10] Richard Delgado, Words That Wound: A Tort Action for Racial Insults, Epithets, and Name-Calling, 17 Harv. C.R.-C.L. L. Rev. 133 (1982).

[11] Mari J. Matsuda, Public Response to Racist Speech: Considering the Victim's Story, 87 Mich. L. Rev. 2320 (1989).

[12] Charles R. Lawrence III, If He Hollers Let Him Go: Regulating Racist Speech on Campus, 1990 Duke L.J. 431.

touchability, there is little (if anything) that can be said to redress either the emotional or the reputational injury.[13]

The impact of hate speech may be felt, moreover, beyond the immediate targets through its capacity to terrorize, immobilize, or demoralize others in the same social group. Because racist speech, even when directed at a particular person, inevitably carries a message about the inferiority of the group, it exposes and reinforces the vulnerability of the group.[14] Beyond suffering emotional distress, this broader class of victims may respond to racist speech by curtailing their activities, withdrawing, or taking other "protective" measures that impose their own costs through social isolation and lost opportunities.

The critical race critique of hate speech uncovers the reverberating effects and silencing impact of racist speech along lines similar to MacKinnon's campaign against pornography. Consideration of the victim's perspective details the full extent of the harms so that when a balance between equality and free speech is struck, minority interests in both equality and free expression will not be invisible or discounted. Additionally, the process of expressing legal harm from a minority point of view challenges the basic categories (physical versus mental, speech versus action) around which traditional analysis of the issue has been organized and reveals the cognitive bias imbedded in these deeper legal structures.

The reconceptualization of harm from the victim's perspective has also led critical scholars to devise new terms to describe some of the distinctive harms associated with social inequality. The term "assaultive speech" is sometimes used instead of "hate speech" to highlight that the harm inflicted resembles a physical assault and does not always emanate from hate-mongering bigots, but from insensitive, ignorant, self-interested, or insecure people. Scholars have also attempted to find more evocative ways to describe the myriad forms of psychological injury caused by racist behaviors, beyond the simple label of "emotional distress." Patricia Williams speaks of "spirit murder" and "spirit injury" to signal that racist actions can damage the spirit of victims through the disabling effect of internalized racism. The term also connotes that it is the perpetrator's own stereotype and demonic image of

---

[13] *Id.* at 452-53.

[14] *See* Lu-in Wang, The Transforming Power of "Hate": Social Cognition Theory and the Harms of Bias-Related Crime, 71 S. Cal. L. Rev. 47, 97-108 (1997).

A. Critical Race Theory

the group, rather than the actions of victims, that incite racist violence. For Williams, the spirit murderer wants to kill that "part of his own mind's image" that has made blacks "large, threatening, powerful, uncontrollable, ubiquitous, and supernatural."[15]

Beyond describing crimes from the viewpoint of the minority victims, critical race scholars have used personal narratives to expose the smaller, but still very painful, "microaggressions" of everyday life. These stories help the reader comprehend how an incident that might seem isolated or minor may be magnified by the larger social context and how difficult it may be to dismiss the contemptuous or mocking views of others. One poignant story told by Patricia Williams tells of an incident involving her sister, who was the only black child in her fourth grade class.

> One Valentine's Day, when the teacher went out of the room, all her white classmates ripped up the valentines she had sent them and dumped them on her desk. It was so traumatic that my sister couldn't speak again in that class, she refused to participate: so completely had they made her feel not part of that group. For a while she stopped performing altogether. Ultimately my mother convinced her that she could "show them" by outperforming them, but I think the joy of education for its own sake was seriously impaired, in both her and me (for I felt it almost as much as she did; we had made the valentines together).[16]

Describing the Valentine Day's incident as offensive or even hateful does not begin to capture the psychic harm inflicted. We sense that the contempt of the white children will invariably take its toll on the self-image of the black child because children learn about themselves and create themselves through their relations with others. Williams defines spirit-murder as "disregard for others whose lives qualitatively depend on our regard."[17] Her definition illuminates a critical aspect of the harm of racist behavior, because it acknowledges human interdependency and does not pretend that only the weak are hurt by disparaging words and other symbols of disapproval and rejection.

---

[15] Patricia J. Williams, *The Alchemy of Race and Rights: Diary of a Law Professor* 72 (1990).

[16] *Id.* at 89.

[17] *Id.* at 73.

4.   Race as a Social Construction

The body of critical race scholarship discussed above is dedicated to uncovering how racial minorities are systematically disadvantaged and exploited through law. To do this, scholars have had to grapple with the importance of race in contemporary life and to break the taboo against speaking openly about race in our purportedly color-blind society. Not surprisingly, the use of race as a central category for analysis has led to a closer scrutiny of the category itself, with the result that many scholars are no longer content to treat race as a given. Similar to those feminist and gay and lesbian scholars who ascribe complicated and multiple meanings to "sex," recent postmodern critical race theorists have delved deeply into the processes of racial categorization and explored how the basic concept of race is given meaning through law and culture.

For the postmodern scholar, the central question is not "what is race?" because that question presupposes that race is a fixed, natural property with clear demarcation lines. Instead, an increasing number of critical race theorists treat race as a social construction. From this postmodernist stance, the more pressing questions relate to how human beings at particular times and in particular places have formed or invented racial categories and have infused them with particular content and meanings. In this brand of scholarship, race is principally an idea, and, as such, is constantly being changed and reformulated. This fluid view of race liberates scholars to search for the ways in which power relations have historically affected our ideas of race and how such relations work today to produce new racial codes and implicit systems of meaning.

In the legal literature, Ian Haney Lopez has provided the most elaborated discussion of race as a social construction. He starts with the compelling observation that "despite the prevalent belief in biological races, overwhelming evidence proves that race is not biological."[18] In everyday speech we may use terms such as "whites," "blacks," "Asians," "Latinos," and "American Indians" to represent separate racial groups. However, modern science is quite clear that there is no genetic basis for such a classification scheme, nor even for

---

[18] Ian F. Haney Lopez, The Social Construction of Race: Some Observations on Illusion, Fabrication, and Choice, 29 Harv. C.R.-C.L. L. Rev. 1, 6 (1994).

A. Critical Race Theory

a simpler scheme dividing the world into white, black, and yellow peoples.

Haney Lopez explains that within small populations, such as the Hmong or the Basques, there may be genetic similarity. This similarity provides no grounding for popular constructions of race, however, because it is geography rather than race that principally accounts for the similarity. For the scientist, "there exists greater genetic distance between the Spaniard and the Swede than between the Spaniard and the North African."[19] Nor is race simply a matter of differences in personal appearance. Some populations may look alike in terms of skin color, hair texture, or facial features, yet be genetically dissimilar. Conversely, some populations—such as Europeans and northern Indians—are quite distinct in appearance, yet close genetically.[20] The paradox is that while science acknowledges the lack of a connection between race and biology, law and popular culture continue to treat race as if it were determined exclusively or primarily by biology. Postmodernists contend that racial differences are not natural in the sense that they are simply a product of the natural world. Instead, they seek to explain how racial differences have been *naturalized* in law and society. This movement away from biological explanations toward explanations that focus on active human agency (whether called social construction, racial formation, or even racial fabrication) represents an important trend in critical race theory.

The social constructionists maintain that law is one of the social forces that gives meaning to racial categories. Particularly in the United States, where white slaveholders once had legal rights to the bodies of black slave women, the law was called upon to decide how to classify the interracial children born as a result of these forced unions. The most common test for defining racial identity was the "one-drop rule" (or "rule of hypodescent"), which mandated that a person with even a drop of "black" blood or any trace of black heritage was to be classified as black. After slavery, states that drew racial distinctions tended to retain similar lopsided definitions of white and black through a variety of odious rules, such as classifying persons as black if they were one-eighth black or had any appreciable black ancestry.[21]

---

[19] *Id.* at 12.

[20] *Id.* at 15-16.

[21] Ian F. Haney Lopez, *White by Law: The Legal Construction of Race* 118 (1996).

Harlon Dalton explains the "logic" and power relationships behind this kind of explicit racial categorization:

> [I]t quickly became settled law everywhere that Black plus White equals Black . . . During slavery, the "one-drop rule" made considerable practical sense; mixed-race offspring of predatory slavemasters became additions to the workforce rather than potential heirs. But practicalities to the side, the "one-drop rule" and the blood metaphor on which it rests transmit a powerful message: Black people are profoundly and unredeemably tainted.[22]

The one-drop rule is a dramatic example of the social construction of race. Through this legal classification scheme, race was structured as a dichotomous category. People were classified as either black or white, not mixed-race or biracial. It is immediately apparent that such a scheme does not function well as a proxy for a person's ancestry or appearance. Conceived in this way, the category of black people is simply too diverse to impart precise information about whether, for example, a person has several ancestors with African heritage, or whether he or she has dark or light skin. The classification scheme is only loosely tied to those biological factors.

Most importantly, under the legal classification scheme, race was also structured as hierarchical. White was defined as a pure category that achieved its superior status because of the absence of black. The classification scheme served principally to police the boundaries of whiteness, not to measure the proportion of each "race" in a person's heritage. This dichotomous and hierarchical concept of race functioned well to support an ideology of white supremacy. As long as the white race remained "pure," there was little concern for race mixing among other groups. This explains why, for example, antimiscegenation laws frequently targeted only marriages between whites and blacks and did not prohibit interracial marriages between blacks and Asians or blacks and Native Americans.[23]

Even though the law no longer uses the one-drop rule to classify people by race, theorists argue that the current meanings attached to race still reflect this history. One burning issue among some critical race scholars is whether the use of race in America invariably leads to

---

[22] Harlon L. Dalton, *Racial Healing: Confronting the Fear Between Blacks and Whites* 74 (1995).

[23] *See Loving v. Virginia*, 388 U.S. 1 (1967).

A. Critical Race Theory

the denigration of anyone who is not white. In contrast to ethnicity, which has been described as the "bearer of culture"[24] and a marker of lineage, language, and community, racial categories tend to tell us more about a person's social position in society, about where a person fits in the social hierarchy. Race thus functions more explicitly as a symbol of power and prestige. For some, the higher value attached to whiteness in our society makes it appropriate to consider whiteness as a form of property. Cheryl Harris, for example, has explained that, until nearly the 1960s, whites had a protectible interest under defamation law not to be labeled as black. Blacks falsely called white, however, had no cause of action because it was presumed that such a mistake caused no harm.[25] In contemporary society, whiteness continues to carry material advantages, as demonstrated by the use of "suburban" as a code word for white, prosperous neighborhoods, while "inner city" is understood to mean nonwhite, impoverished, and unsafe neighborhoods.

Critical race scholars frequently look for strategies to break the link between whiteness, superiority, and privilege on the one hand, and blackness, inferiority, and disadvantage on the other. Because they view race as a social construction rather than a natural fact, the question becomes how to change the social meanings attached to whiteness and blackness. One branch of scholarship addresses whether it is possible to construct a positive white racial identity. Some scholars doubt it and argue that whites should abandon whiteness. Ian Haney Lopez contends, for example, that white racial identity is a "hierarchical fantasy that requires inferior minority identities."[26] He argues that unless and until the category of whiteness is dismantled, there will be little hope of dismantling the systems of racial subordination of people of color. Other scholars, such as Barbara Flagg, do not want to give up on the possibility of reshaping whiteness as an identity that is not formed around the oppression of others.[27] Her prescription for such a change in meaning, however, lies principally in renouncing white privilege. Flagg sees the critical first step for whites as becoming aware of how "neutral" rules and norms have been constructed around the

---

[24] See Dalton, supra note 21, at 107.

[25] Cheryl Harris, Whiteness as Property, 106 Harv. L. Rev. 1709, 1735-37 (1993).

[26] Haney Lopez, supra note 20, at 31.

[27] Barbara J. Flagg, Changing the Rules: Some Preliminary Thoughts on Doctrinal Reform, Indeterminacy, and Whiteness, 11 Berkeley Women's L.J. 250 (1996).

needs of whites. She urges whites to make a commitment either to renounce their privilege or to use their privilege to the advantage of people who are not so positioned. Whether Flagg's vision of such an antiracist identity, however, would ultimately be one we would classify as "white" is debatable, and her proposal tends to merge with Haney Lopez's call for the deconstruction of whiteness.

In addition to investigating whiteness as a category and a basis for racial identity, social constructionists have begun to develop more complex understandings of the meanings of "color" and "blackness" in American life. On an individual level, legal scholars have grappled with the construction of their own personal racial identities. Two compelling memoirs have been written by Gregory Williams and Judy Scales-Trent, each of whom is a light-skinned African-American law professor. The scholarly response to their stories has deepened postmodern understandings of racial identity.[28]

Williams's memoir, *Life on the Color Line: The True Story of a White Boy Who Discovered He Was Black,* is about growing up in Muncie, Indiana in the 1950s and 1960s, and tells the remarkable story of a boy who, at the age of ten, discovered he was black. For the first decade of his life, Williams believed he was white because his mother was white and his light-skinned black father "passed" for an Italian. After his mother abandoned him, Williams was sent to live with his father's family in the impoverished black section of Muncie. The book recounts how Williams gradually repositioned himself as a black person and grew up to identify as a black man despite his white appearance.

In *Notes of a White Black Woman,* Scales-Trent paints a picture of her life that is markedly different from that of Williams, despite their similarity in appearance. As a "colored girl growing up in the protection of a strong family in the segregated South,"[29] Scales-Trent did not experience either crushing poverty or personal rejection. From early life, her identity as a black woman was cemented and she makes it clear to the reader that "white black Americans are still black."[30] Like Williams, however, her essays explore "the dilemma of being black and looking white in a society that does not handle anomalies

---

[28] *See* Martha Chamallas & Peter M. Shane, 46 J. Legal Educ. 121 (1996) (review of Williams); Mary Coombs, Interrogating Identity, 11 Berkeley Women's L.J. 222 (1996) (review essay of Scales-Trent).

[29] Judy Scales-Trent, *Notes of a White Black Woman* 13 (1995).

[30] *Id.* at 9.

A. Critical Race Theory

well."[31] She describes herself as existing at the intersection of race and color and constantly presenting a challenge to the conventional wisdom, which conflates race and color.

In a dramatic way, the life stories of each of these scholars demonstrates the inadequacy of treating blackness as a biological or natural category that is somehow the opposite of whiteness. Both authors identify as black persons, even though they look white to most white Americans. Perhaps more than most of us, they have experienced race as a social construction—whether they are regarded as white or black depends very much on the circumstances: where they are, who they are with, and the knowledge and background of the people making the assessment. One striking point made by both writers is that white people tend not to be attuned to differences in appearance among black people, often mistaking light-skinned blacks for whites. Because of their social position, however, blacks often acquire a more complex understanding of blackness, becoming more sensitized to the heterogeneity within the black community, including the existence of white black people.

Once blackness is severed from color, moreover, it is necessary to search for new understandings of racial identity. Williams and Scales-Trent often speak about personal identity in relational terms—as a way for the individual to show allegiance to or solidarity with the black community. Williams identifies as black in part because it was black people who embraced him and gave him a sense of belonging. One of the most important persons in his life was the woman who took care of him after he moved to Muncie, a remarkably caring person who was not even a blood relative. Scales-Trent identifies strongly with her extended family, a cohesive group whose skin colors range from dark brown to white. Despite the material advantages of being white in the worlds they inhabited, neither author ever wished to "pass" for white. To the contrary, they each describe the pain and discomfort of being misidentified as white and show the reader how they sometimes "pass" for white against their will. Scales-Trent analogizes the difficulty faced by white black people as comparable to that experienced by gay men and lesbians, who repeatedly must decide whether and when to "come out" and how to respond to people who assume they are heterosexual.

---

[31] *Id.* at 11.

These autobiographies also confront the relationship between racial categorization and power. During their lives, each author struggled with self-proclaimed authorities, whether institutions or other individuals, who insisted that they had the right to classify them as either white or black. For example, Scales-Trent recounts the recurring problem of being told by white people she meets at parties that she isn't black. The teachers in Williams's elementary and junior high school policed the color line, passed on the word about his black relatives, and made sure that no one was fooled by his "deceptive" appearance. Reflecting on such presumptuous acts of racial classification, Mary Coombs argues that the construction of personal identity is often contested and requires individuals to struggle against social forces to define themselves within severe constraints.[32] This postmodern conceptualization of identity as a site of struggle bears a resemblance to recent feminist analyses of women's complicated and sometimes contradictory sense of victimization and agency in their lives.

In addition to looking more deeply into the categories of black and white, some recent critical race scholarship explores why the experiences of other racial groups—notably Latinos, Asian-Americans, and Native Americans—have tended to be eclipsed in the discourse about race in America. The construction of race as dichotomous (black or white) and oppositional (white as the opposite of black) has left little space to explore the meaning of racial identity in other communities and the particular ways white domination harms minority groups other than African-Americans. As one scholar explains, "the Black experience tends to become the template against which the experiences of *all* people of color are measured."[33]

Most recently, critical race scholarship has expanded to focus on such topics as language discrimination, of paramount concern to ethnic groups in addition to African-Americans. One particular target of commentators has been employer prohibitions on speaking non-English languages in the workplace and discrimination against workers with foreign accents.[34] The writers have argued that most often

---

[32] Coombs, supra note 27, at 223.

[33] Dalton, supra note 21, at 5.

[34] *See, e.g.*, Juan F. Perea, Ethnicity and Prejudice: Reevaluating "National Origin" Discrimination Under Title VII, 35 Wm. & Mary L. Rev. 805 (1994); Mari J. Matsuda, Voices of America: Accent, Antidiscrimination Law, and a Jurisprudence for a Last Reconstruction, 100 Yale L.J. 1329 (1991); Martha Chamallas, Structuralist and

A. Critical Race Theory

these linguistic practices and traits do not interfere with an employee's job performance and that language restrictions serves mainly to identify or mark businesses as Anglo or white. They contend that requirements such as English-only rules force people to suppress their cultural identity and show little tolerance of difference; that, looked at from the perspective of ethnic minorities, the preference for English is a form of cultural domination; and that language restrictions have the effect of reinforcing the widespread belief that English is superior to, not just different from, other languages, particularly those languages and dialects spoken by groups with lower status. Such restrictions, they say, can also make assimilation to the tacitly white norms of the workplace a requirement of getting and keeping a job.

The branching out of critical race theory to encompass ethnic groups in addition to African-Americans has also led to theorizing about the connections between ethnicity and race. In a process similar to that of dissecting blackness and whiteness, scholars have begun to uncover the social construction of ethnicity and to delve more deeply into why some ethnic groups are sometimes treated as separate racial groups. Juan Perea, for example, employs a definition of ethnicity that intersects with, and to some degree, overlaps with the concept of race. For Perea, ethnicity refers to "physical and cultural characteristics that make a social group distinctive, either in group members' eyes or in the view of outsiders."[35] This definition of ethnicity is considerably broader than the concept of national origin, which focuses solely on the country of origin of a person or his or her ancestors. Ethnicity, in contrast, encompasses a variety of ethnic traits such as race, national origin, ancestry, language, religion, shared history, traditions, values, and symbols. What constitutes ethnicity is the group's internal sense of its distinctive identity and the perceptions of others that the group is distinctive. In this sense, ethnicity is not solely an immutable, natural characteristic, but a more complex social construction that also implicates individual choice and human relationships within a community. Critical theorists such as Perea denounce the tendency of courts to distinguish between permissible language restrictions, which the courts see as harming only those employees who choose not to speak English, and discrimination based on national origin. Social con-

---

Cultural Domination Theories Meet Title VII: Some Contemporary Influences, 92 Mich. L. Rev. 2370, 2385-94, 2407-08 (1994).

[35] Perea, *id.* at 833.

structionists stress the inseparability of language and ethnic identity and regard the impulse to grant a privileged position to the English language as a way of maintaining existing hierarchies in the workplace and other social institutions.

As social constructions, ethnic and racial labels are subject to change over time, sometimes far more rapidly than we might suppose. For example, Haney Lopez's historical research on Mexican Americans supports his thesis that, in the first half of the 19th century, Mexicans in the Southwest were transformed by sociohistorical forces from an ethnic group to a racial group.[36] Haney Lopez explains that in the early 1800s, people in the United States thought of Mexicans as a separate nationality, encompassing people from different races. In this early period, Mexicans could be white, black, Asian, or Indian. By mid-century, however, the Anglo-Mexican conflicts over territory in the Southwest prompted racial stereotyping of Mexicans as "greasers," lazy and unfit to govern. Mexicans then began to be thought of as a separate, non-white racial group. Haney Lopez stresses that the racialization of this group occurred in a specific historical context and was not the inevitable byproduct of the appearance or ancestry of the group. Instead, the racial designation was the product of—and a weapon in—a power struggle, rather than a discoverable, natural fact.

The denaturalization of race and ethnicity that has characterized much of the contemporary critical race scholarship is perhaps the most striking way in which this body of research departs from popular culture and the traditional legal discourses, which regard race and ethnicity as biologically based and immutable. To be sure, the biological paradigm has provided a measure of protection for racial minorities. The classic equal protection doctrine declares that it is unfair to heap disadvantages upon an individual or a group because of an ascribed characteristic over which they have no control. Like feminists, however, critical race theorists argue that the biological paradigm ultimately harms nonprivileged groups because it denies that there is discrimination whenever a policy or practice seems to involve even the barest measure of individual choice, as in the case of regulations relating to language, dress, or residence. Rather than stress the lack of control of the victimized group, critical race theorists highlight the political dimensions of the preferences and choices of policymakers

---

[36] Haney Lopez, supra note 17, at 28-34.

156

and employers. They maintain it is these actions that disproportionately create and recreate the meanings attached to race and ethnicity in our society.

B.   GAY AND LESBIAN STUDIES

The volume of scholarship addressing sexual orientation and discrimination against gay men and lesbians has grown exponentially in the last five years. The growth in gay and lesbian legal studies has been inspired in part by the popularity of "Queer Theory," the term used to describe an intellectual movement centered in English and cultural studies departments which is devoted to analyzing sexuality and the different kinds of sexual desire.[37] Much of the legally-oriented scholarship has been produced by openly gay and lesbian scholars who write from personal experience. Much as the burst of feminist scholarship flowered in the 1980s when the number of women faculty finally became large enough to sustain an intellectual movement, gays and lesbians in the legal academy have recently gathered the strength to make their issues and perspectives visible to the legal academic community.

The major law reviews no longer uniformly shun the topic of sexual orientation, and there are now journals dedicated predominantly to exploring the social meaning of sexuality and sexual orientation. In 1990, the Association of American Law Schools (AALS) took a position condemning discrimination on the basis of sexual orientation. The policy change means that law schools are required to admit students on a nondiscriminatory basis and to exclude any law firm or other recruiter (including the military) that practices discrimination against gay men or lesbians. This measure of tolerance and acceptance in official policy undoubtedly has contributed to the growth of gay and lesbian studies in law schools.

---

[37] Eve Sedgwick and Judith Butler are two theorists often credited with developing the school of Queer Theory and investigating how culture defines and controls sexual desire. *See* Dinitia Smith, "Queer Theory" Is Entering the Literary Mainstream, N.Y. Times, Jan. 17, 1998 at B1. Critical texts are Eve Kosofsky Sedgwick, *The Epistemology of the Closet* (1990); Judith Butler, *Gender Trouble: Feminism and the Subversion of Identity* (1990).

In some ways, the predicament of gay and lesbian scholars is unique. In contrast to women and racial minority groups, gay men and lesbians have not yet been afforded even formal equality under the law. The courts have generally held that the Equal Protection Clause of the Fourteenth Amendment does not prohibit classifications based on sexual orientation. Nor has Title VII or its state counterparts been interpreted to provide protection against discrimination based on sexual orientation, even when the discriminatory acts are explicit and intentional. Perhaps most importantly, the Supreme Court's controversial 1986 decision in *Bowers v. Hardwick*[38] still permits states to criminalize consensual sexual activity engaged in by same-sex partners. At a time when most critical scholars have rejected liberalism as inadequate, most courts have not yet seen fit to apply the tenets of liberalism to recognize equal legal rights for gay men and lesbians.

Faced with this repressive legal regime, recent gay and lesbian scholarship has principally concentrated on analyzing and critiquing the cultural forces that sustain the law. Although there is still some writing detailing how the law is inconsistent in its treatment of gay men and lesbians compared to other minority groups, gay and lesbian theorists now seem most interested in probing why discriminatory attitudes persist. The new theoretical work has also focused on how the repression of gay men and lesbians is reproduced over time, even as ideas about the origin and meaning of homosexuality change.

1.   Connecting Heterosexism to Sexism

Many feminist theorists and gay and lesbian writers share the view that heterosexism reinforces male supremacy. They see the link between the two "isms" not as logically compelled, but as a product of culture and habits of thought. As a matter of pure logic, it is possible to imagine a society in which men and women are treated as equals, but there is still discrimination against gay men and lesbians because homosexual activity is viewed as immoral. Many people in fact believe that we currently live in such a society. However, the prevailing view among critical feminist and gay and lesbian theorists is to regard discrimination on the basis of sexual orientation as a particularly virulent species

---

[38] 478 U.S. 186 (1986).

of sex discrimination. Consistent with the theme of interlocking regimes of discrimination, this view posits that it is impossible to dismantle one form of discrimination without doing serious damage to the other.

The connection between male supremacy and heterosexism was first imported into the legal literature by Sylvia Law. In her 1988 article, Homosexuality and the Social Meaning of Gender,[39] Law argued that the strong cultural endorsement of heterosexuality and corresponding disapproval of same-sex relationships had material and ideological consequences for women. The principal ideological impact of heterosexism was to preserve traditional concepts of masculinity and femininity, the social meaning of "gender." On the material side, heterosexism reinforced the traditional family and those political and market structures that imitated the gender division of labor within the traditional family.

Law's social meaning theory tracked feminist scholarship outside the law which for some time had characterized heterosexuality as "compulsory" in our society, with negative effects for straight women, lesbians, and gay men. The famous essay by poet and theorist Adrienne Rich, Compulsory Heterosexuality and Lesbian Existence, had called upon feminists to examine the myriad societal forces, ranging from the use of physical force to the control of consciousness, by which "women have been convinced that marriage and sexual orientation toward men are inevitable, even if unsatisfying or oppressive components of their lives."[40] Rich dared women to consider the "lesbian possibility,"[41] to ask themselves whether they would choose heterosexual coupling if all other things were equal and women were not punished or ostracized for rejecting male sexual attention.

The basic claim is that our culture's intolerance for sexual diversity has pressured and channeled women into traditional male/female relationships in which men retain the dominant role. Feminists frequently charge that heterosexual marriage entails the economic dependence of wives and that the dependent wife is not a creature of the past. Even though the participation of married women in the work-

---

[39] Sylvia A. Law, Homosexuality and the Social Meaning of Gender, 1988 Wis. L. Rev. 187.

[40] Adrienne Rich, Compulsory Heterosexuality and Lesbian Existence, 5 Signs: J. Women in Culture & Soc'y 631, 640 (1980).

[41] Id. at 647.

force has steadily increased, women continue to be assigned disproportionate responsibility for housework and child care and typically earn less money than their husbands.

Given that women are ordinarily dependent on men even in contemporary versions of heterosexual marriage, the societal hostility towards lesbians becomes more understandable. Lesbians arguably pose a threat to the status quo because of their independence from men. One commentator, for example, has described lesbianism as a kind of insubordination.[42] The connection between lesbianism and independence from men is manifested by the common practice of lesbian-baiting—accusing women who resist discrimination or act assertively of being lesbians, regardless of their sexual preferences or practices. In the popular text, *Homophobia: A Weapon of Sexism*, Suzanne Pharr characterizes the social meaning of "lesbian" in this way:

> [T]he word *lesbian* is still fully charged and carries with it the full threat of loss of power and privilege, the threat of being cut asunder, abandoned, and left outside society's protection. To be a lesbian is to be *perceived* as someone who has stepped out of line, who has moved out of the social/economic dependence on a male, who is woman-identified. A lesbian is perceived as someone who can live without a man, and who is (however illogically) against men . . . She is seen as someone who has no societal institutions to protect her and who is not privileged to the protection of individual males. Many heterosexual women see her as someone who stands in contradiction of the sacrifices they have made to conform to compulsory heterosexuality. A lesbian is perceived as a threat to the nuclear family, to male dominance and control, to the very heart of sexism.[43]

In this feminist account, different attitudes explain the societal hostility against gay men. Hostility toward gay men stems not from their assertion of independence, but from their perceived abdication of the dominant role. Because they are cast as "traitors" to their sex, gay men have been targeted for violence, police harassment, and legal censure. In fact, in some respects, the legal and societal condemnation of gay men has been so prominent that it has eclipsed the issue of the treatment of lesbians. Because of the higher social status of men

---

[42] Andrew Koppleman, Why Discrimination Against Lesbians and Gay Men is Sex Discrimination, 69 N.Y.U. L. Rev. 197, 236 (1994).

[43] Suzanne Pharr, *Homophobia: A Weapon of Sexism* 18 (1988).

generally, the conduct of gay men is subject to intense scrutiny, sending the social message that masculinity should be kept pure from the demeaning influence of femininity.

Recent gay and lesbian legal scholarship has expanded upon and refined the feminist account of the connection between heterosexism and male dominance. A direct descendant of Law's social meaning theory is Andrew Koppleman's interdisciplinary research on the taboo against homosexuality.[44] Koppleman believes that homophobia functions to police the boundaries between the genders. It is important to his theory that women are perceived not only as different from men, but as the "opposite" sex. In this account, gender polarization helps to sustain the cultural association of men as superior and women as inferior. Central to Koppleman's schema is the social meaning he ascribes to sexual intercourse. His historical inquiry leads him to conclude that intercourse has a "hierarchical significance, with penetration expressing the dominance of the man over the woman."[45] The symbolic meaning of intercourse is therefore disrupted whenever people with superior social status, such as men, consent to be penetrated.

Koppleman supported his argument about the homosexual taboo by drawing an analogy to anti-miscegenation laws that formerly had prohibited whites from marrying blacks or other racial minorities. As the Supreme Court finally officially recognized in the 1967 case of *Loving v. Virginia*,[46] such laws were not premised on equal respect for different races, but were designed to maintain the system of white supremacy. Anti-miscegenation laws targeted only marriages in which one partner was white. There was little concern for the sexual practices of "inferior" races. Moreover, the social meaning of the laws was clear to Southerners. The ban was primarily meant to prevent black men from marrying white women, as a way of "protecting" white women against being degraded by having sexual intercourse with an inferior. To allow such interracial marriages would have upset the racial order by affording a measure of social dominance to black men. It also would have diminished white men's exclusive sexual access to and control over white women. For Koppleman, the current ban on gay marriage and the criminalization of sodomy serve a very similar pur-

---

[44] Koppleman, supra note 41, at 197.
[45] *Id.* at 224.
[46] 388 U.S. 1 (1967).

pose. The laws "protect" men from degrading themselves through taking the passive position in sexual intercourse. This is a clear expression of misogyny because it presumes that feminization is inherently degrading. The current laws also assure that women will not be in a dominant (or equal) position in intimate relationships with other women.

2.   Analyzing the Constructs of Sex, Gender, and Sexual Orientation

By examining the cultural meanings attached to homosexuality, gay and lesbian theorists have begun to tease out the connections among three important social constructs: "sex," "gender," and "sexual orientation." Francisco Valdes has extensively analyzed this topic.[47] In his work, Valdes distinguishes them thus:

- "Sex" means a person's biological sex, specifically whether a person has a vagina or a penis.

- "Gender" refers to the "social dimension of personhood,"[48] including personal appearance, personality attributes, and behaviors understood to be masculine or feminine.

- "Sexual orientation" refers to a person's sexual or affectional desire toward members of the same sex, the other sex, or both sexes.[49]

Central to Valdes's theory is that the constructs ought to be considered separately, so that, for example, we should not presume that a person's sex determines either her social style (gender) or her choice of sexual partner (sexual orientation). Valdes argues, however, that in our contemporary culture, there is a strong tendency to "conflate" the three constructs. The cognitive associations among the three constructs are so strong that the constructs have actually become mutually defining and mutually dependent. Thus, for example, courts often pre-

---

[47] Francisco Valdes, Queers, Sissies, Dykes, and Tomboys: Deconstructing the Conflation of "Sex," "Gender" and "Sexual Orientation" in Euro-American Law and Society, 83 Cal. L. Rev. 1 (1995).

[48] Id. at 21.

[49] Id. at 23.

B. Gay and Lesbian Studies

sume a person's sexual orientation (gay) simply from his gendered behavior or appearance (effeminate).

Feminist theorists have also explored the relationship between sex and gender. However, feminist legal theorists have tended to treat sex and gender interchangeably, often downplaying the biological aspect of sex. This strategy was meant to underscore that discrimination against women often results from exaggerating the biological differences between men and women and from mapping socially constructed differences onto the biological framework. Legal feminists thus often regard all discrimination against women as gender discrimination and argue that this is what laws against sex-based discrimination were meant to prohibit.

Valdes's conflation theory cautions that more attention needs to be paid to the interrelationship among the three constructs, including sexual orientation. Under current judicial interpretations, Title VII and the Constitution prohibit only discrimination that is characterized as either sex-based or gender-based. Significantly, discrimination based on sexual orientation is not prohibited under these provisions, creating a loophole in the law.[50] Although the United States Supreme Court has recently held that same-sex harassment is actionable under Title VII,[51] the plaintiff in such a case must still prove that the harassment is sex-based, a requirement most courts regard as distinct from proof of discrimination based on the plaintiff's sexual orientation.

Valdes asserts that courts selectively classify some instances of gender discrimination as discrimination based on sexual orientation. He argues that the sexual orientation loophole serves generally to reinforce traditional gender roles as well as to punish gay men and lesbians for their sexual orientation. It is interesting to note that Valdes ends up in the same place as most feminist and other gay and lesbian theorists. He believes that because discrimination based on sexual orientation is so intertwined with discrimination based on sex and/or gender, in order to be effective and fair, the law must address all three types of discrimination.

A good example of the sexual orientation loophole in operation is the case of *Goluszek v. Smith.*[52] The male plaintiff in *Goluszek* was the target of a campaign of harassment by his co-workers that re-

---

[50] Valdes, supra note 46, at 147.
[51] *Oncale v. Sundowner Offshore Services, Inc.*, 118 S. Ct. 998 (1998).
[52] 697 F. Supp. 1452 (N.D. Ill. 1988).

sembled the kind of sexual harassment often faced by women in hyper-masculinized jobs. Anthony Goluszek worked as a mechanic in a factory that employed mostly men in blue-collar jobs. There was nothing in the record disclosing his sexual orientation. The only "clues" to his sexual orientation were that he had never married and had always lived with his mother. There was also testimony describing Goluszek as "unsophisticated," having "little or no sexual experience," and "blushing easily." Other men at the plant persistently taunted him, targeting his sexuality. The harassment started with jokes and escalated to physical threats. Many of the harassing comments focused on women as sex objects. Goluszek's co-workers showed him pictures of nude women and told him that his problem was that he needed to get married, and that he should go out with a female employee "because she fucks." They also accused him of being gay or bisexual. When Goluszek complained to management, the harassment took on a physical dimension: some men even poked him in the buttocks with a stick and threatened to knock him off a ladder.

Like several other "effeminate" male plaintiffs, Goluszek lost his sexual harassment suit. The court ruled that Goluszek had not experienced sex discrimination because his tormentors were other men and there was no allegation that the working environment was anti-male. In effect, the court treated the claim as if it were a claim for discrimination based on sexual orientation.[53] The ruling exemplifies how courts distinguish between heterosexism and sexism, affording relief only when they believe that the latter is present. The ruling also lends support to the conflation theory, because it is quite possible that the court believed that plaintiff was homosexual based on his demeanor (gender traits) or at least presumed that it was plaintiff's perceived sexual orientation, not his sex or gender, that prompted the harassment.

A feminist analysis of *Goluszek* would have closely examined the connection between heterosexism and sexism. In an article criticizing

[53] Perhaps the ruling might have been different if the case had been decided after *Oncale*, supra note 51, which allows Title VII plaintiffs to sue for same-sex sexual harassment. However, Goluszek would still have had to prove that his discrimination was sex-based and "not merely tinged with offensive sexual connotations." *Oncale*, 118 S. Ct. at 1002. This is difficult to show in cases in which there is no comparative evidence indicating that the other sex is not subjected to similar treatment.

B. Gay and Lesbian Studies

the case,[54] I argued that Goluszek was intimidated by aggressive male behavior in much the same way that a woman would be intimidated in that setting. Goluszek was apparently singled out for harassment because he did not conform to the men's image of male heterosexuality. Like a woman in a male-dominated environment, Goluszek threatened to disrupt the homogeneous quality of the workplace and was punished for possessing attributes of the inferior sex. Because he was feminized and subjected to harassment usually reserved for women, his claim should have been classified as a form of gender discrimination actionable under Title VII.

Mary Ann Case has analyzed cases such as *Goluszek* involving discrimination claims by men perceived to be effeminate. She reads the cases as demonstrating that employers and courts regard traditionally feminine traits as completely unacceptable in men, while they sometimes tolerate traditionally masculine traits in women. With respect to women who are perceived as being too feminine for a job, Case sees the case law as providing little protection. In these cases, employers often successfully argue that the women are not qualified or that their performance is deficient. What rarely gets discussed, however, is whether the employer has merely assumed that certain "masculine" qualities are necessary to perform a job, without carefully analyzing the job to determine whether such assumptions are warranted. In Case's view, we might be shifting from a society that demands separate gender spheres and separate gender styles to "one favoring masculinity pure and simple, whether manifested by men or women."[55] It is doubtful, however, that this updated form of sex discrimination represents progress. Rather, it is an example of how basic discriminatory patterns—sexism and heterosexism—are reproduced over time in somewhat different forms. Like the other theorists who have examined the three constructs, Case ultimately calls for legal prohibition of all three forms of discrimination.

Despite the strong sentiment in the legal literature for closing the sexual orientation loophole, there has not yet been a clear shift in the courts or legislatures in favor of equal rights for gay men and lesbians.

---

[54] Martha Chamallas, Feminist Constructions of Objectivity: Multiple Perspectives in Sexual and Racial Harassment Litigation, 1 Tex. J. Women & Law 95, 126-130 (1992).

[55] Mary Ann Case, Disaggregating Gender from Sex and Sexual Orientation: The Effeminate Man in the Law and Feminist Jurisprudence, 105 Yale L.J. 1, 31 (1995).

The most notable recent legal victory for gay rights advocates is the U.S. Supreme Court's decision in *Evans v. Romer*,[56] which invalidated a Colorado constitutional amendment prohibiting municipalities from enacting gay rights measures. The decision marks the first time the Court has ruled in favor of gay men and lesbians in a civil rights case, but the Court's holding stopped short of treating gay men and lesbians as a suspect or semi-suspect class, comparable to other minority racial or gender groups. Formal legal protection for gay men and lesbians is still restricted to those few states that have included sexual orientation in their anti-discrimination legislation and the greater number of municipalities that have passed local ordinances.

3. Gay Narratives and Pre-Understandings

To bridge this wide gap between conservative political attitudes and critical theory, gay and lesbian scholars, like critical race scholars, have increasingly turned to narrative. Gay and lesbian writers have used narratives to challenge stereotypes about their lives and to break the habit of conflating sex, gender, and sexual orientation. The narrative method seems particularly suited to the gay and lesbian intellectual movement because gay issues have been driven underground and have been considered improper for public discussion. Perhaps more so than other minority groups, gay men and lesbians can be rendered invisible because of the strong societal pressures against coming out and the reluctance to disclose facts about individuals' private lives.

An important article in the storytelling genre is Marc Fajer's Can Two Real Men Eat Quiche Together?[57] Fajer mixes stories with cultural and legal analysis in a deconstructive and reconstructive process. His first step is to uncover the submerged but widely held set of beliefs about gay men and lesbians in our society that structure and distort the dominant cultural image of gay life. The next step is to counter those cultural images with narratives offering a more textured, diverse view of the way gay men and lesbians live.

---

[56] 116 S. Ct. 1620 (1996).

[57] Marc A. Fajer, Can Two Real Men Eat Quiche Together? Storytelling, Gender-Role Stereotypes, and Legal Protection for Lesbians and Gay Men, 46 U. Miami L. Rev. 511 (1992).

B. Gay and Lesbian Studies

For Fajer, the gross societal misunderstanding of gay life is structured around three crucial "pre-understandings." Presaging Valdes's conflation theory, Fajer identifies the commonly held myth that gay men and lesbians will exhibit cross-gender behavior, that is, that gay men are typically effeminate and lesbians are mannish. The gender coding of gay men and lesbians is so strong that it is sometimes inconceivable for heterosexuals to fathom how gay couples arrange their daily lives. For example, Fajer tells the story of a gay man who experienced the emotional trauma of his mother's first visit to the home he shared with his lover. After a few days, the mother asked her son, "I don't quite understand . . . which of you does what?"[58] She was not referring to sex, but was wondering instead how they could possibly decide who would take on the wifely roles of cooking, cleaning, and laundry. The story shows how deeply-ingrained gender role expectations make it difficult to understand something like a gay "marriage" or other intimate relationship, once it is stripped of the organizing principle of gender.

The two other pre-understandings in Fajer's theory that function as conceptual constraints to a deeper understanding of gay life relate more directly to sexual activity. One is the "sex as lifestyle" assumption, which assumes that gay people are defined by and obsessed with sexual activity. Fajer wants to separate the identity formation process from the simple decision to have sex with another man or woman. By telling stories about people who are gay and celibate or people who have same-sex relationships but do not identify as gay, Fajer hopes to counter the common tendency to reduce gay people to exclusively sexual beings. This process of disaggregation is particularly important if people are to see gay men as experiencing sex in the context of love, marriage, and family relationships.

Finally, Fajer challenges the pre-understanding that gay topics and issues are inappropriate for public discussion. Reminiscent of Peggy McIntosh's inventory of daily privileges that attach to white skin, Fajer's stories capture the very real emotional and material costs of having to hide one's intimate relationships while others constantly talk about their family and spouses. The harm of imposed secretiveness is minimized when gay men or lesbians are criticized for not being discreet or for "flaunting" their relationships. Because intimate relation-

---

[58] *Id.* at 611.

ships are "inherently public in nature,"[59] Fajer argues, to censor public discussion of gay life amounts to denying to gay men and lesbians the common privileges that heterosexuals take for granted.

4.   Construction of Group and Personal Identity

The gay and lesbian scholarship discussed above shares with critical race theory and much post-essentialist feminist theory three prominent attributes: an emphasis on the cultural and ideological dimensions of subordination, an analysis of cognitive structures that inhibit understanding of and compassion for difference in our society, and the use of narratives to enable people to bridge the gap of different life experiences. In particular, the body of work focusing on the relationship among sex, gender, and sexual orientation often seems indistinguishable from feminist analysis, given its purpose of expanding the legal conception of gender discrimination.

There is, however, at least one particularly distinctive theme in gay and lesbian scholarship. The theme of the construction of group and personal identity plays an even more crucial role in this work than it does in the feminist and critical race literature. Informed by recent historical work, legal scholars such as William Eskridge have embraced a radical social constructionist view of the category of "homosexual."[60] They date the origin of a group identity for gay men and lesbians to the late Nineteenth Century, at a time when the medical profession began to regard persons who engaged in same-sex relations as suffering from a medical disease or disorder. Before that time, there was condemnation of same-sex intercourse by men, but it was directed more to the sexual acts themselves than to an identifiable class of persons. The idea that sexuality, including same-sex sexual orientation, is a central part of a person's identity is a relatively modern development. Moreover, it was not until the modern field of sexology acknowledged the existence of women's sexuality that relationships we might characterize today as lesbian relationships came under scrutiny. Because historians can trace the development of early homosexual communities and date the origin of gay consciousness, it is apparent in this field

[59] *Id.* at 575.

[60] William N. Eskridge, Jr., A Social Constructionist Critique of Posner's *Sex and Reason*: Steps Toward a Gaylegal Agenda, 102 Yale L.J. 333 (1992).

that homosexuality is a socially created construct that is neither natural nor unchanging. Gay and lesbian legal scholars consistently stress this nonessentialist view of group identity to oppose the popular idea of homosexuality as biologically fixed. The strain of cultural feminism that grounds women's perspective on biological difference has no analogue in recent gay and lesbian legal theory.

On a more individual level, gay and lesbian writers have shown great interest in analyzing the "coming out" process, a process critical to the formation of personal identity. Patricia Cain describes the process as first involving discovery. The moment of discovery is so important to identity that Cain views it as "the core experience of lesbianism."[61] For Cain, a woman discovers that she is a lesbian when she feels an emotional and erotic attraction to another woman and recognizes that the attraction has occurred. Even if the attraction never materializes into sexual intimacy, Cain believes that it is still transformative because "women loving women is not supposed to occur." She claims that "[o]nce we realize the truth of our attraction, we realize our difference from the rest of the world, and our lives are different from that moment on."[62] The next step in the process involves sharing "coming out" stories with other lesbians and developing a sense of lesbian community. When the disclosure is more public, William Eskridge regards the coming-out process additionally as a political act, aligning gay and lesbian individuals with other "out" members of their class in a "community of resistance," often with the effect of transforming the "out" person into an activist.[63]

The coming-out process of identity formation is clearly situational and relational; that is, it occurs at a specific time or times, and in relation to specific people. In this respect, "coming out" is a decidedly postmodern phenomenon, where we can see personal identity being constructed as part of an ongoing process. It is also easy to understand the fluidity of gay and lesbian identity and the importance of context. Because a person's sexual orientation is not a physically observable trait, gay men and lesbians must constantly decide when and how much to "come out" to others. Even "out" gay men and lesbians do not disclose their sexual orientation before every social encounter. The

---

[61] Patricia A. Cain, Lesbian Perspective, Lesbian Experience, and the Risk of Essentialism, 2 Va. J. Soc. Pol'y & L. 43, 65 (1994).

[62] *Id.* at 65.

[63] William N. Eskridge, Jr., Gaylegal Narratives, 46 Stan. L. Rev. 607, 636 (1994).

self-conscious act of deciding which self to present to the world is reminiscent of the multiple consciousness experienced by women of color when they are called upon to shift their perspective to fit the context. As postmodern scholars work more at the intersections of different kinds of oppression, the coming-out process experienced by gay men and lesbians could become the model for describing the process of identity formation generally.

At the moment, the body of scholarship treating gay and lesbian legal issues is taking several directions. Some scholars, like William Eskridge and Francisco Valdes, envision a gay and lesbian legal studies that is allied with, but separate from, feminism and critical race theory. Patricia Cain, along with Ruthann Robson,[64] have called for the development of lesbian legal theory, not wholly merged with gay men's scholarship. Conscious of the tendency of even nontraditional discourses to marginalize the experiences of women, these two scholars wish to claim a positive identity for lesbians as a distinct group of women. Finally, the intersectional genre of scholarship exemplified by Stephanie Wildman's writings on heterosexual privilege[65] perhaps is best described as anti-subordination theory with a triple focus on race, gender, and sexual orientation.

[64] Ruthann Robson, *Lesbian (Out) Law* (1992).
[65] *See* supra pp. 109-110.

CHAPTER 7

Applied Feminist Legal Scholarship—Economic Subordination of Women

The chronology of feminist legal theory and allied intellectual movements presented in the prior chapters only begins to suggest the full scope of feminist scholarly developments in the law in the past three decades. Like most legal scholarship, much of the body of feminist legal scholarship is not highly theoretical and can be more accurately described as applied scholarship. In virtually every substantive field, ranging from family law to tax law, writers have applied feminist theory and insights to specific issues, often informing their doctrinal analysis with feminist-oriented historical inquiry and empirical research.

The starting point of much applied feminist research is to retrieve what has been left out of conventional analyses. To gain an understanding of how the law has affected women in their daily lives, feminists have undertaken in-depth analyses of areas of the law that have not always been of pressing concern to mainstream scholars. Applied feminist legal research is often compensatory, in the sense that it compensates for the lack of attention paid to certain topics by male-focused research agendas that have tended to downplay the significance of women's lives, activities and work. In much of this feminist writing, there is the recognition that women's activities, even when conducted in the private sphere, are regulated and shaped by law. For example, to a greater degree than traditional scholars, feminists have examined how the law treats labor done within the home. Because women still perform most of the housework and child care, feminists have been interested in determining the value placed on such work and how such valuations affect women's economic and social status.

Applied feminist scholarship has also concentrated on giving a much fuller account of women's injuries and suffering, particularly in those contexts, such as sexual harassment and domestic violence, where far fewer men have experienced victimization. Even with respect to overdebated "women's issues," such as abortion and motherhood, feminist legal scholars have drawn on women's experience and feminist theory to challenge the conventional wisdom about the basic terms of the debate.

The next three chapters present an overview of a small fraction of this work, principally to give some examples of how many of the recurring themes of feminist legal theory play out in specific contexts. The five feminist moves described in the introductory chapter are very much in evidence in applied feminist research:

- In a variety of contexts, feminist writers have measured harm and argued for legal protection based on *women's experience* of suffering and pain, rather than traditional conceptions of legal injury.

- Feminist scholars have gone beyond the traditional women's domains of family law, constitutional law, and civil rights law to tease out *implicit male bias* in the deep structures of the common law, such as contracts and torts, and in complex statutory schemes such as the tax code.

- Feminist-inspired reforms have often posed *dilemmas of difference* as scholars ponder, for example, whether remedial measures designed to counteract the disadvantages associated with gender segregation in jobs will backfire and end up widening the pay gap between men and women and decreasing the number of women in high-paying, nontraditional fields.

- To show how *patterns of male domination are reproduced* in contemporary marriage and family life, family law scholarship has revisited historical legal doctrines, such as coverture, to examine the system that erased the legal identity of married women and gave husbands exclusive rights to control and manage the property and affairs of the marriage.

- Finally, in virtually every facet of modern life, feminists have argued that *women's choices* whether about work, sexuality, reproduction, or family relationships cannot be taken at face value, but must be unpacked to see the strategy and hidden logic behind constrained choices and restrained resistance.

The new generation of applied feminist scholars is more responsive to the internal critique that emerged in the Diversity Stage of feminist legal theory. Their work is less essentialist than their predecessors and less caught up in dichotomous structures of thought. For example, Reva Siegel,[1] a legal historian who writes about marital property law, domestic violence, and abortion, has examined how legal reforms have differently affected working-class and middle-class women and has explored divisions among feminist activists. Her work is intersectional, treating race and sex discrimination simultaneously and showing how even feminist-inspired changes in the law can sometimes intensify racial oppression through racist selective enforcement of laws. In addressing the subject of social change, Siegel avoids the victimization/agency dichotomy by carefully tracing out how feminists strategically deployed the conservative gender ideology of their times to their own advantage, yet at the same time were limited by the prevailing conventions of thought.

A.   THE COMPONENTS OF WOMEN'S ECONOMIC SUBORDINATION

Feminist visions of a more egalitarian world almost always call for major changes in the distribution and control of wealth. Whether cast as a desire for equality, self-determination, or autonomy, feminists of each generation have decried the relative impoverishment of women

---

[1] *See* Reva B. Siegel, "The Rule of Love": Wife Beating as Prerogative and Privacy, 105 Yale L.J. 2117 (1996); Home as Work: The First Woman's Rights Claims Concerning Wives' Household Labor, 1850-1880, 103 Yale L.J. 1073 (1994); Reasoning From the Body: A Historical Perspective on Abortion Regulation and Questions of Equal Protection, 44 Stan. L. Rev. 261 (1992).

compared to men and targeted economic dependence as a chief cause of women's subordination. Not surprisingly, one important focus of the legal literature on the economic subordination of women asks how the law contributes to women's inferior economic status, either by actively placing obstacles in the path of women's acquisition of wealth or by failing to correct for undervaluations of women's labor by employers, judges and juries, or other institutional actors.

Like women's lives, the scholarship on women's economic subordination straddles the boundary between home and work. Feminist scholarship has simultaneously grappled with women's relationship to individual men and to the market structures dominated by men. Recent articles have continued to examine the barriers to integration of male-dominated work, looking more deeply into workplace patterns, such as tokenism and stereotyping, that limit the advancement of women in a variety of fields. Another recurring theme in the scholarship has been the devaluation of women's work, wherever women perform it. This has led feminists to advocate such reforms as adopting a pay standard based on "comparable worth" of labor to increase pay in predominately female jobs, and other measures designed to recognize the contributions of homemakers. In this genre, scholars must persistently deconstruct the concept of "choice" to counter the claim that when work and family conflict, women voluntarily subordinate their economic interests to that of their husbands and families and willingly accept their status as economic dependents. The feminist explorations of the devaluation of women's work and activities have also spilled over from employment law and family law to generate a critique in areas, such as tort law, that determine which injuries will be legally cognizable and how to measure those injuries in damages. Finally, feminist work in tax law focuses directly on the boundary between home and work in its exploration of how the tax code creates disincentives for some groups of married women to work outside the home, while also penalizing nontraditional families, notably same-sex couples and single mothers with children.

In the 1970s Equality Stage of feminist activism and scholarship, the principal strategy for attacking women's economic subordination was a push for integration of jobs. By that time it had become clear that the 1963 Equal Pay Act's legal mandate of "equal pay for equal work" would do very little to close the pay gap between men

A. The Components of Women's Economic Subordination

and women, for the primary reason that comparatively few women did the same kind of work as men. One of the most salient feature of the American workplace has been the high degree of gender segregation in both jobs and occupations. Even today, most women work in low-paying, low-mobility, mostly female jobs.[2] The skilled trades continue to be heavily dominated by men (e.g., only 1 in 58 carpenters is a woman; 1 in 20 welders is a woman). The professions are more integrated but still are identifiably male occupations (e.g., 79 percent of physicians are men; 87 percent of dentists are men; 76 percent of lawyers are men).[3] While their estimates differ, most researchers agree that a sizable portion of the male/female wage gap is attributable to occupational and job segregation and cannot be explained away by factors such as education, training, experience, or other "human capital" differences between male and female workers.[4] In 1988, for example, the median yearly wages for full-time women workers was only 65 percent of that of men, a meager 6 percent improvement over comparable figures reported in the late 1960s.[5]

Throughout this period, feminists have employed a dual strategy to address the wage gap and women's economic subordination: They have sought ways to increase women's representation in male-dominated jobs, while advocating a revaluation and upgrading of female-dominated work. These two strategies correspond to the major themes of liberal and cultural feminism. The liberal emphasis on equality and inclusion fuels the drive for integration of male jobs; the cultural emphasis on respect for difference provides the philosophical underpinning for comparable worth and other strategies aimed at upgrading female jobs.

---

[2] Women's Bureau, U.S. Dep't of Labor, 20 Leading Occupations of Employed Women, 1990 Annual Averages (Mar. 1991).

[3] For a listing and breakdown of job categories by gender from 1990 census data, see Katherine M. Franke, The Central Mistake of Sex Discrimination Law: The Disaggregation of Sex from Gender, 144 U. Pa. L. Rev. 1, 88 (1995).

[4] *Gender Inequality at Work* (Jerry A. Jacobs ed., 1995).

[5] Sarah M. Evans & Barbara J. Nelson, *Wage Justice: Comparable Worth and the Paradox of Technocratic Reform* 43-44 (1989).

B.   TOKENISM, GENDER STEREOTYPING, AND MALE-DOMINATED WORK

In the 1970s, perhaps more than at any previous time in history, liberal feminists insisted that gender differentiation in the workplace produced women's inequality and fought for greater access to male-dominated work. Since that time, feminist legal scholarship has begun to evaluate and theorize about the experiences of women who now work in these formerly "men-only" domains. With the notable exception of the treatment of sexual harassment, however, the legal literature on women and nontraditional work is not very extensive. In this area, feminist legal scholars have often imported theories from sociology and social psychology to explain resistance to fuller gender integration and to fashion arguments in favor of enlarging the meaning of "discrimination" under laws such as Title VII. In an attempt to educate courts about the dynamics of gender bias in large organizations, social science experts have also testified in lawsuits on behalf of female plaintiffs who claimed that their employers denied them jobs and promotions because of their sex.

The phenomena of tokenism and gender stereotyping have received the most sustained attention by feminist commentators writing in the employment discrimination field. The term "tokenism" was coined during the black civil rights movement and later taken up by feminist and critical race scholars. The first published use of the term appears in a 1962 magazine article by Dr. Martin Luther King criticizing the slow pace of racial integration in schools and factories in the South.[6] At that time, King used "tokenism" in the sense of a "token effort" or a minimal concession to demands for social justice made by blacks. He regarded tokenism as a simple delaying tactic, intentionally designed to halt movement toward racial integration. In those early days of tokenism, there was no occasion to develop a theory to explain the persistence of the phenomenon, the psychology of "tokens," or how to break out of the tokenism pattern.

By the middle to late 1970s, when women began to enter nontraditional fields, most women found themselves in highly skewed set-

---

[6] Martin Luther King, Jr., The Case Against Tokenism, N.Y. Times Mag., Aug. 5, 1962, at 11.

B. Tokenism, Gender Stereotyping, and Male-Dominated Work

tings, where women represented less than 15 to 20 percent of the working group. The sociologist Rosabeth Moss Kanter developed a theory of tokenism to describe the situation of women who belong to a group that is dramatically underrepresented in a given organizational setting.[7] Because of their rarity in the organization, Kanter theorized that tokens were forced into serving as representatives of their social groups, as symbols of their kind. Through ethnographic research in a large corporation, Kanter found that stereotyping was most likely to flourish in these skewed settings. For women, this meant that they were often noticed and rated on a scale applied to women only, which focused selectively on their style of dress, their appearance, their bodies, their social graces, and other traits not directly linked to their ability to perform the job. Token women were also often typecast into role traps that mimicked patterns associated with women outside the workplace, such as mother, little sister, seductress, or militant. Once the token was so cast, her behavior was likely to be perceived as fitting the role. Kanter found a tendency to characterize "mixed" behavior (tough and assertive, yet warm and funny) as being all of one type (tough and assertive), suppressing the interpretation that did not fit the stereotype. In this usage, the token is very much a social construct, the majority's image and distortion of the outsider, with little room left for individuality or diversity within the token group. Kanter hypothesized that until a social group reached a critical mass—somewhere between 15 and 35 percent—they would be unable to form alliances and coalitions and engage in effective strategies to influence the culture of the organization.

Kanter's approach to workplace discrimination has been called "structuralist" because it emphasizes organizational structures and demographics and deemphasizes the mindset or motivation of individual decisionmakers. For the structuralist, discrimination is less the aberrant conduct of prejudiced individuals than it is the byproduct of specific organizational structures, particularly in those contexts where management has not taken active steps to counteract stereotyping or to create opportunities for women in nontraditional jobs.

The significance of tokenism for legal controversies came to the forefront in the case of *Price Waterhouse v. Hopkins*,[8] involving a claim

---

[7] Rosabeth Moss Kanter, *Men and Women of the Corporation* 206-42 (1977).

[8] 490 U.S. 228 (1989), discussed supra at pp. 17-18.

of sex discrimination by a woman in a "Big Eight" accounting firm who was rejected for partnership. Despite Ann Hopkins's proven ability to attract clients and generate billable hours, the partners in the firm claimed that she was unsuited for partner because she lacked social graces and was too harsh on the people working under her supervision. Hopkins was very much the token professional woman—she was the only woman being considered for partner that year in a field of 88 candidates. Price Waterhouse was also a typical elite firm of the era, in that only a handful of partners (7 out of 662) were women. Because the Supreme Court had only recently held that partnership decisions could be challenged under Title VII,[9] *Hopkins* was the first tokenism case to be decided on the merits by the federal courts.

As part of her litigation strategy, Hopkins employed Dr. Susan Fiske, a social psychologist of the Kanter school, as an expert witness to elicit testimony about tokenism and stereotyping in male-dominated workplaces. Fiske emphasized that where women are dramatically underrepresented, the token individuals are much more likely to be thought of in terms of their social category, with the result that evaluators may give biased attention to "feminine" dimensions such as social skills and personality and react negatively to individuals who do not fit the conventional mold. Fiske explained that in such an unbalanced setting, it was predictable that some partners voting on Hopkins would make sex-based comments about her and react with intense dislike to what they perceived to be her overbearing and arrogant "masculine" personality. Fiske's research supported the view, however, that it was the phenomenon of tokenism, as well as Hopkins's individual attributes, which prompted her colleagues' negative perception of her.

Hopkins eventually won her case, including the unusual remedy of a court-ordered partnership. The change in legal doctrine brought about by the case was incremental only: In a narrow class of cases where plaintiffs produce direct evidence of discriminatory motivation by decisionmakers, the burden of proof now shifts to the employer to prove that the taint in the process did not cause a biased result. Inspired by the Kanter/Fiske approach to workplace discrimination, however, feminist legal commentary has gone beyond the precise holding of *Price Waterhouse* to imagine a transformation of foundational Title VII concepts along structuralist lines.

---

[9] *Hishon v. King & Spaulding,* 467 U.S. 69 (1984).

B. Tokenism, Gender Stereotyping, and Male-Dominated Work

In this vein, my articles have focused on reconceptualizing the requirements of causation and intent in cases like *Price Waterhouse* where women seek to break into nontraditional occupations.[10] As in most areas of the law, prevailing Title VII doctrine treats causation as a straightforward matter of objective fact. Under the current law, there are generally only two possible sources of plaintiff's disadvantage: The harm is thought to be caused either by plaintiff's deficiencies or by the intentionally biased attitudes of evaluators. This dichotomous conceptualization of causation, however, leaves little room to consider how workplace demographics may affect the way a plaintiff's personality and performance is perceived by others. Nor does the traditional approach focus directly on the dynamics of tokenism because it presumes that the position of both majority and minority workers in skewed working groups is the same. The traditional approach simply asks the comparative question of whether the plaintiff would have been treated better if she were a man, ignoring the importance of the structural positions of the evaluators and the person who is the object of their judgment.

Drawing upon both feminist and structuralist critiques of objectivity, I have argued for a new approach to causation in anti-discrimination law that starts from the proposition that differences are socially constructed. In cases such as Ann Hopkins's, the process of "finding" the truth is complicated by the realization that the token's personality is shaped and sometimes distorted by her outsider status in the workplace. For example, Dr. Fiske's expert testimony cast doubt on whether there could be a truly objective assessment of Hopkins's personality given the dangers of selective perception and typecasting. Even if the partners sincerely believed that they were being fair to Hopkins, their judgments were likely influenced by an organizational climate which fostered stereotyping and increased the probability that Hopkins was being judged "as a woman."

From a feminist perspective, the search for objective causation is inadequate because it fastens on either the inherent qualities of the plaintiff or the conscious motivations of the evaluators. What is miss-

---

[10] *See* Martha Chamallas, Structuralist and Cultural Domination Theories Meet Title VII: Some Contemporary Influences, 92 Mich. L. Rev. 2370 (1994); Jean Jew's Case: Resisting Sexual Harassment in the Academy, 6 Yale J.L. & Feminism 71 (1994); Listening to Dr. Fiske: The Easy Case of *Price Waterhouse v. Hopkins*, 15 Vt. L. Rev. 89 (1990).

179

ing from this account is how the perceptions of the evaluators construct (rather than simply assess) a plaintiff's personality, and how the evaluation process itself is affected by structural factors aside from the conscious beliefs of the evaluators. In contrast, a structuralist approach shifts the focus from a factual inquiry about whether difference exists to an inquiry about how perceptions of difference originate and are maintained. In this respect, structuralism has much in common with theories such as Martha Minow's relational approach to difference.[11] Both analyze how the relationship between the parties can alter perceptions of reality and look for multiple realities rather than one objective truth.

The concept of "discrimination" under Title VII is open-ended enough to permit a shift in a structuralist direction without need to amend the statute. Title VII law could be revised to take account of phenomena such as tokenism and stereotyping and to incorporate feminist and structuralist insights that challenge the notion of objective causation. Rather than devise elaborate evidentiary structures to ferret out cause and intent, for example, courts could hold employers liable if they relied on subjective assessments of employee performance and did nothing to guard against the dynamics of tokenism.

As I envision such a revised doctrine, plaintiffs would challenge employment decisions by offering evidence of a highly imbalanced workforce and proof that they satisfied the typical "objective" standards for satisfactory job performance. Such a showing would raise a suspicion that a subjective assessment of an employee's performance was unfair because of the high risk that stereotyping might have influenced the evaluation. To avoid liability in such imbalanced workforces, employers could be required to make structural changes, such as giving decision-making authority to a more sexually integrated group or instituting an evaluation process that specified as precisely as possible the criteria to be used in making the decision. If such an approach were used in Title VII cases, employers would have a much greater incentive to hire and promote women in nontraditional jobs.

So far, the structuralist influence has not reshaped Title VII doctrine to the extent of displacing the objective causation framework. Instead, expert testimony on stereotyping and tokenism has been used selectively to bolster arguments for plaintiffs and to provide a back-

[11] *See* supra at pp. 95-97.

B. Tokenism, Gender Stereotyping, and Male-Dominated Work

drop for traditional inquiries into intent and causation. Even these modest developments, however, have intensified interest among feminist scholars in the potential of social science theories to stimulate changes in anti-discrimination law. Scholars are now importing insights from cognitive psychology to provide more reality-based explanations about how employers make decisions relating to hiring, promotions, and the entire range of employment actions. In particular, the phenomenon of stereotyping has been scrutinized and targeted as a pervasive form of discrimination in today's workplace.

A very extensive examination of stereotyping as it relates to employment decisions is Linda Krieger's article setting forth a cognitive bias approach to discrimination.[12] Krieger criticizes current Title VII doctrine for placing too much emphasis on deliberate or conscious discrimination and failing to appreciate how unconscious bias may affect the decision-making process. Particularly in race discrimination cases, courts often require that plaintiffs prove that the employer's stated reason for the decision is a "coverup" for racial bias. This framework presupposes that employers are lying about the true reasons for their actions and that they are aware of all the motives for their decisions. Kreiger states that courts often proceed from a tacit assumption that equates cause and intent; that is, to demonstrate that race or gender played a role in a decision is tantamount to saying that the person making the decision consciously considered race or gender at the moment of the decision. Most significantly, Krieger asserts that even the phenomenon of stereotyping gets interpreted within this framework of intentional discrimination. Courts often assume that only prejudiced people engage in stereotyping and that stereotyping consists principally of the deliberate use of unwarranted generalizations about a minority group—for example, the employer who asserts that female employees are less committed to their careers than male employees.

Krieger argues that the model of employer decision-making that lies beneath current Title VII doctrine reflects outmoded views in psychological theory. Since the 1970s, social cognition theory has changed the thinking about the mechanisms that produce and perpetuate bias against social groups. This newer approach to bias regards stereotyping as a pervasive phenomenon that is not qualitatively different from

---

[12] Linda Hamilton Krieger, The Content of Our Categories: A Cognitive Bias Approach to Discrimination and Equal Employment Opportunity, 47 Stan. L. Rev. 1161 (1995).

"normal" cognitive processes by which all people, not only prejudiced people, make everyday decisions. Social cognition theorists assert that in an attempt to simplify the world, people rely on categories, "person prototypes," and "social schemas," which "function as implicit theories, biasing in predictable ways the perception, interpretation, encoding, retention and recall of information about other people."[13] Stereotypes influence what we remember, how we classify an event, and whether we are likely to attach significance to the event, months or even years later when we are called upon to make an evaluation. This model of stereotyping is broader than the model most often used in employment discrimination litigation. It encompasses biased judgments that occur long before the moment of decision and recognizes that decision-makers are rarely aware of the bias that corrupts their judgments.

Krieger's application of social cognition theory to employment discrimination law bolsters the claims of feminist and critical race theorists who see racism and sexism as pervasive and as intricately connected to unconscious habits of thought. Similar to the movement toward structuralism in sociological theory, social cognition theorists in psychological theory have shifted the focus from motivational prejudice to cognitive bias and have concentrated on explicating the specific cognitive mechanisms by which disparate treatment is produced.

One cognitive mechanism that has considerable potential for influencing Title VII law is what psychologists call "causal attribution." Causal attribution is the process by which people connect cause and effect, by which we assign certain causes to certain outcomes. The term itself highlights how it differs from the notion of objective causation: The process of causal attribution is not a passive discovery of objective fact, but an active process of social construction.

Krieger's article explains how judgments about causation are affected by the content of group stereotypes, and how unconscious bias can imperceptibly creep into and infect the judgments of employers and other decision-makers. The empirical evidence indicates that in making causal judgments, people often ascribe the cause of an action either internally (to the actor herself) or externally (to forces outside the actor). There is a tendency, moreover, to attribute one's own behavior to external causes or *situational* factors that are beyond our con-

---

[13] *Id.* at 1188.

B. Tokenism, Gender Stereotyping, and Male-Dominated Work

trol. When evaluating another's action, however, we are more likely to attribute it to internal factors, such as the actor's personality, attitudes or abilities. We are apt to locate the cause of another's action to internal, *dispositional* factors within the actor's control. This means that we are more likely to blame the victim when we are not the victim.

This situational/dispositional dichotomy also operates in evaluating groups as well as individuals. Krieger explains that when behavior appears to confirm a stereotype about the group, we tend to attribute that behavior to a dispositional factor, that is, one within the control of the actor. Only if the behavior is inconsistent with our stereotype about the group are we apt to seek out an external explanation and then attribute the behavior to situational factors. Thus, for example, if a black employee is late for work, the white supervisor might unconsciously attribute the lateness to lack of commitment or irresponsibility, in conformity with the negative stereotypes about blacks. When a white employee is late for work, however, the same supervisor might assume that something special has happened, such as a car accident or other emergency, that prevented the employee from being on time that particular day. The process by which the supervisor makes such a judgment regarding causation takes place instantaneously and unconsciously, and it is unlikely that he realizes that his judgment is infected by racial stereotypes. At a subsequent time, however, the supervisor may make a salary or promotion decision to the disadvantage of the black employee, because the supervisor sincerely believes that the black employee is unreliable.

In these ordinary cases, the disparate treatment of the black employee may be very difficult to prove. The supervisor probably does not recall his more favorable assessment of the similarly situated white employee, and probably regards the two employees as *not* similarly situated in any event, given that he has not identified the white employee as being irresponsible. The requirement that a Title VII plaintiff prove the employer deliberately covered up racially discriminatory motives is likely not to capture such cases, and thus will fail to eliminate one common mechanism by which cognitive bias translates into disparate treatment.

In the 1990s, it is becoming increasingly clear that the barriers to fuller integration of high-level jobs are different from, and more subtle than, those that were apparent in the 1960s and 1970s when the push for racial and gender integration began. The belief that harmful stereotypes about groups would disappear once there was greater exposure to "different" people has not proved true. In contemporary society, even "affirmative action" employers discriminate, and women who succeed in gaining access to formerly male domains face a "glass ceiling" that allows them to see, but not to obtain, the most prestigious jobs. Although courts in Title VII cases often state that the law prohibits subtle as well as blatant forms of discrimination, for the most part they have created doctrinal models that treat discrimination as if it were the result of consciously biased decisionmaking by prejudiced individuals.

Feminist and critical race scholars have argued that the fundamental pattern of white male domination of the workplace has not changed nearly as rapidly nor as profoundly as popular portrayals in the media would imply. The new scholarship on tokenism and stereotyping suggests that updated versions of occupational and job segregation are held in place in the 1990s by cognitive bias and workplace structures that replicate patterns of the past, even when those in power harbor no antipathy toward excluded groups. Perhaps because these barriers are pervasive and describe the actions of "normal" people and typical institutions, recent critical legal commentary has drawn heavily upon new strains in social science research—notably structuralism and social cognition theory—in a search for concrete ways to revamp the legal definition of discrimination to reach unconscious racism and sexual bias and to provide incentives for more far-reaching integration of the workplace. The newest feminist literature retains the belief that integration of male-dominated work is vital to ending the economic subordination of women, but is more mindful of the difficulty of achieving such integration.

C.   DEVALUATION, COMPARABLE WORTH, AND WOMEN'S WORK

The emphasis in the 1980s on gender difference dispelled any hesitation feminist scholars might have had towards investigating sex-segregated environments, where most women spent most of their time. The rapid increase in the number of women in the paid labor force, which had continued unabated from the 1960s, did not result in a sizable decrease in occupational segregation. Instead, as mothers of

C. Devaluation, Comparable Worth, and Women's Work

young children entered the job market, they tended to work in the growing service sector in predominantly "female" jobs. For these women, a major obstacle to economic independence was not the lack of equal treatment with male co-workers in the same positions, but the low pay scales generally assigned to "women's" jobs or occupations.[14] The few men who worked in women's jobs also tended to receive low pay and suffered a loss of prestige from doing a women's job. The harm stemmed not from the sex of the individual worker, but from the gender categorization of the job itself.

In theoretical terms, the problem faced by workers in female jobs is one of *devaluation*.[15] Devaluation is a kind of bias that affects value judgments about the importance of an activity. Although it does not take the form of the classic case of disparate treatment where an identically situated man is treated better than his female counterpart, the process of devaluation described by feminist scholars is crucially connected to race and gender. At the core of devaluation is the claim that once a type of conduct becomes associated with women or racial minorities, it descends in importance. When a category is devalued, moreover, it affects all individuals within that category. Although the negative impact of such devaluation is suffered disproportionately by women as a group, the process of devaluation is one step removed from the classic case of disparate treatment of individuals based on sex.

The concept of devaluation is intricately connected to cultural feminist approaches, such as Christine Littleton's "acceptance" model,[16] which seek to eliminate the societal penalties that flow from following a female lifestyle, in particular pursuing a traditionally female occupation such as nursing, child care, or clerical work. Applied feminist scholarship on women's work has delved into the process of devaluation as it affects jobs and occupations and has offered new conceptions of gender equity, such as the theory of comparable worth, to expand the meaning of equality beyond that of identical treatment of similarly situated individuals. The feminist legal discussion of women's

---

[14] Jobs that are at least 70 percent female are typically characterized as "women's" jobs. *See* Ruth G. Blumrosen, Wage Discrimination, Job Segregation, and Title VII of the Civil Rights Act of 1964, 12 U. Mich. J.L. Reform 397, 461-62 (1979).

[15] For a fuller discussion of devaluation, see Martha Chamallas, The Architecture of Bias: Deep Structures in Tort Law, 146 U. Pa. L. Rev. 463, 470-489 (1998).

[16] *See* supra at pp. 71-72.

work, like the scholarship on tokenism and stereotyping in male-dominated jobs, has often closely tracked developments in sociological research, particularly those structuralist studies that emphasize power relationships, restraints on individual choice, and the social context in which jobs are performed.

In retrospect, the movement for comparable worth was the practical analogue to cultural feminism. Gaining momentum in the early 1980s, the movement rested on the proposition that work perceived as women's work was downgraded and that the value of work performed in predominately female jobs was systematically underrated, given the relative skill, effort, and responsibility involved. On the technical side, comparable worth relies on a process of job evaluation to measure the worth of a particular job to an employer, beyond simply relying on the market wage for that job. Comparing different jobs is pivotal to comparable worth because without it, there is no way to quantify the degree to which the female status of a job has affected prevailing pay scales.

Most job evaluation methods require precisely defining the job, specifying the factors that are relevant to compensation (such as supervisory responsibility and skill), and assigning points based on the level of each compensable factor. The objective is to construct a hierarchy of jobs within an organization that reflects, to some degree at least, the internal value of those jobs. While job evaluation techniques are often themselves subjective and infected by gender bias, they have the virtue of requiring employers to be consistent in the factors they identify as important in setting the compensation for both male and female jobs, and they limit the tendency to exaggerate the importance of differences among jobs.[17]

Large-scale comparable worth studies of public jobs done in several states in the 1980s documented the existence of substantial disparities in pay—most often on the order of 20 percent—between comparably rated predominantly male and predominantly female jobs. Notably, the empirical research disclosed that the more intensely an occupation was dominated by women, the greater the disparity in wages for both male and female workers in that job category.[18] These

---

[17] Deborah Rhode examines job evaluation, comparable worth, and workplace segregation in Occupational Inequality, 1988 Duke L.J. 1207, 1228-29.

[18] See National Research Council, Women, Work and Wages: Equal Pay for Jobs of Equal Value 28-29 (D. Treiman & Heidi Hartman eds., 1986).

studies served as "proof" of the devaluation of women's work, insofar as they were accepted as a measure of the penalty attributable to the gender coding of jobs.

The conceptual significance of comparable worth lies in its core contention that women's work is judged to be less important, and less worthy of compensation, simply because it is mostly women who do such work. The theory claims that the gender of the majority of job holders, rather than the intrinsic demands of the work, influences a job's place in the hierarchy. According to Ruth Blumrosen, one of the earliest comparable worth scholars who studied both "female" and "minority" jobs, a conceptual vicious cycle operates to perpetuate lower wages for workers in these jobs:

> It is not only that the jobs into which women and minorities have been traditionally segregated are lower paying jobs, but it is that they are lower paying, in part at least, because they are the jobs which have been reserved for minorities and women. The social, historical and economic studies have demonstrated the high degree of likelihood that the jobs of minorities and women are considered to be of lesser worth because they are female or minority jobs, and the analysis of both job evaluation and the general method of setting wages has established how this value judgment is applied in the setting of wages.[19]

The conceptual vicious cycle as it affects wage rates provides an explanation for the phenomenon of "job shifting"—the lowering of pay or prestige when a particular job or occupation changes from being male-dominated to female-dominated. The best known examples involve cross-cultural comparisons: Being a physician is a high-status, high-paying job in the United States, where men dominate the field; in Russia, when women are far more likely to be doctors, the job carries less prestige and money. In the United States, this job-shifting phenomenon took place over time with respect to the occupations of secretary and bank teller, which lost prestige when women entered and began to dominate the field. The influential research of Barbara Reskin and Patricia Roos explains that feminization has occurred in fields that have already started to deteriorate in status.[20] Thus, what might

[19] Blumrosen, supra note 14 at 455-57.
[20] Barbara F. Reskin & Patricia A. Roos, *Job Queues, Gender Queues: Explaining Women's Inroads Into Male-Dominated Occupations* 11-15 (1990).

187

superficially look like gender integration might be more aptly described as male "flight" from fields where pay and opportunity are decreasing. There is also evidence of the development of segregated enclaves within seemingly integrated occupations; for example, women are concentrated in residential real estate sales, while men dominate the more lucrative commercial sales market.

Sociologists explain the devaluation that occurs in female-dominated jobs as a kind of stereotyping in which assessments of the importance of the type of work are fundamentally influenced by the social value of a typical incumbent in the job. This means that predominantly male jobs still carry more prestige than predominantly female jobs, regardless of the specific context of the work. The undervaluation is traceable not directly to the sex of the individual job holder, but indirectly to the sex of the prototypical job holder. In this account, devaluation operates at the cognitive level, influencing and shaping categories. The work itself becomes gendered, even though there may be nothing inherent in the tasks of a particular job that make it more suitable for either women or men. This kind of cognitive bias is similar to the stereotyping and habitual ways of thinking about race that interests critical race theorists who focus on cultural domination. Comparable worth advocates stress that it is extremely difficult to shake the negative value assigned to women's work, in much the same way that it is hard to dismantle the negative cultural associations linked to blackness.[21]

As theories of liability under Title VII, however, devaluation and comparable worth have not yet been accepted by the courts. In the mid-1980s, a few influential decisions in the lower courts[22] had the effect of halting the filing of comparable worth claims and shifting the movement towards implementing comparable worth schemes through legislative action or collective bargaining. The major obstacle to judicial acceptance was the courts' reluctance to displace market rates and their fear that such a project would pose too great an administrative burden in Title VII cases. In wage discrimination cases based on sex, the courts have been slow to accept devaluation as a form of actionable bias and still tend to insist on proof that the employer deliber-

---

[21] *See* supra at p. 139.

[22] The two most important cases were *Spaulding v. University of Washington*, 740 F.2d 686 (9th Cir. 1984) and *American Federation of State, County & Mun. Employees v. Washington*, 770 F.2d 1401 (9th Cir. 1985).

C. Devaluation, Comparable Worth, and Women's Work

ately reduced pay scales in female-dominated jobs because of animus toward women.

The courts' hesitation to recognize devaluation as an unlawful form of bias has meant that the gender pay gap has rarely been directly attacked under the law, with the exception of those unusual instances where women have been able to establish an Equal Pay Act violation by proving that they were paid less than men for doing substantially equal work. This is an area of the law where courts tend to permit any appreciable difference in the tasks performed in male and female jobs or in the conditions of work to cut off inquiry into whether there has been sex discrimination in the setting of wage rates.

A prime example of this tendency is the legal treatment of part-time workers, defined as workers who work fewer than 35 hours per week. In contrast to the position taken by the European Court of Justice, for example, courts in the United States have provided virtually no pay equity protection to part-time workers. The voluntary part-time workforce in the United States is overwhelmingly female, made up largely of mothers who care for children. Like the wages of workers in predominantly female occupations, the wages of part-time workers are depressed. On a pro rata basis, part-timers earn considerably less than their full-time counterparts, particularly because they are frequently denied full-timers' valuable fringe benefits, such as health insurance and pension plans. The disparities persist and are tolerated, even though there is no reliable evidence that, as a group, part-time workers are less productive or less committed to their jobs than full-time workers. This adverse treatment of part-time workers is not often considered to be sex discrimination, despite its obvious negative impact on women.

In my scholarship, I have argued that the insights of the comparable worth theory should be applied to the context of part-time work.[23] My contention is that part-time work has been devalued because it is mostly women who engage in such work. In most cases, the difference in the number of total hours an employee works per week is a distinction that does not justify such a difference in the rate of compensation. My position is that the devaluation of part-time work derives not from its intrinsic worth but from our image of the proto-

---

[23] For a discussion of the legal and economic dilemmas posed by part-time work, see Martha Chamallas, Women and Part-Time Work: The Case For Pay Equity and Equal Access, 64 N.C. L. Rev. 709 (1986).

typical part-time worker, namely, a mother who limits her hours on the job to have more time for her family. This cognitive bias translates into material disadvantage when part-timers discover that their choice to work less than 35 hours per week exacts an economic penalty beyond what could fairly be attributed to actual differences in time spent on the job. The gendering of part-time work as "female" also discourages employers from filling more important jobs on a part-time basis, intensifying the disadvantage associated with such work. Devalued in this way, part-time work perpetuates the economic subordination of women, particularly when the contributions of "working mothers" are compared to their husbands who typically work full-time.

D.   HOUSEHOLD LABOR AND THE WORK/FAMILY CONFLICT

In most contemporary discussions of women's economic subordination, the primary focus has been on paid employment, on women's status within the job labor market. It is still the case that unpaid labor, particularly work done in the home, is not considered to be "work." In common parlance, full-time homemakers are treated as unemployed. Recently, however, legal feminists have renewed their challenge to this conventional wisdom and produced a new body of scholarship on the legal status and political history of housework. The new studies apply theoretical insights from contemporary feminist theory, offering concrete descriptions of the devaluation process and showing how the false dichotomy between work and family has operated to obscure the value of women's productive household labor.

A comprehensive study of the legal treatment of housework by Katharine Silbaugh[24] takes a cultural feminist approach to the subject. To a large extent, Silbaugh accepts the reality of the "second shift," the term that signifies that even women who are employed outside the

---

[24] Katharine Silbaugh, Turning Labor into Love: Housework and the Law, 91 Nw. U. L. Rev. 1 (1996).

D. Household Labor and the Work/Family Conflict

home still perform a vastly disproportionate share of housework.[25] Her starting point is women's experience and the startling fact that women spend more of their productive work hours in unpaid labor.[26] Claiming that the economic subordination of women cannot be addressed solely by upgrading women's status in the workplace, Silbaugh's research is dedicated to improving "the consequences that flow from the uneven distribution of home labor."[27] Thus her primary concern is not with equalizing the distribution of household tasks between men and women, but with identifying mechanisms of devaluation that serve to justify the current low status of this form of unpaid labor. In this respect, Silbaugh's approach departs from that of an earlier generation of feminists who were more likely to address the problem by confronting their husbands and partners with the inequity of not doing their fair share of the housework.[28]

In the 1990s, it is no longer useful to frame the topic of domestic labor as a "homemaker/working woman" dichotomy. Instead, the most common pattern for women is to combine housework and paid work, through part-time employment or alternating periods of full-time wage work with periods spent at home. Moreover, even for women who are full-time wage earners, the responsibilities of homework have a significant impact on their lives. As a result, women have less leisure time than men, and constantly face conflicts between work and family to a greater degree than do men. It cannot be denied that the boundaries between work and home have become increasingly permeable now that most women (and men, for that matter) spend large amounts of their time in both spheres. However, the tendency to speak and think in dichotomous terms about conflicts between work and family has not abated, as evidenced by the unending debate about women "juggling" work and family, as if negotiating the two spheres required the special talents of a circus performer.

---

[25] Silbaugh cites time use studies that indicate that in homes where both men and women work more than 30 hours per week for pay, in 1981, men's share of the housework was only 60 percent of women's. *Id.* at 8. Substantially more than one-half of women's working hours are spent on housework, compared to less than one-quarter of men's hours. *Id.* at 10.

[26] *Id.* at 3.

[27] *Id.* at 14.

[28] In the early 1970s, the classic feminist manifesto on housework was Patricia Mainardi, *The Politics of Housework* (1970), a humorous account of the variety of excuses men commonly give for not doing housework.

The new feminist scholars have set about breaking down the familiar dichotomies that confine the discussion of housework. The basic contention of Silbaugh's study, for example, is that, across a wide spectrum of legal contexts, courts tended to downplay or ignore the economic value of housework, treating women's household labor as if it were merely an expression of love and affection, rather than work. This failure to highlight the similarities between wage work and housework is anomalous in our increasingly commercialized culture where everyday discourse tends to be saturated by market terminology and market ideology. Silbaugh's point is not that loving care and personalized attention have nothing to do with housework. Rather, she contends that the familial context in which housework is performed has erased its economic dimension, most often to the detriment of those who perform such unpaid work.

The major practical consequence of the legal categorization of housework as love and affection, rather than productive labor, is that home labor does not lead to financial security.[29] The problem is not simply that homemakers are not paid for their work, either by the state, family members, or others who derive economic benefit from their labors. It is that the "choice" to devote substantial time to housework, analogous to the choice to work part-time, often results in cumulative economic penalties that may appear only after a marriage or relationship has dissolved or a woman has grown older. Thus, despite the changes in marital property law to recognize a "homemaker's contribution" to the family, women still fare poorly in divorce, in part because courts are reluctant to credit employed women for the disproportionate share of the housework they perform in addition to wage work.[30] Women have also been disadvantaged by a Social Security system that, until very recently, did not permit them to accrue credits in their own right when they worked in the home, forcing them to rely exclusively on benefits they accrue as wage workers or on a modest spousal benefit that stems from credits accrued by the "primary" spouse—in other words, the husband—in his career as a wage worker.[31]

An ideological consequence of categorizing homework as an expression of love and affection is that the value of housework is often

---

[29] Silbaugh, supra note 24, at 51.
[30] *Id.* at 62-63.
[31] *Id.* at 38-39.

D. Household Labor and the Work/Family Conflict

seen as derivative of the social value of the specific family relationship in which the household labor is performed. One of the cruel ironies of the contemporary debate over welfare is that stay-at-home mothers of young children who receive AFDC benefits are portrayed as unproductive women who do not work, in marked contrast to the popular image of the selfless, middle-class mother who stays at home, sacrificing her career ambitions for the welfare of her children. In her books on feminist theory and family law,[32] Martha Fineman has traced the connection between socially valued relationships and women's household labor. She argues that because of the high value placed on male-dominated households in our culture, housework and child care are valorized only when there is a male "head" of the household present. Even the grudging recognition now accorded to homemakers' contributions under the law tends to go disproportionately to those women least in need, namely, full-time homemakers with high-earning husbands.

The lack of recognition of the economic dimension of housework may seem unexceptional in our contemporary culture which regards the market as the primary mechanism for valuing productive activities. In many contexts, the term "work" is used synonymously today with "paid work." Feminist historians, however, have recently reexamined the political struggle surrounding the legal treatment of women's household labor over the past century and uncovered a complex history of resistance and compromise. Reva Siegel's political history of housework documents that many Nineteenth-Century feminists did not regard women's household labor as unproductive and strongly resisted the view of homemakers as dependents who were "supported" by their wage-earning husbands. Particularly in the mid-1800s, there was no consensus that the market was the only measure of the worth of human labor, and even the use of the term "earnings" was not then limited to monetary wages. Siegel explains that when feminists claimed a right on the part of married women to their "earnings," they were arguing "that the law expropriated the value of the work they performed . . . [in] an era when it was still

---

[32] *See* Martha A. Fineman, *The Neutered Mother, The Sexual Family and Other Twentieth Century Tragedies* (1995); Martha A. Fineman, *The Illusion of Equality: The Rhetoric and Reality of Divorce Reform* (1991).

possible to discuss the value of labor in terms that did not refer to its market price."[33]

Nineteenth-Century feminists developed a sophisticated understanding of the mechanisms through which household labor was devalued, including the role of law in the devaluation process. Before 1855, when the first modern earnings statutes were enacted, the common law doctrine of marital service[34] operated to dispossess women of the fruits of their labor. The marital service doctrine vested in the husband the right to any proceeds deriving from his wife's labor, whether performed in or outside the home. This doctrine was an aspect of the regime of *coverture* by which married women lost their legal identities through marriage and had to depend on their husbands to file suit, incur debts, and otherwise act on behalf of the family. By law, a wife was economically dependent on her husband because she had no legal right to secure wealth independently. The earnings statutes reformed the law only to the degree of allowing married women the right to retain what they earned outside the home. The husband, however, continued to "own" his wife's labor in the home. In this way, the law helped sharpen the distinction between paid labor and housework, at a time when few women earned substantial amounts in the workplace. By separating the legal effects of paid and unpaid labor, the law operated as one of the social forces which obscured the economic value of housework and perpetuated women's socially constructed economic dependence on men.

Prior to the Civil War, feminists sought a remedy for their husbands' expropriation of the value of their household services by demanding joint property rights in all the assets of the marriage, somewhat akin to contemporary community property rights. This strategy resonates with cultural feminism in that it seeks not to end the differentiation between the types of labor men and women perform, but to revalue women's work in the home. This earlier generation of feminists was skeptical about reforms that permitted women to seek independence only through selling their labor in the market because, as Siegel explains, the "market valued women's labor in accordance with the same system of caste that gave rise to the doctrine of marital

---

[33] Reva Siegel, Home As Work: The First Woman's Rights Claims Concerning Wives' Household Labor, 1850-1880, 103 Yale L.J. 1073, 1112 (1994).

[34] *Id.* at 1117.

service."[35] The critique of market systems of valuation resembles the critique by advocates of comparable worth more than a century later, who argued that the wages of women in predominantly female jobs were still artificially depressed. Perhaps most telling is the persistent dramatic devaluation of household services, disproportionately performed by women of color and immigrant women who work for wages in other people's homes. Silbaugh argues that "housework is not fully dignified as labor even when it is performed for pay."[36]

Feminist insights about the devaluation of women's market labor and the lack of value afforded home labor are connected in the scholarship of Joan Williams, who writes about the work/family conflict in contemporary society.[37] The portrait she paints of the "dominant family ecology" of the 1990s—referring to the dominant patterns of wage labor and domestic labor in families with children—is not so far removed from male-dominated structures under coverture.

Williams's description starts with the observation that most high-status work is organized around a model of the "ideal worker" who is away from home nine to twelve hours per day and consequently has virtually no time for the daily demands of housework and child care. To succeed in this world and meet the expectations of employers, ideal workers "command a flow of domestic services from their spouses"[38] and delegate most of the child care. The gendered structure of wage labor is reproduced because even women who are trained to be ideal workers in high-powered jobs simply cannot bring themselves to delegate this much child care to others. Instead, they find themselves compromising and marginalizing their workforce participation to assume child care and other household responsibilities. Even though the stay-at-home mother is no longer typical, Williams contends that the contemporary ideology of gender equality has obscured the degree to which women's family roles continue to produce women's marginalized employment status:

> The truism that "most mothers now work" actually ignores the nearly one-third of married mothers with minor children who do no market

---

[35] *Id.* at 1079.

[36] Silbaugh, supra note 24, at 73.

[37] Joan Williams, Is Coverture Dead? Beyond a New Theory of Alimony, 82 Geo. L.J. 2227 (1994).

[38] *Id.* at 2239.

work, the roughly one-third of all employed women who mainly work part-time, and the many full-time working women on the "mommy track."[39]

To explain why men are more willing to delegate child care to others and less likely to marginalize their participation in wage work, Williams emphasizes the importance of personal identity, particularly the "gender pressures" on men to conform to traditional roles. Williams contends that, for high-status men, their "sense of themselves, their success as human beings, and even their sexual attractiveness"[40] is tied to their perceived success at work. For working-class men, whose status at work tends to threaten, rather than to enhance, their sense of masculinity, clinging to a traditional allocation of gender roles in the home may become a matter of "personal dignity."[41] Even women often come to regard male domination of the working-class family as a way to compensate for men's sense of disempowerment on the job.

The updated version of coverture described by Williams relies more on women's choices and cultural and ideological pressures than on formal legal rules or total exclusion. The net effect, however, is not radically different from the more rigid common law regime, when husbands owned their wives' household labor and for most women, earning a living wage through market work was not a realistic possibility. Given this dominant structure, it is not surprisingly that, like antebellum feminists, Williams proposes granting the non-earning spouse a joint property right in the income stream generated by the wage earner.

The feminist literature in this area stresses that underlying structures of the workplace and complexities of gendered identities render the concept of "choice" problematic. The applied feminist scholarship on women's employment, housework, and work/family conflicts is also highly critical of the dichotomous structures of thought that position "work" as the opposite of "family," missing both the emotional dimension of employment and the economic dimension of family. The scholarship of Siegel, Silbaugh, and Williams elaborately traces out the gender consequences of such dichotomous thinking: Women's economic subordination is reproduced as women make the pre-

---

[39] *Id.* at 2237 (footnotes omitted).
[40] *Id.* at 2238.
[41] *Id.* at 2245.

dictable "choice" to try to combine work and family, which renders them vulnerable to devaluation in both spheres.

E.   REINFORCING ECONOMIC SUBORDINATION THROUGH TORT LAW

The devaluation of women's work and activities has consequences beyond employment and family law. In particular, feminist scholars have argued that devaluation affects recovery in tort, an important context for determining which type of harms are worthy of legal protection and the value of such injuries. These judgments of value are of considerable importance to tort plaintiffs because tort settlements and awards may represent their principal avenue to economic security. Even for individuals who never have a tort claim, however, tort law performs a function of expressing the relative importance placed on certain interests and on certain kinds of relationships. For these reasons, a growing body of feminist scholarship devoted to tort law has emerged in the past ten years,[42] applying the several schools of feminist theory to critique specific tort doctrines and basic tort concepts and structures in this foundational area of private law.

Given the inferior structural position of women in the workplace and the undervaluation of housework, it is perhaps not surprising that in the aggregate women receive less compensation in tort than men. To some extent, tort law simply recapitulates the valuation placed on women's labor in other contexts, particularly because the goal of compensation is to place the parties in the position they would have occupied if the accident or other tortious event had never occurred. Most empirical studies indicate that women of all races receive significantly lower damage awards than white men in personal injury and wrongful death suits. Some of these data have been generated by the movement to study gender and race bias in the courts,[43] and confirm that in the realm of torts a higher value is placed upon the lives of white men and

---

[42] *See* Leslie Bender, An Overview of Feminist Torts Scholarship, 78 Cornell L. Rev. 575 (1993).

[43] The final reports of state and federal task forces on gender and race bias represent a body of practical scholarship that integrates feminist theory, empirical re-

that injuries suffered by this group are worth more than injuries suffered by other less privileged groups in society.

For example, my calculations from tort judgments and settlements reported in a 1995 guide for personal injury lawyers indicated that awards to male plaintiffs were 27 percent higher than those for female plaintiffs. Similarly, a study of wrongful death cases between 1984 and 1988 conducted by the Washington State Task Force on Gender and Justice in the Courts found that the mean damage award for a male decedent was $332,166, compared to $214,923 for a woman. A nationwide study of jury awards in personal injury cases, conducted by Jury Research, Inc., showed that in virtually all age groups, women received lower mean and median awards for compensatory damages than did men.[44]

The disparity in tort awards cannot be explained on the basis of formal legal rules that differentiate between men and women. The old tort common law doctrines that explicitly limited recovery to one sex only have either been abolished or have been extended on a gender-neutral basis. Like so many other areas of contemporary law, gender bias finds its way into tort law through more subtle means. I have devoted my scholarship in this area to uncovering the deep cognitive structures in tort law that function to devalue women's interests and injuries, or more precisely, those harms that tend to hurt women more often than men or which tend to have a greater significance in women's lives. As was the pattern with women and work, the devaluation processes in tort law do not affect women exclusively, but tend also to disadvantage men whose lives and activities follow "female" patterns.

My primary contention is that tort law devalues the lives, activities, and potential of women, and that one can see this at work both in substantive rules governing liability and in common methods for calculating damages. One important mechanism by which devaluation is accomplished is through the construction of legal categories that pur-

---

search and advocacy of reform. *See* The Effects of Gender in the Federal Courts: The Final Report of the Ninth Circuit Gender Bias Task Force, 67 S. Cal. L. Rev. 745 (1994); Judith Resnik, Asking About Gender in Courts, 21 Signs: J. Women in Culture & Soc'y 952 (1996).

[44] The empirical studies are discussed in Martha Chamallas, Questioning the Use of Race-Specific and Gender-Specific Economic Data in Tort Litigation: A Constitutional Argument, 63 Fordham L. Rev. 73, 84-89 (1994); Martha Chamallas, The Architecture of Bias: Deep Structures in Tort Law, 146 U. Pa. L. Rev. 463, 465-66 (1998).

port to describe types of injuries and types of damages. In contemporary law, these types of injuries and damages are ranked in importance, with higher-ranked injuries receiving more extensive legal protection than lower-ranked injuries. Although the hierarchies of values purport to rank injuries and damages neutrally, they end up having a disparate negative effect on women plaintiffs as a class. Injuries of low value are more often associated with women, while injuries of high value are more often linked to men.

Although the standard texts do not always explicitly state so, there is little question that a higher value is placed on physical injury and property loss than on emotional or relational harm. This implicit hierarchy of value was even more apparent in an earlier era when the scope of recovery in tort was more restricted and there were even fewer possibilities for recovering for marginal harms. Despite the liberalization of tort law, the basic hierarchy has remained intact. Recently, moreover, an implicit hierarchy of types of damages has been constructed that complements the hierarchy of types of injury. The trend is toward favoring or privileging pecuniary or economic losses, such as lost wages or medical expenses, as opposed to nonpecuniary or noneconomic damages, a large category of damages encompassing recoveries for pain and suffering, mental distress, lost companionship and society, loss of enjoyment of life, and punitive damages.

In the abstract, the implicit hierarchies of value look neutral in the sense that they are not tied to any gender or other social group. Because all persons have a body, emotions, and personal relationships, it is often assumed that people possess "privileged" and "nonprivileged" interests in equal proportions. As they operate in social contexts, however, the hierarchies of value tend to place women at a disadvantage. The important and recurring injuries in women's lives tend more often to be classified as lower-ranked emotional or relational harm, or as noneconomic loss. The ranking thus assigned to women's injuries makes it more likely that relief will be denied or that recoveries will be devalued.

In a variety of contexts, applied feminist scholarship on tort recovery has explored how the implicit hierarchies of value negatively affect women. To convey a sense of this scholarship, the following discussion offers two examples of devaluation: one involving the devaluation of relational injury, and one that addresses the devaluation of nonpecuniary damages.

First, let us consider the legal treatment of injuries suffered by caretakers of children. When a child suffers injury or death, people who have special responsibility for caring for the child typically also suffer a grievous injury. Particularly after a serious nonfatal accident, the caretaker must learn to deal with the child's resulting physical disability and the enormous change in daily routine that this often causes. Such an injury is likely to change the relationship significantly, and the caretaker will often feel grief, guilt, and anxiety. For both the caretaker and the child, such an accident can be a life-altering event.[45]

However, tort law most often treats the caretaker's losses as derivative or secondary, failing to recognize the full extent of the caretaker's relational and emotional loss. In an early critique of tort law, Lucinda Finley noted the law's reluctance to recognize a cause of action for what is known as "filial consortium"—the loss of a child's society and companionship which the parent suffers as a result of the reverberating effects of the child's serious injury.[46] Denying this kind of relational claim largely affects women in their roles as the primary caretakers of children. In our culture, the care of children has been disproportionately assigned to women, so much so that mothers, grandmothers, other female relatives and hired female nannies and babysitters tend to spend more time with children than do their male counterparts. As their primary caretakers, women have a greater responsibility for the safety and happiness of children on a daily basis and are likely to place a very high value on the emotional and relational ties to the children under their charge.[47]

Under current law, the child has a "primary" tort claim for the injury suffered, including an amount for medical or other rehabilitative expenses associated with the child's physical injury and the mental and relational injury suffered by the child. The devastating impact of the accident on the daily life of the caretaker, however, is eclipsed because there is no separate claim for the caretaker's loss of consor-

[45] For a description of the hardships of a mother entrusted with the care of her disabled daughter, see Regina Graycar, Before the High Court: Women's Work: Who Cares?, 14 Sydney L. Rev. 86, 86-87 (1992).

[46] Lucinda M. Finley, A Break in the Silence: Including Women's Issues in a Torts Course, 1 Yale J.L. & Feminism 41, 50 (1989).

[47] See Mary Becker, Maternal Feelings: Myth, Taboo, and Child Custody, 1 S. Cal. Rev. L. & Women's Stud. 135, 152-58 (1992).

E. Reinforcing Economic Subordination Through Tort Law

tium. Popular culture valorizes the role of the "soccer mom" and places much importance on middle-class women staying home to raise children. However, the hierarchy of tort claims does not place so high a value on the contributions of parents and other caretakers: The most painful event in a caretaker's life may not be actionable in tort.

Similar to the effect of devaluation in the contexts of employment and family law, devaluation of child raising in tort law harms individuals of both sexes who devote a significant portion of their lives to this activity. This gender-linked devaluation of an activity traditionally associated with women, and still carried on disproportionately by women, contributes to the economic subordination of women by reinforcing the inferior status of "women's work," increasing the chances that child care will remain a predominantly female activity.

The second example of devaluation is linked to the movement for "tort reform." The term tort reform is now most often used to mean initiatives to *limit* tort liability. Reform in this area has been spurred by what business representatives and other groups regard as a litigation explosion, composed of frivolous suits and excessive jury awards. Despite several very convincing studies and arguments disputing the existence of such a crisis and defending the jury system, the pressure to cut back on plaintiffs' rights has not abated for almost two decades. Starting at the state level and now gaining momentum at the federal level, proponents of tort reform have targeted the areas of products liability and medical malpractice for reform, with a particular focus on noneconomic and punitive damages. By 1990, some kind of cap or limit on noneconomic damages had been enacted in well over half the states, some extending beyond health care and products liability actions to encompass all personal injury suits.

Critics of these cutbacks are now beginning to assess the negative gender impact of tort reform. An empirical study by Thomas Koenig and Michael Rustad[48] demonstrates that women stand to lose more when "nonprivileged" types of damages are curtailed, particularly noneconomic damages in actions involving health care. Their study revealed that two out of three plaintiffs receiving punitive damages in medical malpractice litigation are women, often in gender-linked cases involving mismanaged childbirth, cosmetic surgery, sexual abuse, and

---

[48] Thomas Koenig & Michael Rustad, His and Her Tort Reform: Gender Injustice in Disguise, 70 Wash. L. Rev. 1, 64-77 (1995).

neglect in nursing homes.[49] Because so much mass tort litigation has centered on women's reproductive health and other gender-linked injuries—from the Dalkon Shield and Norplant birth-control methods to super-absorbent tampons and breast implants—reforms that would curb noneconomic awards for health care liability also threaten to curtail this new focus on gender-specific injuries.

The Koenig and Rustad study further showed that capping noneconomic damages for pain and suffering and loss of enjoyment of life would disproportionately affect women. This is because the noneconomic portion of the tort award is crucial for women plaintiffs. Since women tend to earn lower wages and bear greater unpaid responsibility for child care and housekeeping, as a group women plaintiffs tend to have smaller economic losses than men of the same age. Even physical injuries to women may not translate into large awards for medical expenses, particularly if there is no current treatment for the condition. Thus, when a housewife suffers reproductive injury from being forced to undergo a hysterectomy caused by damage from an intrauterine device (IUD), the primary measure of her injuries will be noneconomic. Caps on noneconomic damages in health care actions thus would double the disadvantage for women, by restricting an important element of damages in those very cases women tend to bring.

In general, noneconomic damages are particularly significant to women because they serve to offset the disproportionately low value placed on women's claims when the measures of value are solely economic. The nonmarket character of pain and suffering and other kinds of noneconomic damages provides a modest corrective to the current system of tort damages, which generally replicates the market. For feminists who maintain that the market reflects and reinforces cultural biases and systems of privilege, changing tort law to curtail noneconomic damages seems misguided. They argue that such reform solidifies the tendency to privilege economic losses over noneconomic ones, and intensifies the implicit gender bias in tort law.

In tort law, as in many other areas of contemporary law, the mechanisms that maintain the gendered hierarchies of value are cognitive processes that influence the thinking of even people who be-

---

[49] *Id.* at 64-77.

E. Reinforcing Economic Subordination Through Tort Law

lieve they are unbiased. In my research on structural biases in tort law, I argue that there is a conceptual vicious cycle at work, similar to the processes that devalue predominantly female jobs.[50] This perceptual process categorizes injury sustained by women as emotional, relational, or nonpecuniary, even when the same injury could, as a matter of logic, be characterized as physical, property-like, or pecuniary. In this way, types of injury and damages are themselves gendered by being assigned to a gender-appropriate category. My contention is that in deciding how to categorize a loss, we consider not only the nature of the injury, but also *who* we believe suffers the loss; the gender of the prototypical plaintiff affects the way we categorize the nature of the harm. By this theory, the basic legal categories in tort law are not objective entities, but socially constructed. Cognitive bias finds its way into tort law through the legal categorization process itself.

I first understood this process behind the social construction of basic tort categories, such as "emotional harm" and "pecuniary loss," when I read the opinions in *Lynch v. Knight*,[51] the old English case that established the proposition that mental disturbance alone does not qualify as a legally cognizable harm. I found Lord Campbell's opinion most revealing. He discusses the question of why men, but not women, were given the right to sue for "criminal conversation," the adultery-type claim brought by a husband against a man who had intercourse with the plaintiff's wife. Lord Campbell sincerely believed that when a wife was unfaithful to her husband, the husband suffered a loss akin to a permanent loss of property. To him, the husband's loss of exclusive sexual access to his wife was a material harm, property-like in nature. However, when Lord Campbell analyzed the losses the wife suffered from her husband's sexual betrayal, he saw only hurt feelings and emotional harm. Harm to the wife in such a comparable situation was described as subjective, intangible, and transitory. What we would now describe as the same harm—the harm stemming from adultery—was then conceptualized in gender-specific terms, with the man's loss treated as a property loss, while the woman's loss was cast as emotional and relational.

---

[50] Chamallas, supra note 15, at 521-31 (1998).
[51] IX H.L. Cas. 576, 11 Eng. Rep. 854 (1861).

I have argued that the conceptual vicious cycle is still at work in the social construction of tort categories, as evidenced by my study of fright-based injuries. In collaboration with feminist historian Linda K. Kerber, I analyzed the classic "mental distress" cases involving female plaintiffs who suffered miscarriages and stillbirths as a result of emotional trauma.[52] In a very real sense, these plaintiffs suffered physical injuries and, as many early commentators pointed out, their cases could easily have been determined by the same principles and doctrines applied to ordinary negligence litigation. Instead, their claims were categorized as "emotional harm" cases. In this one class of litigation, the law fixed on fright, the mechanism of the injury, rather than on the ultimate physical consequences of the defendant's actions. Once classified as emotional harm, moreover, the various restrictive doctrines governing this unprivileged category of harm came into play to reduce the chances of recovery. To some extent, the classification of fright-based physical harms as "mental distress" persists to this day, as the organization of the basic torts casebooks and treatises attest. When faced with a choice—a choice that is always present when we construct categories—the law matched the type of injury (emotional) to the prototypical plaintiff (pregnant woman).

The concept of the vicious cycle attempts to explain how gender bias can be pervasive in the law of torts, at a time when gender has disappeared from the face of tort law. Like feminist criticism of the valuation of women's work, contemporary feminist critiques of tort law tend to be highly skeptical of the use of dichotomies—such as emotional/physical, property/relational, and economic/noneconomic—that have obscured the full measure of women's suffering and provided an ostensibly neutral justification for diminished recoveries. In this area of law, the processes of women's economic subordination are hidden from view, buried within categories that appear natural, static, and essential. Feminist scholarship has just begun to excavate the deep structures of tort law to tease out implicit male bias and to make room for a feminist reassessment of the basic hierarchies of value.

---

[52] *See* Martha Chamallas with Linda K. Kerber, Women, Mothers and the Law of Fright: A History, 88 Mich. L. Rev. 814 (1990).

F. IMPLICIT GENDER BIAS IN THE
TAX CODE

Particularly in the last decade, feminism has expanded into areas of law that were once thought to have little or nothing to do with gender, but everything to do with money. Recently, scholars in specialties like tax and bankruptcy have become interested in investigating the roots of women's economic subordination and determining whether ostensibly neutral statutory schemes in their fields can somehow be said to be biased against women. Much of this scholarship has been written by legal academics whose primary expertise is in commercial or tax law,[53] but who have been drawn to feminist theory because of its capacity to explain the hidden "logic" behind complex statutory rules and to connect the legal doctrine to broader societal forces and policies. This newer genre of applied feminist scholarship looks at women as economic actors (and as objects of economic legislation) beyond the workplace and the family, implicitly recognizing that women's acquisition and control of wealth depends in part on their treatment as debtors, shareholders, consumers, and taxpayers. In tandem with the recent importation of feminist theory, some authors in the commercial/tax realm have also begun to grapple with issues of race and sexual orientation, in keeping with the 1990s theme of diversity in critical scholarship.

The slice of feminist tax law scholarship I have selected to discuss here bears a close relationship to feminist literature on the work/family dilemma. One of its main themes is how the tax laws influence women's decisions about whether to work outside the home, and how they affect power relationships within the family, particularly between

---

[53] Marjorie Kornhauser notes that, with the notable exception of Patricia Cain, few feminist tax scholars write about feminist issues outside the tax field. Marjorie E. Kornhauser, A Taxing Woman*: The Relationship of Feminist Tax Scholarship to Tax, 6 So. Cal Rev. of L. & Women's Studies 301, 318 (1997). The same seems to be true of bankruptcy scholars. See Peter C. Alexander, Divorce and the Dischargeability of Debts: Focusing on Women as Creditors in Bankruptcy, 43 Cath. U. L. Rev. 351 (1994); Karen Gross, Re-Vision of the Bankruptcy System: New Images of Individual Debtors, 88 Mich. L. Rev. 1506 (1990) (review of Teresa A. Sullivan, Elizabeth Warren & Jay Lawrence Westbrook, As We Forgive Our Debtors: Bankruptcy and Consumer Credit in America (1989)).

husbands and wives in heterosexual marriages. As a subfield, feminist-oriented tax scholarship covers a much broader terrain, from documenting women's attitudes about tax policy to providing detailed critiques of particular estate or gift tax schemes.[54] However, I have chosen to focus on the debate surrounding the joint return for married couples because it has already generated a variety of feminist positions and is a good example of the feminist move of teasing out implicit male bias in a highly technical area of the law.

Except perhaps for tax specialists, few people thoroughly understand the effects of the tax rate structure that specifies rates for the vast majority of married couples who file joint returns.[55] There is public awareness of a "marriage penalty" built into our tax code and periodic calls upon Congress to end it. However, the complexity of the current scheme prevents most of us from realizing precisely which groups of taxpayers are advantaged and which are disadvantaged. Strictly speaking, the feminist-oriented tax scholarship focused on the joint return is not principally concerned with the marriage penalty, that is, the fact that some couples pay more in taxes after getting married than they did when they were single. In assessing the marriage penalty, the couple is treated as a unit and a comparison is made between the combined taxes each would have paid when they were single and their joint tax liability as married persons. Surprisingly, only approximately one-third of married couples face such a tax penalty upon marrying,[56] and the empirical evidence indicates that the financial penalty does not operate to deter people from getting married.[57]

---

[54] *See, e.g.,* Mary Louise Fellows, Wills and Trusts: "The Kingdom of the Fathers," 10 Law & Ineq. J. 137, 157 (1991).

[55] Amy Christian reports that in 1993 an estimated 97.5 percent of all married couples filed jointly. Amy C. Christian, The Joint Rate Structure: Identifying and Addressing the Gendered Nature of the Tax Law, 13 J. of L. & Politics 241, 271 n.112 (1997).

[56] Edward J. McCaffrey, Equality, of the Right Sort, 6 U.C.L.A. Women's L.J. 289, 308 (1996). However, it is important to recognize that the marriage penalty falls disproportionately on African-American couples. Dorothy A. Brown, Race, Class, and Gender Essentialism in Tax Literature: The Joint Return, 54 Wash. & Lee L. Rev. 1469, 1498 (1997).

[57] Anne L. Alstott, Tax Policy and Feminism: Competing Goals and Institutional Choices, 96 Colum. L. Rev. 2001, 2011 & n.36 (1996) (citing study finding that marriage penalty did not influence marriage rates but may lead some individuals to postpone marriage for a short period).

F. Implicit Gender Bias in the Tax Code

Instead, the key issue that many scholars have recently analyzed in connection with the joint return is its built-in-bias against "secondary earners." The problem was first identified by Grace Blumberg in 1971,[58] but it has become a hot topic only in the late 1990s since feminist theory found its way into tax scholarship and Edward McCaffrey's book *Taxing Women*[59] began to reach a more general audience. The term "secondary earner" is used in this literature to refer to the spouse whose wages are viewed as less important than the "primary" breadwinner's. The general assumption is that married women will most often be relegated to the "secondary" position, principally because, as a group, their wages tend to be appreciably lower than their husbands' wages.[60]

The bias against secondary earners is said to be a byproduct of our progressive, marginal tax rate structure, which taxes successive amounts of income at a higher rate. For example, the first $10,000 of income might be taxed at 10 percent, while the second $10,000 of income, from $10,001 to $20,000, would be taxed at a higher rate of 15 percent. Progressivity in a tax rate structure, of course, was not designed to harm those who earn less, such as married women. It instead reflects the judgment that because more affluent persons feel the sting of taxes less sharply than poorer persons, they should shoulder a greater share of the tax burden. The secondary earner bias only comes into play when and if the married woman's earnings are treated by the couple as somehow coming *after* that of her husband's, so that his earnings are regarded by the couple as being taxed first at the lower initial brackets, while her earnings, because they come second, are subject to the higher marginal tax rate. Arguably, this kind of thinking leads some couples to believe that it makes little economic sense for the secondary earner to work, particularly if the costs of child care and expenses of working are mentally "deducted" from that worker's paycheck. Edward McCaffrey claims, for example, that the average working wife in a middle- or upper-income household "sees two-thirds of her salary lost to taxes and work-related expenses."[61] He worries

---

[58] Grace Blumberg, Sexism in the Code: A Comparative Study of Income Taxation of Working Wives and Mothers, 21 Buff. L. Rev. 49 (1971-72).

[59] Edward J. McCaffrey, *Taxing Women* (1997).

[60] *Id.* at 21 ("[m]arried women make about 60 percent of what married men do").

[61] *Id.* at 12.

that this feature of our tax laws discourages married women from entering the labor market and makes it particularly undesirable for such women to work part-time.

As described, the secondary-earner bias is intimately connected to the joint return as it currently functions. One of the great benefits of using the joint return is that it affords couples the advantage of income shifting for tax purposes. Income shifting is a good tax avoidance strategy when it allows a high-earning taxpayer to shift income to a low-earning taxpayer who pays taxes at a lower marginal rate. Not surprisingly, income shifting is generally not permitted, except as it is authorized by the tax rate structure prescribed for married couples filing jointly. When the married couple is viewed as a unit, the joint return operates to lower the couple's taxes because it allows the higher-earning spouse (most often, the husband) to shift some of his income to the lower-earning spouse (most often, the wife). The conventional wisdom is that because their total tax liability is likely to be lower if they file jointly, most couples do not avail themselves of the opportunity to file separate returns.[62]

Even this simplistic rendition of the ramifications of the joint return should be enough to suggest why the topic provides a rich ground for feminist analysis. One important theme of the feminist scholarship centers on the impact taxes have on women's employment. There is disagreement as to whether the secondary-earner bias does in fact discourage married women from working and, if so, whether this disincentive is socially undesirable. As scholars take a closer look at the large category of married working women, they are forced to grapple with the heterogeneity of that category and find it necessary to limit their conclusions to only *some* groups of married women.

Anne Alstott, for example, notes that for married women already in the labor market, eliminating the secondary-earner bias would probably have little effect, because this group of women would likely continue working without appreciably increasing the amount of hours they work. She speculates that changing the current joint income filing scheme might create an incentive to enter the labor force for women in middle- or upper-income households who are not currently employed. However, she is ambivalent about the value of such a change

[62] Because the rates for married persons filing separately are not identical to the rates for single persons, the marriage penalty incurred by some couples would not be eliminated by having the spouses file separately.

insofar as it might ultimately take resources away from homemakers who act as "caregivers" for children, elderly parents, and other dependents.

On this point, the discussion in the tax literature very much parallels the different emphases of liberal, cultural, and anti-essentialist feminism. Put in oversimplified terms, liberal feminists tend to fasten on the secondary-earner bias because of its capacity to produce different patterns of employment for married women versus married men. From this position, it is worth noting that, despite the steady increase of married women's labor force participation, approximately 40 percent of married women with children under age six do not work outside the home, while the comparable figure for men is only 5 percent.[63] Liberal feminists worry that this difference provides employers with an excuse for the continuing disparity in wages between men and women, and could be used to justify tokenism and the glass ceiling. In the contemporary workplace, the fact that mothers more often than fathers interrupt their careers and jobs to care for family members is the difference often seized upon to justify women's economic marginalization.

From a cultural feminist perspective, however, the "secondary earner" bias may not look so pernicious. The argument is that, by giving a tax advantage to one-earner couples, the current structure supports the enterprise of homemaking. To some extent, this subsidy offsets society's devaluation of uncompensated work done in the home.

Finally, from a diversity or anti-essentialist perspective, the controversy over the joint return misses the mark unless it takes account of the very different social positions of various groups of women. Dorothy Brown, for example, has cautioned that in trying to assess the equity of the joint return, it is important to acknowledge race and class differences among married women.[64] She uses the most recent census data to show that African-American married women are more likely to be hurt by the marriage penalty, rather than by the secondary-earner bias, because they are more likely than white women to contribute roughly equal amounts to their households. The "secondary earners" whom the literature has so intensely studied are most likely to be white

[63] Edward J. McCaffrey, supra note 59, at 22.
[64] Brown, supra note 56.

women married to upper-income men. Brown concludes that, for African-American women, it is simply not true that the tax laws encourage them to remain at home.[65]

In addition to looking outward to the employment market, an innovative theme in the new feminist tax scholarship looks inward to examine how tax laws affect the relationship between married men and women. The dimension of power within the family is crucial because, regardless of whether the tax laws actually discourage married women from working, they might nevertheless harm women if they create or reinforce the belief that women's work is marginal. However precisely it is defined, the label "secondary earner" carries a negative connotation and the language suggests a hierarchy with respect to the spouses' material contributions to the household. In particular, the term *mis*describes and eclipses the situation of egalitarian couples where both spouses are committed to working outside the home and neither is regarded as the "secondary" earner, regardless of their respective salaries. Particularly now that it is no longer commonplace for women to quit work when they marry, it may well be that their status does not become "secondary" at the moment they marry simply because they make less money than their husbands. Rather, I suspect that the mindset that encourages couples to ask whether it "makes sense" for the wife to work comes into play only after a child (or more likely, the second child) is born and the couple assumes that the mother is the most appropriate caretaker for the baby. To the extent that it is rare or even odd for young married women to stay at home before they have children, there is little cultural impetus at that moment for labeling one spouse the primary breadwinner and the other the secondary earner. The hierarchical ordering is not simply a matter of economics, but a function of prescribed gender roles and gender stereotyping. This means that "secondary earner" status is a cultural construction and that there is no logic which requires the higher-earner's salary to be regarded as "fixed" and coming first. To test this hypothesis, it would be interesting to study couples in which the woman earns considerably more than her husband to see whether "secondary earner" status has the same meaning when it is attached to a man.

Beyond the debate about "secondary earners," some of the feminist literature on the joint tax return looks critically at the law's deci-

---

[65] *Id.* at 1503.

sion to treat the married couple as a unit for tax purposes. Testing the assumption that couples act as if "what's mine is yours," feminist scholars have been interested in the extent to which couples actually pool their resources and the degree to which each spouse exercises control over money brought into the household. Marjorie Kornhauser's review of empirical studies on the allocation of resources within households begins by recognizing the complexity of the concept of "pooling" assets and emphasizes that power relationships between husband and wife may affect how the couple spends its money. She speculates that many couples say that they pool their assets, even when, in practice, one partner may exercise more power over decision-making.

> Is it pooling when one person makes all the decisions? Is it pooling when both partners nominally make the decisions, but in reality one partner is so subservient that she always yields—consciously or unconsciously —to the dominant partner? Is it really pooling if he says "my assets are your assets," but meanwhile they are all titled in his name so that legally he can do whatever he wishes with them? Is it really pooling when she does not even know what all the assets are?[66]

Kornhauser concludes from the limited available empirical evidence that a significant percentage of married couples—from 30 to 50 percent—do not share all of their income. Instead, it is still often the case that the person who earns the money controls the finances, even if it is the other spouse who manages the checkbook and pays the bills. What is most interesting from a feminist perspective is Kornhauser's notion of the "psychological ownership" of money that prevents many women from feeling entitled to spend money that their husbands earn or to determine how some of it will be spent. Contrary to the stereotype of the wife as the inveterate spender, the studies indicate that many married women feel guilty about spending "their husbands' money," despite the couple's professed belief in sharing or pooling. Kornhauser believes that "[b]ehind the facade of sharing is a deep-seated, though often subtle, control of the income by the earner spouse."[67] Significantly, in those households in which married women contribute substantial amounts to joint income, women are more likely to choose to keep their earnings separate. Thus, the professed commit-

---

[66] Marjorie E. Kornhauser, Love, Money, and the IRS: Family, Income-Sharing, and the Joint Income Tax Return, 45 Hastings L.J. 63, 81-82 (1993).
[67] *Id.* at 91.

ment to sharing may in many cases reflect married women's relative lack of power, particularly if "sharing" in the household does not encompass equality in decision-making.

The new feminist tax scholarship calls into question the underlying assumption of the joint return—namely, that it is fair to treat married couples as a unit because they share their income. The critique also suggests that the basic structure of coverture has not been entirely dismantled.[68] Reminiscent of an older era when "husband and wife were one and that one was the husband," the legal device of the joint return continues to regard the couple as a single entity, often with the effect of reinforcing the husband's control over the finances and reinforcing the wife's secondary or inferior status. It appears that the patterns of domination that once were explicit on the face of the law have been updated to take on more subtle forms, masking women's real-life experiences with the control of money within their own families.

Once the fiction of the unity of married couples is challenged, moreover, it makes sense to ask whether the "savings" that a married couple purportedly experiences from filing a joint return is indeed realized by each spouse. Amy Christian's recent scholarship is perhaps the most critical of the joint return.[69] She contends that the joint return substantially harms large groups of women by coercing a transfer of wealth from women to men. Her argument proceeds from the assumption that not all couples share their income and that each spouse should be treated as an individual to determine when he or she benefits from filing a joint return. Recall that it is the higher-earner who wants to shift his income to a lower-earner who pays at a lower marginal rate. The current joint rate structure tends to benefit the higher-earning husband, as opposed to the lower-earning wife, because it is the former who realizes the benefit from income-shifting. Christian calculates that many wives would be better off (that is, their individual tax liability would be lower)[70] if they filed separately rather than jointly.

---

[68] *See* discussion of coverture in connection with household labor and the work/family conflict supra at pp. 194-96.

[69] Christian, supra note 55.

[70] Currently both spouses are jointly and severally liable for taxes owed by the couple from filing a joint return, meaning that each owes the government the full amount if the other does not pay. Christian's calculations that the lower-earning spouse (most often the wife) would be better off filing separately is based on an as-

F. Implicit Gender Bias in the Tax Code

By filing jointly, it is true, the couple often pays a lower combined tax. As a legal matter, however, the tax saving generally belongs to the husband. Except in a few community property states, a wife has no legal recourse if, for example, her husband chooses to use the tax savings to buy property in his own name, or even to give the money away. In this respect, the joint return scheme resembles coverture in that the "joint" asset (i.e., the tax savings from filing jointly) is legally owned by the husband and the law merely presumes that the wife will derive a benefit.

Christian's analysis also uncovers a contemporary paradox centering on women's choice: Why do the vast majority of married women "choose" to file jointly when they could advance their own interests by filing separate returns? Christian's explanation exposes the constraints under which such a choice is made. Her analysis stresses that the structure of the joint return pressures lower-earning women into acting for the good of the "family" (by reducing the couple's combined taxes) at their own individual expense. Christian argues that such a choice amounts to a coerced transfer of wealth from women to men; what would have been a tax savings for the lower earner if she had filed separately becomes a tax savings for the higher-earning spouse when the couple files jointly. In contrast, under the current structure, the interests of the higher-earning spouse are aligned with that of the family, giving that spouse an easy choice.[71] He does not have to weigh his individual interest against that of the "family," but can simply elect to file a joint return, saving on taxes himself and benefiting the family unit in the process.

The skewed choice offered to married persons under the joint return is not simply an accidental byproduct of the federal tax scheme but results from more deliberate congressional policy decisions made when the joint return was adopted in 1948. At that time, Congress set out to address a disparity in treatment between taxpayers in common law property states and those who resided in the few community property states. Community property states allowed husbands and wives to split income, because each spouse under such a regime held a present property interest in half of the marital assets. The theory was that be-

---

sumption that, as between the spouses, the wife's share of the taxes is considered either to be 50 percent or some lower percentage based on her respective salary compared to her husband's. Christian, supra note 55, at 343.

[71] *Id.* at 352.

cause the earner did not retain sole legal ownership of his salary, it was appropriate to allow the couple to split the earnings 50-50 for federal tax purposes. In common law states, however, the earner of income from labor was not allowed to shift income to his spouse to gain a tax advantage because in those states, the nonearner had no present legal interest in money earned by the other spouse. Legal historian and tax scholar Carolyn Jones discovered that, despite the considerable tax advantage at stake, some states may have refused to convert from a common law to a community property system in part *because* of hostility toward giving wives greater property interests and control of money during the marriage.[72] In any event, states were spared such a difficult choice by the enactment of the joint return in 1948. In effect, the joint return allowed husbands to gain the benefits of income shifting without actually having to cede control of half their earnings to their wives. Adoption of the joint return stemmed what might have become a movement toward community property, a system that gives greater formal recognition to the value of work done in the home and potentially accords women more control over household finances.[73]

Jones's feminist history of the joint return adds a new dimension to the complex legal history of women's household labor and deepens our understanding of the mechanisms through which household labor has been devalued.[74] Seen in this light, the implicit gender bias of the tax code is doubly harmful; at the same time that the secondary-earner bias marginalizes women's wage work, the joint return works to assure that women's household labor does not translate into an equal right to control how money is spent.

The critiques of the joint return discussed above suggest that the law is too quick to treat the married couple as a single unit, and that it fails to take due regard for the interests of women as individuals. Additionally, there is one more aspect of the joint return worth mentioning in connection with feminist critiques of the tax code. It focuses on the legal treatment of same-sex couples and takes a very different point

---

[72] Carolyn C. Jones, Split Income and Separate Spheres: Tax Law and Gender Roles in the 1940s, 6 L. & History Rev. 259, 270 (1988).

[73] However, until quite recently, even in community property states, men were given the right to manage the assets of the community as its "head and master." The feminist vision of equality of decision-making between the spouses was not fully realized in either common law or community property states.

[74] *See* supra at pp. 193-95, discussing Reva Siegel's political history of housework.

of departure. In her article detailing tax problems faced by lesbian and gay couples, Patricia Cain faults the tax code for what she calls its "fallacy of individualism."[75] Under the current scheme, same-sex couples are treated simply as unrelated individuals—they cannot file joint returns and do not receive the benefits of income shifting. This makes it extraordinarily difficult for one partner to provide substantial financial support to the other without risking additional burdensome taxes. It is not only that the higher earner in the same-sex couple will be required to pay tax on her income at the higher, single-person, marginal rate. Cain also points out that it is unclear whether the higher earner may even transfer money to her partner without incurring gift tax liability or, alternatively, subjecting her partner to liability for income tax upon receipt of the support payment. In Cain's view, the problem stems from the law's refusal to recognize the interdependency of partners in the same-sex context, making it hard for these couples to pool their assets without incurring a financial penalty. Cain argues for various reforms of the tax law that would put same-sex couples on a more equal footing with heterosexual married couples.

At first it may seem striking that a feminist scholar such as Cain would fault the tax code for excessive individualism, while another feminist scholar such as Christian would argue for more individual treatment through the filing of separate returns. To some extent, however, their difference in focus simply reflects the different interests of the women at the center of each one's analysis: Cain's point of reference is the lesbian taxpayer, while Christian is primarily concerned with the married woman who earns less than her husband. Taken together, their scholarship underscores the point of diversity feminism, which stresses that women constitute a heterogenous group and that there is no single policy solution that inevitably benefits all women.

At a deeper level, however, I find their analyses to be complementary and reinforcing. Christian shows how tax law reinforces wives' economic dependency upon their husbands, while Cain shows how the law undercuts lesbian relationships where women's economic dependency is not tied to men, but to other women. In terms of the theme of this chapter, both scholars show how women's economic subordination *to men* is reinforced. Like many of the other articles discussed in

[75] Patricia A. Cain, Same-Sex Couples and the Federal Tax Laws, 1 Law & Sexuality 97, 101 (1991).

this section, their work demonstrates how implicit gender bias in the tax code subtly privileges traditional marriages, while taxing the non-traditional (lesbian couples, married women who work outside the home, couples who earn approximately the same income) in a variety of complex and often hidden ways.

CHAPTER 8

Applied Feminist Scholarship—
Sexual Subordination
of Women

The substantive topics that continue to attract the most attention from feminist legal writers—particularly rape, sexual harassment and domestic violence—all involve the general subject of the sexual subordination of women. Often inspired by Catharine MacKinnon's writings, feminists have examined and reexamined legal regulations governing sexual conduct with the twin goals of reducing sexual violence and exploitation and increasing women's sexual autonomy and integrity. The applied feminist scholarship on the sexual subordination of women does not draw a sharp line between the "bread and butter" issues of economic subordination discussed in the last chapter and issues of sexual abuse. Especially in contexts such as sexual harassment, there is often an inseparable mixture of economic and sexual power, and the resulting injuries to women cannot be neatly categorized as either economic or sexual. Since the mid-1980s, moreover, legal feminists have understood that sexualized injuries have a devastating impact on women's lives, even though the infliction of such injuries is not always considered to be gender discrimination under prevailing law, as evidenced by the debate as to whether date rape and domestic violence constitute "gender-motivated" violence under the new federal Violence Against Women Act.[1]

Feminist critiques of legal regulations governing sexual conduct have targeted laws that emanate from both traditional and liberal view-

---

[1] 42 U.S.C. § 13981 (1994).

points.[2] Despite its intimate character, sexual conduct is highly regulated activity, and the laws governing sex have been an especially active site of struggle over the boundary between acceptable and legally sanctionable conduct. Because the regulation of sex includes civil as well as criminal penalties and may extend to the ethical behavior of professionals such as physicians, lawyers, and university professors, feminist scholars have also faced difficult questions regarding the selection of appropriate remedies in specific contexts.

Traditional sex regulations express the familiar moralistic notion that the only sexual conduct that is acceptable is sex that occurs within heterosexual marriage. Legal regulation in the traditional mode regards sex within marriage as qualitatively different from other sexual conduct and treats even consensual nonmarital sex, such as sodomy or adultery, as properly subject to legal penalties.

Feminists have contested both the immunity accorded to sex within marriage and the justice of condemning nonmarital sex in every context. A prime target of the feminist campaign for reform of rape law, for example, has been the marital rape exemption[3] which until recently made it impossible for husbands to be charged with raping their wives, even when the husband used physical force and the wife clearly did not consent. The exemption's total disregard of the sexual autonomy of married women underscored that the law was primarily interested in regulating "property" interests among men, rather than in protecting the personal integrity of the rape victims. Feminists argued that because marriage as an institution is not free from male domination, the fact that the participants are married is no safeguard against violence or exploitation.

Additionally, the legal disapproval of nonmarital sex has also been criticized for perpetuating the subordination of women. The near universal ban on same-sex marriage[4] and the criminalization of sodomy in many states means that "privileged" sex is still confined to the paradigmatic male/female relationship, with its legacy of gender inequality. On these issues, feminists have argued for the lifting of legal prohibitions against "nontraditional" sexual activity. This strain of

---

[2] *See* Martha Chamallas, Consent, Equality and the Legal Control of Sexual Conduct, 61 S. Cal. L. Rev. 777 (1988).

[3] *See* Robin West, Equality Theory, Marital Rape, and the Promise of the Fourteenth Amendment, 42 Fla. L. Rev. 45 (1990).

[4] *See* infra pp. 266-67 regarding developments in Hawaii.

feminist criticism maintains that traditional regulations can oppress women not only by denying protection against coercive sex, but also by repressing women's sexuality, especially lesbian sexuality.

The bulk of the applied feminist criticism, however, has been directed at legal regulations that express a liberal philosophy. Under the liberal view, sexual conduct is quintessentially private conduct with which the law should not interfere. Taking the place of marital status, the concept of *consent* becomes the central demarcation line separating lawful from unlawful conduct. In the liberal view, the phrase "consenting adults in private" signals acceptable conduct that ought to be immune from legal intervention.

As described earlier,[5] the feminist critique of consent and privacy focused primarily on the failure of these liberal legal principles to protect women against widespread male sexual violence. In practice, consent tended to be watered down to mean no more than acquiescence or nonresistance and presupposed a system of unequal sexual relationships in which men actively initiated sexual encounters and women were relegated to the more passive role of consenting or not consenting. This led to feminist attempts to construct a more protective notion of consent and to devise legal formulas that concentrated on the actions of the defendant rather than on the response of the woman. In my scholarship, for example, I have sought to reconstruct consent by first identifying those physical, economic, and psychological pressures that should serve to vitiate consent to sex, in effect to declare which "bargains" are so skewed as to amount to offers that women cannot afford to refuse.[6]

In contrast to other consensual transactions, the law has often permitted men to use fraud, economic coercion, and even a degree of physical force to pressure women into unwelcome sexual encounters which they would not have initiated had they been given the opportunity. This exceptional treatment of sexual encounters not only permeates criminal prosecutions for rape but continues to affect standards in civil cases, such that few plaintiffs recover for injuries from sex induced by deception or threats of economic reprisals. Many of the feminist-inspired reforms in areas such as sexual harassment and tort

---

[5] *See* MacKinnon's critique of consent, supra pp. 55-56.
[6] Chamallas, supra note 2, at 814-35.

law are attempts to delineate which exploitive practices, short of over-powering physical force, should trigger legal sanctions.

In addition to advocating specific causes of action targeting ex-ploitive sexual practices, feminists have also tried to articulate a posi-tive, egalitarian ideal of heterosexual conduct that is more respectful of women's autonomy. As a replacement for consent, commentators have suggested new concepts of "mutuality"[7] or "communicative sexu-ality"[8] to describe encounters in which each person tries to under-stand the other's desires and feelings and takes care not to treat the other as a sexual object. Under such formulations, it is not enough that a woman did not physically resist or even that she voiced no ex-press verbal objections to the sex. Instead, the touchstone of mutuality is that each person must actually welcome the encounter—the sex is not mutual if one person simply gives up or decides that resistance is futile or not worth the cost.[9]

Particularly since the controversy in the mid-1980s sparked by MacKinnon's and Dworkin's model ordinance on pornography,[10] how-ever, the feminist literature on sexual subordination has been marked by divisions not only about the desirability of specific legal reforms, but about visions for the future as well. Although the goal of reducing sexual violence is shared by all, some feminists doubt that pursuing an ideal such as "mutuality" in heterosexual relationships is the best strat-egy. The paramount fear for these "pro-sex" writers is that promoting mutuality in male/female sexual relations might reinforce Victorian views of women as asexual beings who are not interested in sex, but only in the traditionally feminine virtues of intimacy, caring, and nur-turing. Arguing strongly against legal prohibition of pornography, for example, Carlin Meyer expresses concern that mutuality discourse can "trap women in fantasies of an unrealizable, idealized future, rather

[7] Stephen Schulhofer, for example, would criminalize nonviolent interference with sexual autonomy in cases in which a woman's silence or ambivalent conduct does not provide assurance of her desire to engage in sexual intercourse. Stephen J. Schul-hofer, Taking Sexual Autonomy Seriously: Rape Law & Beyond, 11 Law & Phil. 35, 77 (1992).

[8] Lois Pineau's model of communicative sexuality would seek evidence of an on-going positive and encouraging response on the part of the woman to assure that the sex was not coercive. Lois Pineau, Date Rape: A Feminist Analysis, 8 Law & Phil. 217, 233-37 (1989).

[9] I elaborate on the concept of mutuality in Chamallas, supra note 2, at 835-43.

[10] See supra at pp. 59-62.

than enabling them to cope with the reality of uncertain desire, of ne-
gotiated terms and confusing communication, and of the difficulty in
ascertaining one's own arousal—let alone someone else's."[11] The writers who oppose regulations on pornography echo critics of cultural
feminism who see the greatest danger in the law's reinforcement of
social control over women's bodies and activities, rather than its failure to protect women from private violence. Often their prescription
for change is to promote new images of women and women's sexuality
in the mass media, advertising, and other cultural sites to challenge
both the Victorian image of the "good girl" and the pornographic image of the male sex object.

Much of the applied feminist scholarship on sexual subordination addresses why a male-centered view of consent, rather than more
feminist-oriented concepts like mutuality, continues to dominate the
law in action, even when feminists have been successful in arguing for
changes in formal legal doctrine. The persistence of myths about rape
and sexuality, the significantly different perceptions and experiences
of men and women, and the confounding factors of race and sexual
orientation all complicate efforts to afford women greater security and
autonomy in matters relating to sex. This is an area where feminists
generally agree that the state of the law is bad, but are split as to
whether they trust that legal intervention will ultimately make matters
better. The liberal belief that cautions against the repressive aspects of
laws governing sex, particularly as they affect lesbians, bisexual persons and gay men, operates as a limit on feminists' enthusiasm for legal reform.

This chapter first takes a glimpse at three key topics—rape, sexual
harassment, and domestic violence—in the burgeoning feminist legal
literature on sexual violence and exploitation. These three areas were
chosen because they have so thoroughly captured media attention that
the popular discourse about feminism is principally embedded in daily
news accounts of date rapes, sexual harassment allegations, and, to a
lesser degree, stories about domestic violence. The discussion here is
necessarily very abbreviated and incomplete,[12] with the modest goal

[11] Carlin Meyer, Sex, Sin and Women's Liberation: Against Porn-Suppression, 72
Tex. L. Rev. 1097, 1132-33 (1994).

[12] A more extensive treatment, for example, would certainly cover the topics of
pornography, prostitution, child sexual abuse, and the sexual exploitation of women
by professionals.

of developing some of the themes raised in the chronological treatment of feminist legal theory. To sample feminist writings directed more towards sexual freedom and choice, the chapter ends with a synopsis of some of the feminist scholarship on same-sex marriage. It emphasizes heterosexism as an important mechanism of the sexual subordination of women, and the importance of recognizing a legal right to enter into a "nontraditional" intimate relationship.

A.   PROTOTYPES OF RAPE

Rape law is most often the centerpiece of contemporary discussions of women's sexual subordination. Since the groundbreaking works of feminist writers in the 1970s,[13] rape has been acknowledged as a serious threat to women's safety, not only because rapes are common but because the fear of rape severely curtails women's freedom of movement and their ability to act with confidence in negotiating the risks of everyday life. Given the growing awareness of the harms of rape, feminist writers have sought to unravel the paradox of apparent legal condemnation of rape, with the law's failure either to cut down substantially on the incidence of rape or to prosecute most rapists. Commentators on rape frequently start their analyses with a set of observations about the social reality of rape in the United States. They commonly note that the incidence of rape is unacceptably high,[14] a high percentage of women do not report that they have been raped, police and prosecutors often decline to move a case forward, conviction rates in rape cases are lower than for other serious crimes, and

---

[13] *See* Susan Brownmiller, *Against Our Will: Men, Women and Rape* (1975) and Kate Millett, *Sexual Politics* (1970). A particularly influential article was Susan Griffin, Rape: The All-American Crime, in *Forcible Rape: The Crime, the Victim, and the Offender* 47 (Duncan Chappell, Robley Geis & Gilbert Geis eds., 1977).

[14] In the United States, 1 out of every 8 women (or approximately 12.1 million women) has been a victim of forcible rape at some time in her life. National Victims Center & Crime Victims Research and Treatment Center, Rape in America: A Report to the Nation 2 (April 23, 1992).

A. Prototypes of Rape

judges and juries remain suspicious about the motivations and credibility of rape victims.[15]

1. Strangers and Racism

One explanation offered by many feminist scholars to account for the disparity between the formal condemnation of rape and the inadequacy of rape law enforcement emphasizes the importance of stock images and common misperceptions surrounding the crime of rape. As in the case of workplace discrimination, cognitive bias operates within rape law to limit the protective reach of legal prohibitions. However, in this context, cognitive bias does not devalue activities associated with women. Instead, it operates to construct a prototype of rape and of the prototypical rapist that bears little resemblance to most rape victims' experience. The result is that a large portion of behavior that fits the legal definition of rape—forcible penetration without the consent of the victim—is often not regarded or treated as "real rape," sometimes even by the victims themselves.

One writer who has had a great impact by exposing the limitations of the rape prototype is Susan Estrich,[16] whose book, *Real Rape*, popularized the view that only a very narrow class of rape cases were taken seriously under the law in both the past and the present. Estrich's basic claim is that unless a rape is committed by a stranger who inflicts or threatens physical injury, it will rarely be treated as a criminal act.

> At one end of the spectrum is the "real" rape . . . A stranger puts a gun to the head of the victim, threatens to kill her or beats her, and then engages in intercourse. In that case, the law—judges, statutes, prosecutors, and all—generally acknowledge that a serious crime has been committed. But most cases deviate in one or many respects from this clear picture, making interpretation far more complex. Where less force is used or no other physical injury is inflicted, where threats are inarticulate, where the two know each other, where the setting is not an alley

---

[15] *See, e.g.*, Lynne Henderson, Rape and Responsibility, 11 Law & Phil. 127, 128-29 (1992).

[16] Estrich first presented her analysis in Susan Estrich, Rape, 95 Yale L.J. 1087 (1986). The popular version is *Real Rape: How the Legal System Victimizes Women Who Say No* (1987).

but a bedroom, where the initial contact was not a kidnapping but a
date, where the woman says no but does not fight, the understanding is
different. In such cases, the law, as reflected in the opinions of the
courts, the interpretation, if not the words, of the statutes, and the decisions of those within the criminal justice system, often tell us that no
crime has taken place and that fault, if any is to be recognized, belongs
with the woman.[17]

The harm of the "stranger rape" prototype is not simply that it
does not include all the situations that qualify as rape. The prototype
is harmful because it misdescribes the vast majority of rapes,[18] erasing
those date, acquaintance, and marital rapes that make rape a pervasive rather than an isolated phenomenon. As long as rape is conceptualized as being committed by a violent stranger, encounters that do
not fit the prototype will tend to be categorized as "consensual," even
when there is little evidence that the woman wanted to have sexual
intercourse. Much of the feminist writing describing the pain women
experience when they are raped by men they trust seeks to break down
the real rape/consensual sex dichotomy by showing how forced sex,
whether by strangers or "intimates," equally destroys a woman's sense
of personal autonomy and bodily integrity. Mary Lou Fellows and Beverly Balos have also pointed out an irony in the current law of rape
which allows a rape defendant to use a preexisting relationship to bolster a defense of consent. In other legal contexts, in contrast, such preexisting confidential relationships give rise to a heightened duty to
take care to respect the wishes and interests of the other party.[19]

The critique of the stranger rape prototype described by Estrich
and others, however, is inadequate unless the racial dimensions of the
constructs are also extracted and analyzed. Starting with Jennifer Wriggins's law review note in 1983,[20] feminist legal writers have realized
that the pattern of enforcement of rape laws has been permeated by
race. When the offender is black and the victim is white, the rape is
much more likely to result in a conviction. Black men convicted of

---

[17] 95 Yale L.J. at 1092.

[18] An estimated 60 to 80 percent of rapes do not fit the "paradigm of the violent
stranger rape." Lani Anne Remick, Read Her Lips: An Argument for a Verbal Consent Standard in Rape, 141 U. Pa. L. Rev. 1103, 1104 (1993).

[19] Beverly Balos & Mary Louise Fellows, Guilty of the Crime of Trust: Nonstranger
Rape, 75 Minn. L. Rev. 599, 601 (1991).

[20] Jennifer Wriggins, Rape, Racism, and the Law, 6 Harv. Women's L.J. 103 (1983).

A. Prototypes of Rape

rape also continue to receive harsher punishments than other sexual assault defendants. Simply by being black, offenders in interracial rapes are often cast as "strangers," as the prototypical rape evokes an implicit racialized image. Again, the problem with the prototype is not simply one of underenforcement, but the creation and perpetuation of harmful myths that threaten to undermine feminist anti-rape goals. Wriggins explains that in addition to promoting false accusations against black men, the prototype harms white and black women by "implicitly condoning" all but the paradigmatic rapes and contributing to a cultural denial that "rape is painful and degrading to both Black and white victims regardless of the attacker's race."[21] Black feminist writers such as Angela Harris[22] assert that the selective focus of rape laws poses a distinctive hardship for black women who mistrust the racism in the law and never "benefit" from the racialized prototype when they are victimized by black men.

The rape prototype may also serve to exceptionalize rape by suggesting that only certain types of men are likely to rape; that is, the prototype of the action becomes linked to a specific kind of perpetrator (prototypical rapist). In a recent article criticizing the passage of special evidentiary rules for federal sexual assault cases, Katharine Baker characterizes the prevailing view as based on the belief that "rape is different from other crimes because rapists are 'crazy.'"[23] She contends that this psychopathological model of the rapist oversimplifies the multiple motivations that cause men to rape. Trying to unpack the term "rapist," Baker argues that "all rapes are not alike," in that "some rapes are predominantly about sex, some rapes are predominantly about masculinity, and some rapes are predominantly about domination."[24] In a gang rape, for example, men may rape to impress the other men and bring unity to the group. The motivation for a young date rapist, however, may be more directly linked to a desire for sex, combined with a commodified view of sex that minimizes the harm to the unwilling woman. Baker's point is congruent with Estrich's analysis—the tendency to reduce rapists to mentally ill sadists who have an urge to rape increases the risk of missing the more com-

---

[21] *Id.* at 117.

[22] *See* supra at pp. 90-91.

[23] Katharine K. Baker, Once A Rapist? Motivational Evidence and Relevancy in Rape Law, 110 Harv. L. Rev. 563, 565 (1997).

[24] *Id.* at 566.

mon scenarios of victimization. To capture the pervasiveness and complexity of rape, feminists have stressed that rapists are not always deviant individuals. Often they are "normal" persons who have committed a serious crime.

Applied feminist scholarship examining the relationship between legal doctrine and the persistence of the rape prototype is especially well developed. As a matter of formal legal doctrine, a distinction between violent stranger rapes and other rapes is seldom made. The one prominent exception is that several states still place marital rape in a separate category, either immunizing nonviolent marital rapes altogether or treating marital rape as a less serious offense. For the most part, however, the basic doctrinal elements of the crime of rape—penetration, force, and nonconsent—are the same for all kinds of rape and the law no longer permits explicit disparate treatment of black offenders. Instead, the less serious treatment of rapes that do not match the prototype is effectuated by the myriad interpretations of judges, juries, police, and others who share responsibility for enforcing the law. It is these informal understandings about the nature of rape and the harms of rape that have recently drawn the attention of most feminist writers.

2. Causal Attribution, Victim Responsibility, and Rape Justification

In some cases—embodied in the popular "he said/she said" schematic of gender interactions—the credibility of the accused and the alleged victim is at the heart of the case. Who is telling the truth (or lying) may be the principal issue to be resolved. In fact, one of the earliest targets for feminist reforms of evidentiary rules in rape cases was the infamous cautionary instruction fashioned in the Eighteenth Century by Lord Matthew Hale. The instruction warned jurors to be especially skeptical about charges of rape, characterizing rape as "an accusation easily to be made and hard to be proved and harder to be defended by the party accused, tho' never so innocent."[25]

---

[25] Sir Matthew Hale, *The History of the Pleas of the Crown*, I (London: Professional Books, 1971) LVIII: *635.

A. Prototypes of Rape

In their scholarship, feminists have sought to counter the myth that women's accusations of rape are more likely to be false than charges brought by other crime victims, and often emphasize that the ordeal of the investigation and rape trial itself operates as a deterrent to spurious charges.[26] In the 1990s, defendants are not as likely to claim that women falsely charge rape to defend their honor and reputation, a common narrative prior to the sexual revolution of the 1970s. However, they are more likely to assert that the victim is lying because she wants attention or sympathy or stands to gain financially by proceeding with her case. Such credibility contests require the fact finder not only to assess the trustworthiness of each individual but to make a prediction about the plausibility of the defendant's explanation. At this point, general attitudes about women's credibility and the prevalence of rape may play a crucial role in judgment. Whenever the account of the rape victim is not believed, this tends to place responsibility for the sexual encounter on the victim and sends the message that the woman is the cause of her own injury.

Contrary to popular beliefs, feminist legal scholars do not maintain that women who charge rape should always be believed simply because they are women. What concerns many feminist legal scholars, however, is not only the problem of gender bias in gauging women's credibility, but the closely related question of causal attribution. Even when the victim's story is believed, including her claim that she did not consent, responsibility for the sex may still be placed on the woman. Police, jurors, and the general public may blame the victim for provoking or not preventing the rape, often by focusing on her "provocative" dress, appearance, or behavior. By shifting the focus away from the defendant's behavior, this approach treats the woman as the primary causal agent. Although formal legal doctrine does not recognize "justification" as a defense in rape cases, in some contexts, the practice of placing causal responsibility on the woman for failing to control the man operates informally to justify forced sex.

Lynne Henderson has described this causal attribution process as the construction of a narrative of "male innocence and female guilt." In the dominant narrative, "women control sex, but men lose control, and it is 'only natural.'" Despite feminist-inspired changes in the law,

---

[26] *See* Morrison Torrey, When Will We Be Believed? Rape Myths and the Idea of a Fair Trial in Rape Prosecutions, 24 U.C. Davis L. Rev. 1013 (1991).

such as the elimination of the resistance requirement and the passage of rape shield laws that limit inquiry into the victim's sexual history, cultural attitudes about causal responsibility in sexual matters are notoriously resistant to change. Henderson contends that

> [w]e as a society still see women as responsible for "controlling" heterosexuality, and blame them when they do not, despite a concomitant belief that emphasizes male initiation and persistence in sexual matters. In bourgeois culture, in a bizarre distortion of causality, girls are raised to believe that their dress, makeup, hairstyle, walk, and talk determine male reactions.[27]

Even the feminist victory in getting date rape recognized as a genuine type of sexual assault has sometimes been transmuted into a warning to college-age women to prevent date rape by not drinking too much, "carefully check[ing] to see if the man is listening to and interested in them," and refraining from any conduct that might be interpreted by a man as "an invitation to intercourse."[28]

These judgments about causality and responsibility are often played out under the rubric of "consent," even though they may have little to do with whether a woman actually desired to have intercourse with a particular man on a particular occasion. The familiar catalogue of behaviors that jurors have regarded as proof of a woman's consent include drinking, dancing, agreeing to drive home with a man, or even just being sexually experienced, as evidenced by having a live-in boyfriend or taking the Pill. One feminist commentator points out that these behaviors are ambiguous in that they may have "other meanings wholly unrelated to sex. A woman may drink for purposes of celebration; she may take oral contraceptives for health reasons; she may dress provocatively because it makes her feel confident."[29] The struggle in these cases is over the interpretation of the encounter, as jurors ask themselves whether it was reasonable for the man to press for sex, given the woman's conduct. The ambiguity is often construed against the woman who offers no physical resistance to a man's aggressive ac-

---

[27] Henderson, supra note 15, at 138.
[28] *Id.* at 139.
[29] Remick, supra note 18, at 1125.

tions, resurrecting resistance as a "ghost element of rape"[30] long after the reform of rape statutes.

An interesting vein in the feminist literature has explored why causal responsibility for rape continues to be placed on women, despite nearly a generation of feminist anti-rape initiatives, from "take back the night" marches to rape crisis hot lines. Several scholars have stressed differences in perceptions between men and women, what Kim Scheppele calls a "perceptual fault line."[31] In this postmodern account of sexual encounters, there is no single truth about what happened; lawsuits function more to decide "*which* true version of a particular story should be adopted as the official version of what happened."[32] The competing versions or scripts, however, are structured predictably along gender lines. Social science research indicates that men tend to interpret women's behavior in a sexualized way, seeing seductiveness and sexual receptivity when women are likely to see only friendliness and sociability. Particularly when the meaning of nonverbal behavior is in question, the potential for misinterpreting "cues" is great, generating a vigorous debate among legal scholars about whether rape defendants should be held criminally responsible for negligence, for not taking care to ascertain whether the woman is truly consenting.

In an approach reminiscent of the debate about the "reasonable woman" standard in sexual harassment cases,[33] feminist writers have looked for ways to make a rape victim's construction of events more coherent and visible in the law, to develop counternarratives that redefine "force" and "consent" from the victim's perspective. One important doctrinal development, for example, has been the willingness of some courts to consider the force necessary to accomplish penetration against the wishes of a woman as sufficient "physical force" to satisfy the statutory requirement in rape cases.[34] This viewpoint has been regarded as a feminist interpretation of rape law because it appreciates that "lack-of-consent intercourse" is a serious harm, often

---

[30] Dana Berliner, Note, Rethinking the Reasonable Belief Defense to Rape, 100 Yale L.J. 2687, 2691 (1991).

[31] Kim Lane Scheppele, The Re-Vision of Rape Law, 54 U. Chi. L. Rev. 1095, 1104 (1987).

[32] *Id.* at 1111.

[33] *See* supra pp. 97-98.

[34] The leading case is *State ex rel. M.T.S.*, 609 A.2d 1266 (N.J. 1992).

described by victims as "degrading," "scary," and "excruciatingly pain-ful."[35] Requiring that the victim prove that she was subjected to addi-tional violence beyond forced penetration reflects a male-oriented view that defines force only as "the sort of punching, kicking, brawling vio-lence that is required to get a conventionally socialized man to do something against his will."[36]

The understanding of sexual encounters from the victim's per-spective is closely linked to judgments about causal attribution. The more palpable the victim's pain and lack of sexual desire, the easier it is to perceive callousness and aggression in the defendant's behavior and to regard it as the precipitating cause of the sexual encounter. The difficulty for many victims of date and acquaintance rape lies in convincing others that it is unfair to assign them responsibility for their own victimization, simply because they might possibly have prevented the rape by being more cautious, reserved, or modest. Even female jurors who may have had the experience of being pressured for un-wanted sex may nevertheless "subjugate" their knowledge,[37] apply Vic-torian standards in the name of following the law, and distance themselves from the powerlessness of a rape victim. In this second gen-eration of feminist legal scholarship on rape, the question of how to change basic cultural attitudes and the terms of the discourse about rape and consensual sex remains a high priority.

3.   Commodification, Devaluation, and New Feminist Discourses

Most feminists resist speaking about women's sexuality as if it were a thing to be possessed or given away. The commodification of sex seems to resonate with older notions of women as the property of their hus-bands or fathers and with a system of rape laws that has as its primary objective the regulation of men's sexual access to women. For ex-ample, a classic article in feminist theory by anthropologist Gayle Rubin—The Traffic in Women: Notes on a "Political Economy" of

---

[35] *See* Lynne Henderson, Getting to Know: Honoring Women in Law and in Fact, 2 Tex. J. Women & Law 41, 58, 64-65 (1993); Robin L. West, Legitimating the Illegiti-mate: A Comment on *Beyond Rape*, 93 Colum. L. Rev. 1442, 1448 (1993).

[36] Scheppele, supra note 31, at 1103.

[37] *Id.* at 1112.

A. Prototypes of Rape

Sex (1975)—analyzed the social systems by which women have been exchanged by men in marriage, war, prostitution, and other contexts. These systems commodified women by treating them as sexual objects and gifts, according men the status of sexual subjects or exchangers.

Feminists have argued that the commodification of women puts them at a disadvantage and defames them. Discussions of rape that draw an analogy between the harm of forced intercourse and the theft of property tend to minimize the enormous psychological and spiritual injury felt by rape victims. Such discourse often ends up by reducing rape to a bad "bargain," especially when nonviolent means, such as fear of losing one's job, are used to coerce the woman to have sex.

The commodified view of sex, however, is still very prevalent, not only in the increasing use of sex and sexual images of women's (and men's) bodies to sell products, but in the vocabulary popular among young men and women. In an article discussing what she calls the "property theory of rape," Alexandra Wald explains how property metaphors influence cultural perceptions of rape:

> This metaphorical market uses fictions of exchange to provide a narrative in which sex appears not to have been forced but to have been "traded." Women seeking justice for sexual violation must combat "quid pro quo" rape justification stories such as the view that a man is entitled to have sex with a woman if he has spent money on her . . . Market terminology permeates descriptions of rape. For example, the phrases "breach of contract" and "date fraud" have been used in describing rapes. One rapist asked "[W]hy should a man rape if he can get it for free?" The prevalence of sex market imagery suggests that women are embroiled in a coercive sexual "market" in which their sexuality is regarded as a bargaining chip . . .[38]

A similar point is made with respect to the commodified language commonly used by teenagers to discuss sex, such as "Did you get some?" "Did you give it up?"[39] Katharine Baker argues that many teenage males regard date rape as an infraction on the same order as shoplifting: "They know it is wrong, but it is not *that* bad." Because they view sex as a commodity, taking sex without the consent of the

[38] Alexandra Wald, What's Rightfully Ours: Toward a Property Theory of Rape, 30 Colum. J.L. & Soc. Probs. 459, 483-85 (1997) (footnotes omitted).
[39] Baker, supra note 23, at 603 n.224.

woman becomes a kind of petty theft, what Baker calls a violation of a "little rule."[40]

As applied to sex, commodified discourse tends not to be gender neutral. Instead, most often it is women's sexuality which is commodified and treated as a thing to be taken or given away. Men's sexuality, on the other hand, is not thought to be depleted or alienated by having sex. Frances Olsen has described this "double standard" as deeply gendered: "For males, sex is an accomplishment; they gain something through intercourse. For women, sex entails giving something up."[41] In the commodified discourse about sex and rape, moreover, women's sexuality is objectified, treated as a thing distinct from the women themselves. Men's sexuality, in contrast, is part of their personhood. Men are discussed as subjects who retain the right to control their bodies.

One irony of the commodified discourse of rape and sex is that, although women's sexuality has been treated as property, it has not been protected as fully as other types of property. That is, as property, women's sexuality has been devalued. Several feminist commentators, for example, have criticized the law of rape for presuming women's consent to sexual intercourse in situations where consent to property crimes, such as robbery or theft, would never be presumed. Susan Estrich argues that "if a thief stripped his victim, flattened that victim on the floor, lay down on top, and took the victim's wallet or jewelry, few would pause before concluding forcible robbery."[42] The disparity in treatment stems from the lingering belief that women secretly desire to be forced to have sex, placing them in the paradoxical position of wishing to give their "property" away. This implies that the "property" is not of high value and, as Alexandra Wald argues, inflicts a "double injury" on women. "First, it devalues claims of sexual expropriation relative to property crimes. Second, this devaluation conveys to the female victim that her loss of sexual autonomy does not count as a loss at all."[43] Treating women's sexuality as a commodity not only has the potential to damage women by reducing them to sex objects, but may intensify the injury by discounting the value of that object.

---

[40] *Id.* at 604-05.

[41] Frances Olsen, Statutory Rape: A Feminist Critique of Rights Analysis, 63 Tex. L. Rev. 387, 405 (1984).

[42] Susan Estrich, *Real Rape: How the System Victimizes Women Who Say No* 59 (1987).

[43] Wald, supra note 38, at 483.

A. Prototypes of Rape

The most familiar response of feminists to the injuries associated with commodified discourse is to resist the discourse and reject a property approach to sex and rape. A strong theme in the feminist literature is that rape law should protect women's sexual autonomy, not men's property interest in sexual access to women. Dorothy Roberts regards this reorientation of the object of rape law as "one of feminism's most dramatic contributions to legal culture."[44] Through concepts such as "mutuality" in sexual relations, feminists have sought to develop a discourse that regards both men and women as subjects who engage in sexual relations, hopefully freeing women from the devaluative aspects of treating their sexuality as a not-so-special object to be traded or bargained away. By substituting a noncommodified language that emphasizes relationships, reciprocity, and response, feminist writers seek to redescribe sex in a way not dissimilar to Carol Gilligan's description of a different voice in moral reasoning. This feminist description of sex also helps to identify and define the central harm of rape, namely, the disregard of women as sexual subjects (women's subjectivity) and right to sexual autonomy.

Robin West has provided an eloquent defense of a noncommodified vision of sexual relationships. Compared to scholars such as Baker and Wald, West downplays the prevalence of commodified views of sexuality, claiming that "for vast numbers of women and men, sex is not experienced as a commodity . . ."[45] For West, the exchange analogy fundamentally misdescribes those common experiences of sex to which people refer when they talk about "making love." In an exchange of goods, West argues, we must "separate our selves from that which is commodified."[46] In fact, the object of an exchange is to hold back one's self, to give the "thing" away and ultimately get something else in return. This process, however, bears little resemblance to the experience of "lovemaking," in which the point is *not* to differentiate between the person who "gives" the sex and the sex itself. In this vision, the person in love wants to connect with the other person, not take something away from him.

Feminist writers who criticize the commodified view of sex, such as West and Henderson, realize that many sexual encounters do not fit

---

[44] Dorothy E. Roberts, Rape, Violence and Women's Autonomy, 69 Chi.-Kent L. Rev. 359 (1993).

[45] West, supra note 35, at 1449.

[46] *Id.* at 1451.

the vision of mutual lovemaking described above, yet may not amount to rape. In attempting to describe a range of sexual experiences from women's perspectives, feminist writers sometimes use the term "bad sex" to refer to "intercourse that was not particularly pleasurable but was not scary, or deadening, or shaming."[47] In such situations, women may later regret having sex, but they do not suffer the trauma of rape victims. According to Henderson, "women who have experienced bad sex do not feel raped, because they were exercising some agency, and their partner did not abuse them, ignore them, or deny their humanity."[48] These distinctions are often obscured in contemporary case law and discourse, largely because legal categories are not built around women's experiences. The paucity of legal language means that the law often fails to capture the denial of sexual autonomy that many feminists see as central to the harm of rape.

In addition to developing a noncommodified discourse that emphasizes sexual agency, subjectivity, and human relationships, some feminist scholars have also experimented with giving a new meaning to "property" in the context of sexual relationships. As mentioned before, a principal difficulty with the commodified view of sex is that, traditionally, women's bodies have been viewed as the "property" and men have competed for women's bodies in their capacity as potential "property owners." What is lost in this gendered account is an appreciation that a woman could possess a valuable interest in controlling the right of access to her own body. In proposing a new property theory of rape, Alexandra Wald has argued that we should shift our thinking from identifying women's sexuality as the object of property to locating a property interest in women's right to consent to sex. By so appropriating for women "the protections of the talismanic concept of property,"[49] women might come to be seen as property owners, an identity that protects women's subjectivity by recognizing their right of self-ownership in their bodies. One key difference in Wald's approach from the more masculine versions of commodified sex is that Wald emphasizes women's right to *retain*—not to *give away*—their valuable property interest. She argues that:

[47] Henderson, supra note 35, at 59.
[48] *Id.*
[49] Wald, supra note 38, at 463-64.

A. Prototypes of Rape

In terms of the feminist debate on commodification, such an attitude to property would be equivalent to saying: "I'll preserve what I want to preserve, because I own it." This does not preclude saying "I'll share what I want to share," (as owning possessions does not preclude lending or giving them away), but it does establish a right of possession whose enjoyment women have long been denied.[50]

A great value of Wald's argument is that it demonstrates that devaluation of women's sexuality and sexual autonomy is not inherent in every conception of property as it relates to sex and rape. To be sure, the transformation in the discourse that Wald urges is no more likely to take hold than noncommodified feminist models of sex that do not rely on property concepts. Nonetheless it deepens our analysis by exposing the flexibility of both models of discourse.

Much of the writing about rape has been constructed around the sexualized dichotomy of property/personhood. In traditional discourse, women represented sexual property, while men's sexuality was considered a vital aspect of their personhood. Many feminist writers, myself included, have tried to resist the gendering of the dichotomy and have discussed issues of sexuality and rape by stressing the personhood of both women and men. Wald's analysis takes a different tack by attacking the property pole of the dichotomy and articulating a property interest in women's sexual autonomy. These two discourses, however, are both feminist in approach because each challenges the devaluation of women's sexuality and the trivialization of the injury of rape.

Taken together, the new feminist discourses constitute an attempt to break the habit of dichotomous thinking about rape. They recognize that dichotomous structures of thinking limit the possibilities for making convincing arguments to change the status quo. The "personhood" strain of the new feminist discourse is important to show the insult and injury of treating women's sexuality as property, the disposition of which is ultimately controlled by men. It also provides a vision of noncommodified sex that repudiates the treatment of people as sex objects. The property strain of the new feminist discourse, however, is also necessary to underscore that owning property is an important attribute of being a person and that property itself is a social construction. Without some attention to how we construct property

---

[50] *Id.* at 500.

interests in the context of sex, it will be difficult to reposition women as sexual agents rather than sexual objects.

The major outcome of the feminist debate on commodification may well be to fashion a strategy that regards the property/personhood dualism not as expressing a dichotomy, but as mutually defining. Both of the new feminist discourses, for example, could be deployed to urge a jury to see how date rape is a violation of women's agency to control her own body on her own terms, to be sexually active without fear of sexual violation. Women need a new conception of responsibility in sexual relationships, one that is neither Victorian nor pornographic. Because the goal of sexual autonomy for women is so far from being realized, the need for creativity in changing the terms of the debate is particularly pressing.

B.   SEXUAL HARASSMENT

1.   A Feminist Cause of Action

In comparison to other forms of legal regulation of sexual conduct, the claim for sexual harassment is notable for its distinctively feminist origins. It is the quintessential feminist harm. Born in the mid-1970s, the term was invented by feminist activists, given content by feminist litigators and scholars, and sustained by a wide-ranging body of scholarship generated largely by feminist academics.[51] The cause of action for sexual harassment represents, in Catharine MacKinnon's words, "the first time in history . . . that women have defined women's injuries in a law."[52]

With this beginning came hope that this new claim not only would give women who had been harassed some recourse under the law but might also bring about a change in the cultural understanding of what constitutes sexualized misconduct in the workplace. The goal has al-

---

[51] *See* Martha Chamallas, Writing About Sexual Harassment: A Guide to the Literature, 4 UCLA Women's L. Rev. 37 (1993).

[52] Catharine MacKinnon, Sexual Harassment: Its First Decade in Court (1986), in *Feminism Unmodified: Discourses on Life and Law* 103, 105 (1987).

ways been to prevent harassment, because once the harm has occurred, it is not easily remedied. Like a rape prosecution, the ordeal
of a sexual harassment trial can often produce a "second injury,"
which sexual harassment victims experience when they bring their
claims to court.

After two decades of enforcement of sexual harassment laws, the
results are decidedly mixed. There can be little question that, for many
people, particularly the targets of harassment, a change in consciousness has occurred. What was once quite universally regarded as private, petty conduct (for which the target herself was often deemed
responsible) can now be argued to be a serious infringement of a worker's civil rights. On the other hand, the development of the law of
sexual harassment has not escaped some of the stultifying influences
of the law of rape. There is a persistent tension between the courts'
inclination to domesticate (in every sense of the term) the cause of
action, and the radical feminist origins of the claim. In the early stages
of the campaign against sexual harassment, Catharine MacKinnon observed that "[t]he law against sexual harassment often seems to turn
women's demand to control our own sexuality into a request for pater-
nal protection, leaving the impression that it is more traditional morality and less women's power that is vindicated."[53] Her concern was
prescient. Many opinions in this unusually active area of litigation embody traditional views of proper behavior for men and women and fail
to see the connection between sexual harassment and women's subordination. The tendency to attribute causality to women's "provocative" dress or behavior and to credit myths about the motivations and
credibility of complainants can sometimes make sexual harassment litigation look like the civil version of a rape trial.

2.   Feminist Doctrinal Critiques

In first recognizing the claim of sexual harassment in 1986,[54] the
United States Supreme Court held unanimously for the plaintiff, a notable occurrence given the ideological differences on the Court. However, in refining the details of proof required in sexual harassment

---

[53] Catharine A. MacKinnon, Introduction, Symposium: Sexual Harassment, 10
Cap. U. L. Rev. i, viii (1981).
[54] *Meritor Savings Bank v. Vinson*, 477 U.S. 57 (1986).

suits, the Court created special obstacles for the harassment plaintiff that make it possible for many claims to be dismissed on motions for summary judgment prior to trial. Even with the 1991 amendments to Title VII, giving sexual harassment victims the right to a jury trial and limited rights to compensatory and punitive damages, only the most egregious claims cases, involving physical touching or exceedingly gross name-calling, are likely to be tried. In establishing the specific elements of the legal claim for harassment, it has proven difficult to match the emerging legal categories to feminist conceptions of the harms women actually suffer when they are harassed at work.

One eloquent critic of the fast-developing law on sexual harassment law has been Susan Estrich, who has applied many of the same arguments she developed in her work on rape law.[55] At the heart of Estrich's critique is her assessment that the response of the sexual harassment victim, rather than the conduct of the harasser, is often scrutinized during the course of the litigation. The victim who does not behave the way a court or jury believes a woman should behave may be penalized. Estrich claims that because so few real women measure up to these expectations, it is exceedingly difficult to secure legal protection.

> One judges the woman's injury from a perspective which ignores women's views; or one compares her view to that of some ideal reasonable woman, or that of women afraid to speak out against harassment for fear of losing their jobs; and thus one applies a standard that the victim cannot and does not meet.[56]

A particularly problematic element of proof is the requirement that the plaintiff prove that the harasser's conduct was "unwelcome," regardless of how objectionable the conduct may appear. Estrich argues that "[u]nwelcomeness has emerged as the doctrinal stepchild of the rape standards of consent and resistance, and shares virtually all of their problems."[57] As she reads the cases, Estrich sees the harassment victim caught in a familiar double bind when the courts evaluate whether she welcomed the behavior about which she now complains:

---

[55] *See* supra at pp. 223-24.
[56] Susan Estrich, Sex at Work, 43 Stan. L. Rev. 813, 815-16 (1991).
[57] *Id.* at 827.

B. Sexual Harassment

> In practice, both traditional and nontraditional women may find that their own actions are used against them in the unwelcomeness analysis. A woman who behaves in the most stereotypical way—complimenting men, straightening their ties, "mov[ing] her body in a provocative manner," let alone eating dinner with the boss on a business trip, or remaining friendly even after rejecting his advances—may find that the sexual advances she rejects are, as a matter of law, not unwelcome. Similarly, women who act too much like men—who use "crude and vulgar language," or choose to eat with men in the employee lunchroom—cannot be heard to complain. . . .[58]

Another recurring theme of writers who have studied sexual harassment cases is that, like rape victims, sexual harassment victims lack credibility. One writer concluded that the "overwhelming impression created by hostile work environment sexual harassment cases is that, regardless of the standard applied, women simply are not trusted. This is true for decisions that find for plaintiffs as well as those which find against them."[59] There is also discussion in the commentary of causal attribution, focusing on when and why victims are held responsible for inciting harassment or at least not preventing it.

The literature contains a rich discussion of the reasons women are not accorded credibility in this context. Susan Deller Ross,[60] for example, explored the case of Richard Berendzen, the former president of American University, who was forced to resign after pleading guilty to making obscene phone calls. She makes the point that absent hard evidence (like the tape recordings in the Berendzen case), most people will tend to believe the more highly-ranked and credentialed person, particularly if there are some readily available myths about women that can be used to discredit the lower-ranking woman. Reflecting upon the thousands of letters she received after the confirmation hearings, Anita Hill described the "most disheartening stories" as those involving mothers who did not believe their own daughters' accounts of sexual harassment. Hill speculated that these instances of distrust may represent "attempts to distance ourselves

---

[58] *Id.* at 830.

[59] Wendy Pollack, Sexual Harassment: Women's Experience vs. Legal Definitions, 13 Harv. Women's L.J. 35, 69 (1990).

[60] Susan Deller Ross, Proving Sexual Harassment: The Hurdles, 65 S. Cal. L. Rev. 1451, 1452-63 (1992).

from the pain of the harassment experience,"[61] to convince our-selves that, because it didn't really happen to her, it couldn't happen to me.

A key defense strategy in both sexual harassment and rape trials is to discredit the complainant by introducing evidence bearing on her dress, sexual history, or other sexual conduct outside of work. Such evidence of "provocative" dress or other sexualized conduct purports to bear on whether plaintiff "welcomed" the advances, much in the same way that the use of such evidence purports to be relevant to the issue of consent in rape trials. However, as feminist commentators have recognized, the real issue is often one of causal attribution: The portrayal of the harassment victim as a "bad girl" tends to justify a denial of protection, even when it is clear that the plaintiff did not subjectively desire the sexual conduct directed toward her. In an article about the gulf between women's experience of harassment and the legal categories used to address the claim, Wendy Pollack described her experience as an apprentice carpenter. Starting with the question, "What is provocative?" Pollack challenged a conclusion by the Supreme Court that how a plaintiff dresses for work is "obviously relevant" to whether she was sexually harassed.[62] She unpacked the male-biased notion of "provocative" dress by using a story to convey a sense of what it was like to be a token woman in the apprentice program:

> Every day the cafeteria served lunch to 300 to 400 apprentices, all men except for three or four women. Whenever a woman walked through the cafeteria, especially a young woman, the place would go wild. The men would shout, whistle, and howl until the woman left the room. One woman in particular was a favorite target for this behavior. She was an apprentice painter. She wore the same white painters' pants that all the other painters wore. There was nothing in her dress or manner that welcomed the men's behavior. The only possible cause of this attention that I could identify was that she had blond hair.[63]

The story suggests that it is futile to search for a societal consensus about what constitutes sexually provocative dress. An important element is always going to be context, particularly the gender de-

---

[61] Anita F. Hill, Sexual Harassment: The Nature of the Beast, 65 S. Cal. L. Rev. 1445, 1446 (1992).

[62] *Meritor Savings Bank v. Vinson*, 477 U.S. 57, 69 (1986).

[63] Pollack, supra note 59, at 57 n.73.

B. Sexual Harassment

mographics and gender dynamics underlying the interactions. For example, a kind of gang mentality may have provoked the men in the apprentice program to taunt the women. It is likely that the catcalls and other displays were less reactions to a specific message "sent" by the particular woman than rituals signaling the masculine nature of the work culture. The story suggests that the segregated character of the workplace itself "sexualized" the women and underlined their "outsider" status. When the focus is on how an individual woman dressed or acted, however, it is easy to miss the structural factors that frame the backdrop for the harassing behavior. This is why feminist scholars have borrowed structuralist theories from sociology[64] to explain the dynamics underlying sexual harassment, hoping to shift the focus from the behavior of the targets to the function that harassment serves for the dominant group.

In an effort to make the victim's experience more salient to the court and jury, plaintiffs' attorneys have also generally found it advantageous to urge adoption of an explicitly gendered standard—the *reasonable woman* standard—to judge whether defendant's conduct qualifies as harassment. As discussed earlier,[65] this move to reintroduce explicit gender categories into formal doctrine has prompted a vigorous debate among feminist scholars. Advocates of this approach typically stress the importance of articulating how and why sexualized conduct differentially harms women. They maintain that judging harassment from the perspective of the victim or target is crucial in order to purge the law of the implicit male bias lodged in familiar legal concepts such as the "reasonable person" standard.

In an influential article,[66] for example, Kathryn Abrams relied on social science data to explain why women often define sexual harassment more broadly than men and are more likely to find sexualized conduct in the workplace offensive or threatening. The first explanation centered on personal safety. As a group, women are more likely to be the targets of sexual assault and thus, understandably, are more "wary of sexual encounters."[67] This fear of sexual coercion means that

---

[64] *See* text supra at pp. 177-78.

[65] *See* text supra at pp. 97-98.

[66] Kathryn Abrams, Gender Discrimination and the Transformation of Workplace Norms, 42 Vand. L. Rev. 1183 (1989).

[67] *Id.* at 1204-05.

women may more readily interpret sexual propositioning and sexual pursuit as a prelude to force and coercion.

The second explanation is linked to the structural position of women in the workplace, particularly that of women in male-dominated jobs and occupations. In these settings, Abrams explains, women still find that they are "comparative newcomers," who have greater difficulty than majority group members cultivating mentors and allies, being recognized for their accomplishments, and generally being accepted in the informal culture of the workplace. Sexual joking, taunts, and other offensive behaviors are often taken very seriously by women workers because they see such conduct as jeopardizing their already precarious position and sending a message that they are incapable of succeeding in that job environment. Abrams asserts that women experience such harassment as creating a sense of "devaluative sexualization," emphasizing the role that sexualized conduct plays in devaluing women as workers. Her analysis is predicated on a radical feminist understanding of sexual harassment as a mechanism for perpetuating male domination of the workplace, refining and applying MacKinnon's dominance theory in the specific context of hostile-environment claims.

One of the most prominent decisions to endorse the reasonable woman standard and support Abrams's analysis is *Ellison v. Brady*, decided by the Ninth Circuit Court of Appeals in 1991.[68] Depending on one's choice of perspective, the case could be called the "love letters" case or the case of the "delusional romance." The plaintiff, Kerry Ellison, received three letters from Sterling Gray, a male co-worker in her office at the IRS. The letters described Gray's intense feelings for Ellison. He confessed that "I cried over you last night and I'm totally drained today. I have never been in such constant term oil [sic]."[69] They also contained several statements that seemed to assume that the two had formed a genuine and mutual relationship. "I know that you are worth knowing with or without the sex," Gray wrote. "Leaving aside the hassles and disasters of recent weeks . . . [d]on't you think it odd that two people who have never even talked together, alone, are striking off such intense sparks . . . ."[70] This pursuit frightened Ellison because, as far as she was concerned, no such relationship existed.

---

[68] 924 F.2d 872 (9th Cir. 1991).
[69] *Id.* at 874.
[70] *Id.*

B. Sexual Harassment

Gray seemed oblivious to her lack of interest in him and ignored her requests to stop. Gray argued, however, that his actions were harmless and noncoercive, best characterized merely as love letters designed to win Ellison's affections.

In ruling for Ellison and embracing the reasonable woman standard, the court cited Abrams to explain why a female employee might reasonably regard Gray's conduct as a "prelude to [a] violent sexual assault"[71] and why such a woman might have good reason to regard sexual conduct at work as a threat to maintaining her image as a serious professional. The court justified its choice of the reasonable woman standard by accepting a core feminist criticism of objectivity: that a "sex-blind reasonable person standard tends to be male-biased and tends to systematically ignore the experiences of women."[72] In tune with the approach of dominance theorists, proponents of the reasonable woman standard believe it is important to highlight gender in order to capture the full nature and extent of the plaintiff's sexualized injury. For example, unless the judge took account of Ellison's social position as a woman trying to establish her credentials as a competent worker, he might miss the danger lurking behind Gray's professions of love.

Proponents of the reasonable woman standard have suggested refining it to encourage courts to put a feminist gloss on reasonableness. I have argued, for example, that the "reasonable woman" should not be equated to the average or typical woman who has found a way to cope with, but not to challenge, sexually harassing conduct. Instead, my variant of the reasonable woman standard posits a woman who is interested in advancing at her workplace and who offers a reasoned account of how the conduct complained of functions to deprive women of employment opportunities.[73] Feminist economist Gillian Hadfield has proposed a similar construct of the "rational woman" and would have the court or jury ask whether defendant's conduct would induce a rational woman to change her workplace behavior (such as refusing an opportunity to travel or work on a project) because of the prospect of harassment.[74]

---

[71] *Id.* at 879.

[72] *Id.*

[73] Martha Chamallas, Feminist Constructions of Objectivity: Multiple Perspectives in Sexual and Racial Harassment Litigation, 1 Tex. J. Women & L. 95, 135 (1992).

[74] Gillian K. Hadfield, Rational Women: A Test for Sex-Based Harassment, 83 Cal. L. Rev. 1151 (1995).

It is still not clear whether the courts will ultimately embrace such a "reasonable woman" standard. The Supreme Court has not yet spoken definitively on the issue, although dicta in *Harris v. Forklift Systems, Inc.*[75] suggest that the Court is adhering to the unmodified "reasonable person" standard. Future cases will have to confront the specifics of how juries should be instructed in hostile environment cases, specifically whether they may be told that it is appropriate to consider a plaintiff's sex when they decide whether a plaintiff's response to defendant's conduct was reasonable.

To some extent, of course, the precise formulation of the legal standard may not matter—in each case, the jury will be well aware of the sex of the parties and will undoubtedly take this social fact into account, regardless of the wording of the jury instructions. Feminists who oppose use of the reasonable woman standard, however, often express ideological concerns about the standard. They fear that courts and others will give a conservative reading to it, with the effect of further "naturalizing" differences between men and women. They worry that traditionally minded judges are likely to interpret women's broader definition of sexual harassment as evidence that women simply do not like sex as much as men do, missing the structural factors that account for the different responses of men and women. Instead of making the law more responsive to the multiple perspectives of women workers, an explicitly gendered standard could end up backfiring and reinscribing Victorian notions of morality into Title VII law. In addition to the serious problem of essentialism discussed earlier,[76] there is always the danger, most often expressed by liberal commentators, that any standard that highlights gender *difference* will be abstracted from its feminist origins and will simply lend support to antifeminist forces who argue that the presence of women in certain work settings is inappropriate or generates too many problems. Such a fear is not groundless. For example, the discourse surrounding the recent

---

[75] 510 U.S. 17 (1993). Specifically, the Supreme Court stated that "[c]onduct that is not severe or pervasive enough to create an objectively hostile or abusive work environment—an environment that a reasonable person would find hostile or abusive—is beyond Title VII's purview." *Id.* at 21. The Court still left open the question of whether the reasonable person standard might be further refined to take into account plaintiff's sex or race, that is, whether it should be expressed in terms of a reasonable person of the plaintiff's sex or race.

[76] *See* supra pp. 97-98.

sex scandals in the military, coupled with calls for resegregating men and women during basic training, conveys an implicit threat that the "experiment" with women in the military might be declared a failure.[77]

As even critics of the reasonable woman standard generally acknowledge, however, there is no alternative standard likely to be adopted by the courts that totally eliminates the risk either of submerging women's perspectives or reinforcing stereotypes about women. This dilemma of difference forces feminist scholars to make a strategic choice about the lesser of the evils, as they try to redirect the law once more toward recognizing the legitimacy of women's perspectives and the systemic nature of women's subordination. This challenge arises because a feminist cause of action, such as the claim for sexual harassment, is a rarity in American law and does not comfortably fit in a system designed principally to reflect the experiences and needs of dominant groups.

3. Intersectionality: The Legacy of the Hill/Thomas Hearings

The confirmation hearing of Justice Clarence Thomas marked the most intense moment of public awareness and public debate about sexual harassment—Carol Sanger declared 1991 to be a "seismic year for sexual harassment."[78] The scholarship generated in the aftermath of the hearings displays a sophisticated understanding of the intersection of race and gender discrimination that is unmatched in applied feminist research. Since 1991, scholars have gone beyond commenting on the fact that black women have brought a disproportionate number of sexual harassment suits, to examining the ways in which harassment of women of color is distinctive and cannot be fully understood simply as a more virulent form of harassment faced by white women.

---

[77] See Martha Chamallas, The New Gender Panic: Reflections on Sex Scandals in the Military, forthcoming Minn. L. Rev. (1998).

[78] Carol Sanger, The Reasonable Woman and the Ordinary Man, 65 S. Cal. L. Rev. 1411 (1992).

Chapter 8.   Applied Feminist Scholarship—Sexual Subordination of Women

Kimberlé Crenshaw's intersectionality theory[79] has been particularly useful in explaining why so many people found Anita Hill's claim hard to accept. As a black woman, Hill was "situated within at least two systems of subordination: racism and sexism."[80] This meant that Hill was doubly burdened. Not only did she have to overcome the stereotypes and credibility issues typically faced by white women and black men; additionally, Hill was forced to confront obstacles that are unique to black women when they attempt to create a context in which charges of sexualized racism and racialized sexism can be comprehended.

In reflecting on her experiences before the Senate hearing, Anita Hill identified barriers created by racism and sexism that also might well have hampered a black man or white woman in a similar situation.[81] On the racial front, Hill believed that one reason the Senators mistrusted her was that she came before them without a "patron," specifically a powerful white person who was willing to vouch for her trustworthiness and worthiness.[82] In political circles, of course, having a sponsor is often critical for anyone who wants to influence the decision-making process. However, Hill reads American history as imposing a special patronage obligation on African-Americans. During slavery, survival for slaves often depended on white patronage; a slave could not engage in ordinary commerce and did not even have rights to his or her own ideas or inventions. According to Hill, the legacy of the compulsory patronage system persists to this day, as evidenced by the mistreatment of African-Americans by police who require some showing of affiliation with white persons or white institutions before releasing a "suspect." Lacking such a patron, Hill was vulnerable to charges that she was "an incompetent product of affirmative action,"[83] despite her elite credentials and high-level jobs.

On the gender front, Hill's predicament very much resembled that of a victim of date or acquaintance rape, particularly before the

[79] *See* supra pp. 89-90.

[80] Kimberlé Crenshaw, Race, Gender and Sexual Harassment, 65 S. Cal. L. Rev. 1467, 1468 (1992).

[81] Anita Faye Hill, Marriage and Patronage in the Empowerment and Disempowerment of African American Women, in *Race, Gender and Power in America: The Legacy of the Hill-Thomas Hearing* 271 (Anita Faye Hill & Emma Coleman Jordan eds., 1995).

[82] *Id.* at 276-78.

[83] *Id.* at 275.

246

latest wave of feminist-inspired evidentiary reforms. Hill believed that because Thomas did not fit the prototype of the "depraved" harasser, the focus immediately turned toward her. A variety of sexist myths then surfaced in the Senators' questions to explain why Hill's account was false—she was alternatively portrayed as vindictive, delusional, a spurned woman suffering from a romantic fantasy, and a political pawn of radical feminists.[84] Notably, Hill also believed that she suffered a loss of credibility simply by not being married. Questions were raised about her sexual "proclivities," which some took to mean that Hill was a lesbian.[85] As Hill saw it, the Senators constructed a narrative that she was single because she was "unmarriageable or opposed to marriage, the fantasizing spinster or the man-hater."[86] Her opponents also invoked her unmarried status to argue that she lacked "traditional values," obscuring the fact that, as the youngest of thirteen children, Hill felt connected to her family and its values, as well as to the larger African-American community. Writer Toni Morrison has contended that because neither the press nor the Senate Judiciary Committee seriously examined the truth of her accusations, Hill could be called

> any number or pair of discrediting terms and the contradictions would never be called into question, because, as a black woman, she was contradiction itself, irrationality in the flesh. She was portrayed as a lesbian who hated men *and* a vamp who could be ensnared and painfully rejected by them. She was a mixture heretofore not recognized in the glossary of racial tropes: an *intellectual* daughter of black *farmers*; a *black female* taking *offense*; a black *lady* repeating *dirty words.*[87]

Other commentators have elaborated on the intersectional aspects of Hill's experience of discrimination. In a widely cited essay on the hearings,[88] Kimberlé Crenshaw stressed that as a black woman, Hill's experience did not match the "available and widely

---

[84] *Id.* at 274-75.

[85] *Id.* at 283, 290 n.46.

[86] *Id.* at 274.

[87] Toni Morrison, Introduction: Friday on the Potomac, in *Race-ing Justice, En-gendering Power: Essays on Anita Hill, Clarence Thomas, and the Construction of Social Reality* xvi (Toni Morrison ed., 1992).

[88] Kimberlé Crenshaw, Whose Story Is It, Anyway: Feminist and Antiracist Appropriations of Anita Hill, in *Race-ing Justice, En-gendering Power: Essays on Anita Hill, Clarence Thomas, and the Construction of Social Reality* 402 (Toni Morrison ed., 1992).

comprehended narratives"[89] used to describe discrimination against white women and black men, respectively. The "rape trope" invoked by white feminists may have highlighted many of the myths about rape victims that contributed to Hill's credibility problems. It nevertheless understated the historical legacy distinctive to black women, which stripped Hill of her sexual respectability and exacerbated her inability to persuade others that she was telling the truth. Despite Hill's modest appearance, prestigious career, and traditional upbringing, she was still vulnerable to being treated like a whore. As Crenshaw analyzes it:

> For black women the issue is not the precariousness of holding on to the protection that the madonna image provides or the manner in which the madonna image works to regulate and thereby constrain black women's sexuality. Instead, it is the denial of the presumption of "madonna-hood" that shapes responses to black women's sexual victimization.[90]

When the all-important question was raised about why Hill did not press her complaint earlier, the feminist response centered on the potential damage such a charge often inflicts on a professional's career. At least at the time of the hearings, there was less appreciation for the special barriers faced by black women when they charge a black man with sexual abuse. Crenshaw argued that white feminists did not fully understand the reluctance of many black women to press charges and run the risk of reinforcing stereotypes about the dangerous nature of black male sexuality. She stressed that black women comprehend the coercive power behind silence; they realize that black women who publicly complain about intraracial harassment are likely to be perceived as traitors who lack racial solidarity. The black woman's dilemma, described by Angela Harris and Jennifer Wriggins in their articles on the intersection of race and rape,[91] was enacted on the national stage in the Hill/Thomas hearings when initial opinion polls showed that Thomas had far greater support in the black community than Hill.

---

[89] *Id.* at 404.
[90] *Id.* at 414.
[91] *See* supra at pp. 91, 224-25.

B. Sexual Harassment

Perhaps the most striking aspect of Hill's "intersectional disempowerment"[92] was her inability as a black woman to invoke a common narrative to express her vulnerability to sexualized racism. The story of the professional black woman degraded by her boss's sexual baiting was not a familiar script. In contrast, Thomas was very effective in mobilizing antiracist rhetoric, by calling upon the "lynching trope" to establish himself as a victim of race discrimination. Thomas convinced the public that he was the victim of a "high-tech lynching," even though no black man had ever been lynched for raping a black woman. In an incisive essay, Emma Coleman Jordan showed how Thomas and his supporters were successful in casting Anita Hill as the "'white' feminist who happened to be black," thereby stripping her of her racial identity and working-class background.[93] Hill was initially unable to make the public understand that her race also contributed to her abusive treatment in the workplace.

Adrienne Davis and Stephanie Wildman argued that in the hearings race as a symbol was gendered, and that the symbol "black" equaled "male." This form of cognitive bias, which renders visible only the harm of the relatively privileged group within a minority group, is at the heart of black women's intersectional disadvantage. The authors observed that "in a stunning sleight of hand, [Thomas] managed to convince all involved, including the Senate, that white racism, rather than a Black woman, had accused him of harassment. Thus, race became something Professor Hill did not have."[94] This transformed the hearings for many into a contest between feminism and anti-racism, thereby erasing black women from the picture.

The deracialization of Anita Hill was not the first time that the racial dimensions of black women's sexual victimization had been eclipsed. For example, social historian Estelle Freedman has written about cases in which black women were lynched, particularly when they named a white man as their assailant.[95] Rather than being a racist

[92] Crenshaw, supra note 88, at 406.

[93] Emma C. Jordan, Race, Gender and Social Class in the Thomas Sexual Harassment Hearings: The Hidden Fault Lines in Political Discourse, 15 Harv. Women's L.J. 1, 12-13 (1992).

[94] Adrienne D. Davis & Stephanie M. Wildman, The Legacy of Doubt: Treatment of Sex and Race in the Hill-Thomas Hearings, 65 S. Cal. L. Rev. 1367, 1381-82 (1992).

[95] Estelle B. Freedman, The Manipulation of History at the Clarence Thomas Hearings, 65 S. Cal. L. Rev. 1361, 1363 (1992).

practice that affected men only, lynching actually served to punish both sexes for their resistance to white supremacy. The erasure of black women's resistance in the historical record, however, has made it harder for women like Anita Hill to prove that they are vulnerable to abuse because of their race as well as their sex. Lynching became something done exclusively to black men, leaving no metaphor or word to describe what happened to black women.

The dominant tendency to think in dichotomous ways about race and gender had a devastating effect in the Hill/Thomas hearings. For many, the hearings indicated that racism "trumps" sexism in the hierarchy of oppressions—that Thomas's charges of racism won over Hill's claims of sexism. This reasoning, however, fails to grasp the importance of intersectional oppression. Because Hill is also black and alleged a racialized form of sexual harassment, it is just as appropriate to assert that Thomas's male gender privilege prevailed over Hill's allegation of racial oppression. The commentary on the hearings thus presented a unique, if painful, opportunity to analyze how these structures of discourse affect real conflicts by limiting how we talk and think about race and gender discrimination.

C. DOMESTIC VIOLENCE

Particularly because domestic violence is now recognized as the leading cause of injury to women in the United States, it is worth noting that the contemporary conceptualization of the problem can be traced to the battered women's movement, a grassroots offshoot of second-wave feminism that gained momentum only in the late 1970s and early 1980s. The now familiar constructs of the "battered woman" and "battered woman syndrome" are also of very recent origin; the latter is generally traced to psychologist Lenore Walker's first book on the subject, published in 1979.[96] Not surprisingly, the concept of domestic violence has no fixed boundaries, but is still in the process of being reconfigured by feminist practitioners and theorists.

---

[96] Lenore Walker, *The Battered Woman* (1979).

C. Domestic Violence

1. Feminist Terms and Descriptions

As is often the case with fast-moving issues connected to social movements, writers struggle to formulate basic terminology. Some feminists prefer to use the term "woman abuse" or "male battering of women" to highlight the fact that women are most often the victims of the violence. These writers also wish to signal a break with the tradition in the social sciences of addressing domestic violence from a "family systems" perspective, insofar as it implies that each person in a "violent marriage" bears some responsibility for the violence directed at the woman. There has also been a concern that the adjective "domestic" is problematic, because it obscures the political dimension of domestic violence by suggesting that domestic violence is private in nature. Isabel Marcus has further deconstructed the adjective "domestic," analyzing how it "tends to remove domestic violence from a national civil rights agenda" and further signals that this worldwide phenomenon should be treated as a matter "internal to the nation-state, rather than a matter subject to scrutiny and review by the international community."[97]

A major objective of feminist scholarship in this area has been to de-privatize the harm and make visible the systemic, as opposed to the individual, dynamics of domestic violence. In tune with the contemporary emphasis on diversity among women, recent feminist scholars have also been careful to note that domestic violence is not exclusively tied to heterosexual relationships, and have established that battering in lesbian relationships is a serious problem for some women.

Despite these linguistic disputes, the naming of domestic violence has been enormously important because it unearthed a harm that defies conventional categories. Although here discussed as an aspect of the sexual subordination of women, domestic violence could just as easily be considered to be economic subordination. Economic realities often constrain battered women who might otherwise leave their abusers, and the abuse may make it impossible for them to keep their jobs and be self-sufficient. Domestic violence is also intimately connected to motherhood and pregnancy—abused women tend to evalu-

---

[97] Isabel Marcus, Reframing "Domestic Violence": Terrorism in the Home, in Martha Fineman & Roxanne Mykitijuk, *The Public Nature of Private Violence: The Discovery of Domestic Abuse* 11, 27 (1994).

ate their options in connection with the likely fate of their children, making strategic choices they might not have made if they had only themselves to consider.

The sexual dimension of domestic violence stems largely from the social meaning of wife-beating. As Catharine MacKinnon argues, male violence against women has been sexualized in our society, even when the violence does not include specific sexual acts such as marital rape. Particularly when the violence is perpetuated by a husband against his wife, it is understood as taking place within a sex-defined system that immunizes male domination from legal penalties. The recent "discovery" of lesbian battering,[98] moreover, has not undercut the meaning of domestic violence as sexual. As Christine Littleton explains it, lesbian battering does not make domestic violence "non-sexual" but rather underscores that "sexual roles are non-biological." She makes a radical feminist argument that battering, like rape, is a "socially male" activity, "even though occasionally practiced by biological females."[99]

The most significant contribution feminist writers have made toward our understanding of women's experience of domestic violence has been to explain domestic violence as a mechanism of male power and control. One of the richest early accounts of domestic violence from the perspective of an activist in the battered women's movement is contained in Susan Schechter's 1982 book, *Women and Male Violence*. Schechter described how many batterers start with a sense of entitlement. They see themselves as rightfully in control of their wives or partners, and feel aggrieved and victimized when these women try to assert independence. One of Schechter's important conclusions is that "[w]omen's self assertion through jobs or school particularly infuriates some [abusive] men."[100] Battering may begin or escalate when women try to become more autonomous or receive recognition for their work. Women are often forced to leave jobs and training programs and go back on welfare when the men in their lives pressure or

---

[98] An early book on lesbian battering was *Naming the Violence: Speaking Out Against Lesbian Battering* (Kerry Lobel ed., 1986).

[99] Christine A. Littleton, Women's Experience and the Problem of Transition: Perspectives on Male Battering of Women, 1989 U. Chi. Legal F. 23, 28 n.20 (1989).

[100] Susan Schechter, *Women and Male Violence: The Visions and Struggles of the Battered Women's Movement* 220 (1982).

C. Domestic Violence

intimidate them because the men are jealous of the freedom and money that even minimum-wage jobs seem to offer these women.[101]

Explaining domestic violence as a specific type of gender power also helps us to fathom how men who otherwise do not seem out of control or dangerous may nevertheless pose a grave risk to one woman. A man who batters his wife may not be violent toward others; he may be deferential to his boss, pleasant to the women at work, and nice to his neighbors. In Schechter's view, "[e]ven though the motivations of individual abusers are unique, through battering men are making a statement to women about the kind of relationship they believe they are entitled to. In this sense, battering is a way of organizing a relationship so that men continue to feel superior to women."[102]

Once domestic violence is viewed as a form of power and control, the definition enlarges to encompass acts of intimidation, aggression and cruelty that may not fall within the traditional categories of criminal or tort law. The firsthand accounts of victims indicate that a regime of domestic domination may take many forms, some of which are not yet recognized as unlawful or treated only as petty offenses. To intimidate and humiliate his partner, an abusive man may kill a woman's pet, destroy her favorite objects, or verbally abuse her in front of children and others. Without a feminist theory of domination, these injuries might be discounted as simple trespass to property or hurt feelings, missing the role they play in the batterer's overall course of conduct.

What is striking about many situations of domestic violence is the infliction of harms other than physical battering, although the implicit threat of violence may well underlie seemingly nonviolent acts. In many cases of domestic abuse, the denial of a woman's autonomy may be as significant as the use of physical force. Many batterers set out to deprive a woman of any voice or vote on important matters in her life, setting restrictions on dress, food, mobility, and friendships. Domestic violence often also produces relational harms. It is not uncommon for the abusing spouse to isolate his partner from the support of friends and family, sometimes causing an especially virulent form of false imprisonment.

---

[101] On the connection between welfare and domestic violence, *see* Lisa D. Brush, Harm, Moralism, and the Struggle for the Soul of Feminism, 3 Violence Against Women 237, 248-50 (1997).

[102] Schechter, supra note 100, at 224.

Chapter 8. Applied Feminist Scholarship—Sexual Subordination of Women

The legal categories used to criminalize or otherwise sanction domestic violence often do not match feminist descriptions of the central dynamics of the battering process. In her major article identifying "separation assault" as a specific kind of attack on a woman's autonomy that occurs when a woman decides to separate from her abuser, Martha Mahoney analyzed why the law often misses the mark. In the legal context, the definition of domestic violence most often tends to be "incident-focused, looking to the types of assaultive or coercive incidents and the number of times these occurred."[103] This formulation is convenient in that it allows lawyers to "prove" a case of domestic violence in the same way most other crimes are proven, zeroing in on a discrete number of events and highlighting the impact of those events on the victim. The problem with these definitions is that they tend to shift the focus away from the batterer and onto the victim—the inquiry becomes *whether* and *when* the woman was battered, instead of *how* and *why* the batterer acted as he did.

The more feminist "control-focused" definitions of domestic violence, on the other hand, emphasize the batterer's motivation and strategies. In these accounts, there is no sharp distinction between occasions of battering and other types of power struggles in which women confront men's attempts to dictate their actions or movements. Mahoney argues that this conceptualization of the process fits women's understandings of their own situation far better than incident-driven definitions. Many women resist being labeled a "battered woman," in part because such a characterization tends to filter out all their attempts to resist the coercion and violence and to reduce them to the status of abject victim. Mahoney believes that if domestic violence were situated within a system of male control, women would be better able to identify with victims of violence.

> Attacks on our autonomy are one point at which women can—without stereotyping or invoking the likelihood of denial—locate our own experiences and those of our sisters and friends on a continuum of control attempts that includes those extremes of violence that become known through the sensational cases covered by the press. Women may find the current terminology of battering stigmatizing or alienating, yet be willing to admit that they have experienced inappropriate control at-

---

[103] Martha R. Mahoney, Legal Images of Battered Women: Redefining the Issue of Separation, 90 Mich. L. Rev. 1, 28 (1991).

C. Domestic Violence

> tempts by their partners, including assaults on their capacity to separate from "bad" marriages. Exposing control attempts reveals the woman's struggle, rather than defining her according to the behavior of her assailant.[104]

Feminist definitions of domestic violence, like similar efforts to describe date and acquaintance rape and sexual harassment, expose the texture and details of male sexual subordination of women and connect these abusive patterns to more "normal" patterns of interactions between men and women. Feminist writers tend to view domestic violence and abuse as pervasive and potentially lethal, but not exceptional, and consequently try to prevent battered women from being discussed or treated as if they were qualitatively different from ordinary women. Like the scholarship on rape prototypes, much of the applied feminist scholarship on domestic violence tackles the distorting effects of the prototypes and images that dominate the discourse in this area of law.

2. *Prototypes of the Battered Woman: Syndromes and Self-Defense*

The legal literature on domestic violence is marked by the disproportionate attention it gives to an unusual type of case—cases in which battered women kill their abusers. Although it is far more likely that a battered woman will eventually be killed than kill her assailant, commentators and the public imagination seem fixated on exploring what makes battered women kill and whether they should be punished for their actions. It may even be that the "battered woman who kills" has become the prototype for victims of domestic violence. Martha Mahoney believes that the book *The Burning Bed,* and the movie based on it, in which a woman killed her husband in his sleep after years of enduring torture at his hands, had an enormous impact on public consciousness. The story was based on the real-life case of Francine Hughes. However, feminist scholars have recently tried to analyze the precise ways in which such a case is atypical and fails to express the experience of the majority of domestic violence victims.

---

[104] *Id.* at 69.

In the prototype, the battered woman commits her act in a non-confrontational setting, such as when her husband is sleeping or there is otherwise a lull in the violence. The image is one of a desperate—but, to some degree, still passive—person who can see no other way out of her misery. She is like a sleepwalker killing the sleeping victim in a dream. The emphasis is on the woman's victimization, ironically obscuring the woman's agency in taking the life of another. Holly Maguigan's extensive survey of cases involving battered women who kill, however, indicates that the prototype is unrepresentative. She found that at least 75 percent of the cases involve confrontations,[105] that is, situations in which the man was engaged in an ongoing attack or posed an imminent threat of death or serious bodily injury. The women in these more representative cases met force with force, taking active steps to defend their lives.

Another feature of the prototype that may promote misunderstanding of the lives of ordinary battered women is through its suggestion that homicide is the only way out of a violent marriage for battered women. This scenario presumes that the batterer cannot change, the woman is too powerless to leave, and that the only "solution" is to eliminate the batterer. This masks the reality that women respond to and cope with violence in various ways, including the important fact that battered women often leave home, at least temporarily, in an effort not only to change their lives, but to induce changes in the conduct of the batterer. Mahoney points out that, despite the risk of "separation assault,"[106] many experts advocate the "credible attempt to leave" as the best strategy for women who seek to end the violence, but who also wish ultimately to maintain the relationship with their spouses or partners.[107] The difficulties such women confront stem in large part from the lack of social support for their decision to leave: the unavailability of shelters; the disapproval of family, friends, or counselors; and the risk that their actions might later jeopardize their right to custody of their children. The prototype hides the efforts women make to change the terms of the relationship, implying that violence is inevitable and making it seem that initiatives for social change would be futile.

[105] Holly Maguigan, Battered Women and Self Defense: Myths and Misconceptions in Current Reform Proposals, 140 U. Pa. L. Rev. 379, 397 (1991).

[106] For a description of separation assault, see supra p. 254.

[107] Mahoney, supra note 103, at 62.

C. Domestic Violence

In the legal context, the image of the battered woman has been encased within the term "battered woman syndrome."[108] As used by feminist litigators and psychologists, battered woman syndrome refers to the long-term effects of violence on battered women, as evidenced by a set of characteristics displayed by many (but not all) victims. Popularized by Lenore Walker, the core of the syndrome is most often taken to be the psychological theory of "learned helplessness"—the victim's feeling that she cannot control what happens to her and that resistance or escape is impossible. Walker analogized the situation of battered women to the behavior of dogs exposed to random electrical shocks. Once the dogs learned that there was nothing they could do to prevent the shocks, they "ceased any further voluntary activity and became compliant, passive, submissive." Their helplessness prevented escape even when escape was possible—"even when the door was left open and the dogs were shown the way out, they remained passive, refused to leave, and did not avoid the shock."[109]

Expert testimony about battered woman syndrome and the social context within which battering takes place has proven useful to expose judges and juries to dilemmas facing domestic violence victims, particularly in giving a sense of why the victim did not simply solve her problems by leaving. The significant negative consequence of the discourse about battered woman syndrome and learned helplessness, however, is that it again implies that the problem lies with the woman. The feminist conception of domestic violence as a manifestation of male power and control can easily get lost in psychologizing about the victim, sometimes amounting to speculation about whether the woman qualifies as an "authentic" battered woman. Christine Littleton traced how feminist accounts of male violence can be transformed in legal discourse into statements about women's weakness or inferiority:

> In Walker's account of learned helplessness, the *cause* (random, uncontrollable violence inflicted by men) is at least part of the "syndrome." In the case law, the cause disappears while the "syndrome" remains. In neither case, however, is the focus explicitly and continuously placed where it belongs—on the intolerable conditions under which women live.[110]

---

[108] *See* supra at p. 105.
[109] Walker, supra note 96, at 45-46.
[110] Littleton, supra note 99, at 42.

Chapter 8. Applied Feminist Scholarship—Sexual Subordination of Women

Feminist litigators have had to resist the prototypical image of the battered woman as suffering from a psychological disorder. If a battered woman is seen as "sick," it may be difficult for her to plead self-defense, reducing her chances of convincing a judge or jury that her actions were reasonable. The dilemma for defense counsel in a case charging a battered woman with homicide is that evidence relating to the social context of battering, originally designed to enlarge the fact finder's understanding of what was reasonable conduct under the circumstances, may be received principally as proof of the woman's diminished capacity to make a reasonable judgment. Rather than seek an acquittal on grounds of self-defense, the defense may have to settle for a strategy of defending a lesser charge of manslaughter, stressing the irrationality of the woman's impulsive actions.

Battered women who do not fit the prototype because they are perceived to be too strong, competent, or independent also run the risk of gender bias. Commentators have remarked that some trial judges are affected by a "vigilante stereotype" in which they assume that battered women must be out for revenge, unless they cry or behave in stereotypically feminine ways. For example, Holly Maguigan argues that in circumstances in which men's actions would be interpreted as reasonable self-defense, women's actions are more likely to be understood as impermissible retaliation for past abuses.[111] Dichotomous portrayals of battered women as totally helpless victims or avenging agents miss the complexity of the lives of many survivors who strategically resist and cope with domestic violence and do not see themselves as either deranged or malicious.

Ironically, the prototype of the battered woman who kills in desperation may also have obscured the visibility of a recurring type of case in which the woman is the homicide victim. These are instances in which a man kills his wife, his ex-wife, his lover, or even a third party who happens to be in the way, because he is enraged over her decision to leave him or break up the relationship. Victoria Nourse's important new study of intimate homicide cases involving male defendants found that 65 percent of these cases involved situations of "departure"—where the relationship was over or coming to an end, or the victim sought to leave.[112] Supporting Mahoney's observations

[111] Maguigan, supra note 105, at 435.
[112] Victoria Nourse, Passion's Progress: Modern Reform and the Provocation Defense, 106 Yale L.J. 1331, 1345 (1997).

C. Domestic Violence

about separation assault, her research shows that it was women's assertions of independence, rather than discovery of their adultery or sexual betrayal, that most often triggered the deadly assaults. Instead of unequivocally condemning such violent attempts at control, however, the law of provocation in some states has been "reformed" to permit the defendant in such instances to argue "extreme emotional distress" to mitigate his crime to manslaughter.

Applied feminist scholarship, such as Mahoney's and Nourse's, displays a sophisticated understanding of the ways that narrow prototypes and cultural images can infuse male bias into legal categories such as self-defense and provocation, even when the law purports to be engaged in feminist reform. The experience with domestic violence, rape, and sexual harassment cases over the last two decades shows that the resistance to thinking of sexual violence in terms of gender inequality runs deep, as new scenarios emerge to make ordinary cases of domestic violence appear to be exceptional.

3. The Rhetoric of Privacy and Relationships: Historical Insights

The enormous difficulty activists have encountered in trying to implement strategies that would prevent and punish domestic violence has inspired scholars to explore why the basic pattern of male domination seems to persist over the long term, despite substantial reform initiatives. There is widespread agreement among feminist scholars that notions of "privacy" and "private relationships" have stifled change. Elizabeth Schneider, for example, talks of the "violence of privacy" to indicate how the conception of male battering as a private issue continues to exert a "powerful ideological pull on our consciousness" and leads many to deny the pervasiveness and seriousness of domestic violence as a political issue.[113] Victoria Nourse argues that the "veil of relationship" surrounding date and marital rape and domestic violence still has the ability to lessen or diminish these crimes in the pub-

---

[113] Elizabeth Schneider, The Violence of Privacy, 23 Conn. L. Rev. 973, 983 (1991).

lic's view, perpetuating the attitude that the "violence was chosen by choosing a relationship."[114]

Reva Siegel's "The Rule of Love": Wife Beating as Prerogative and Privacy provides a comprehensive legal history of domestic violence.[115] Siegel explains that the concept of privacy as it relates to domestic violence has a history—that the origins of contemporary discourse can be located in a specific cultural context and have not always existed in their current form. Until the mid-Nineteenth Century, husbands had an explicit right of "chastisement" over their wives—in effect, the husband had a legal right or prerogative to inflict corporal punishment on his wife to force her to submit to his authority. Even at this time, however, the right to beat was purportedly limited: "Violence" was not to be condoned except as a means of inducing submission. This formulation of the husband's prerogative dramatically illustrates the roots of the conceptual separation between domestic violence and other kinds of violence. As long as the husband was acting within his rights as the head of the household, use of force against his wife was legitimated and not likely to be seen as "violence."

Siegel explains that even in the late Eighteenth Century when Blackstone wrote his famous *Commentaries*, there was judicial uneasiness about the propriety of wife-beating. Jurists tended to characterize chastisement as an antiquated institution and to take the view that only men from the lower classes would insist on exercising this brutal privilege. One of Siegel's major themes is that class and race bias has long infected attitudes about the prevalence of domestic violence and produced a pattern of selective enforcement. The denial that domestic violence exists in middle-class and upper-class households was present from our nation's founding, and this misconception has obscured the links between gender violence and the assertion of male authority and control.

When attitudes about the nature of marriage began to change in the mid- to late Nineteenth Century as a result of first-wave feminist agitation and other social forces, the idea of wife-beating as a legal right no longer made sense. As women began to acquire formal

---

[114] Victoria F. Nourse, Where Violence, Relationship, and Equality Meet: The Violence Against Women Act's Civil Rights Remedy, 11 Wisc. Women's L.J. 1, 4 (1996).

[115] Reva B. Siegel, "The Rule of Love": Wife Beating as Prerogative and Privacy, 105 Yale L.J. 2117 (1996).

C. Domestic Violence

rights to act as independent persons, the concept of marriage as a hierarchy, with the husband as the master and the wife as the subordinate, slowly gave way to a more egalitarian conception of companionate marriage. Siegel's major insight, however, is that this ideal of equality never managed radically to change the power relationships within marriage and did not bring an end to domestic violence. She argues that instead, domestic violence was shielded precisely by transforming and modernizing the rules and rhetoric surrounding it. Legal prerogative was replaced by legal privacy as the rule governing judicial decisions; the rhetoric shifted from the right of chastisement to what Siegel calls the "rule of love." In this discourse of affective privacy, wives were not forced into submission, but willingly yielded to their husband's wishes, in accord with their more altruistic and virtuous nature.

In the modern cases of the late Nineteenth and Twentieth centuries, courts often condemned the use of physical force, but nevertheless refused to intervene in domestic disputes, expressing concerns about the privacy of the marital relationship and the evil of government intrusion into the private sphere. Husbands no longer had a legal right to hit their wives, but they were often afforded legal immunity when they did so. Siegel carefully qualifies this point, however, underlining the selectivity of the new privacy regime. Particularly in the late Nineteenth Century, some lower-class men, mostly immigrants and African-Americans, were criminally prosecuted for wife-beating. There was even a campaign in the 1880s to bring back the whipping post for wife-beaters. Upper- and middle-class men, in contrast, were not likely to be charged in criminal court. Their greatest vulnerability was in civil court, where they might face a tort claim for battery brought by their abused wives. At this point, the legal doctrines of intraspousal immunity and marital privacy functioned quite efficiently to deny liability, generating the impression that domestic violence was a class-specific problem.

By the 1920s, the protection afforded to domestic violence in civil suits spread to the criminal arena. Special domestic relations courts were established, and a therapeutic approach to family conflict gained acceptance in legal circles. As a result, battered women were encouraged to drop criminal charges against their spouses, couples were urged to reconcile, and violence was reconfigured as "an expression of emotions that needed to be adjusted and rechanneled into marriage."[116] This was the environment against which feminist activists in the battered women's movement of the 1970s first struggled to develop a system of shelters, enact more protective criminal and civil laws, and generally try to alter the public consciousness about domestic violence.

Siegel's history goes a long way toward explaining the resilience of the concepts of privacy and relationship in this area of the law. The pernicious legacy of chastisement and coverture may be found in the batterer's sense that he is entitled to use force within his own family, coupled with society's continuing reluctance to equate domestic violence with violence inflicted in other contexts. In her capacity as a facilitator of court-mandated educational groups for batterers, Isabel Marcus has noted that the regime of coverture lives on in the minds and attitudes of batterers:

> I have repeatedly heard revealing statements of deeply held beliefs made by batterers which speak to the daily life practices of coverture—the muting or denying of a separate and separable identity for a partner or spouse. Men are "in charge" of a relationship; it must be structured to their liking or comfort; abuse and violence are among the means to "ensure" these outcomes and to control a partner or spouse who challenges the ordering of domestic life. "She provokes me because she knows what I like and what I don't like"; "she needs to be reminded who is in charge"; "a little violence clears the air between us." These statements speak to the well developed notions of sex-based power, control, and hierarchy. These men rely on strong gender-based differences in a clear, hierarchically ordered relationship which are supportive of and essential to coverture. As I listen to them, I envision a chorus of men at any point in history chanting a version of this litany.[117]

In contemporary discourse, privacy can still function selectively to hide violence perpetrated by those men who have the resources to avoid public scrutiny. The rhetoric of intimate relationships and affection also makes it difficult to discuss marital conflicts as conflicts about power, because of its tendency to focus the discussion on the pathology of the victim. Finally, the selective enforcement—or, more accurately, selective *non*enforcement—of laws prohibiting domestic

[116] *Id.* at 2170.
[117] Marcus, supra note 97, at 23.

C. Domestic Violence

violence encourages the development of narrow prototypes of victimization, which make it easier to deny the extent of the problem.

One important recent struggle involving domestic violence has centered on the Violence Against Women Act (VAWA), finally passed by Congress in 1994 after four years of debate. The most controversial aspect of the federal legislation is a provision that establishes a civil cause of action on behalf of any person who has been a victim of a crime of violence "motivated by gender." The provision is patterned after civil rights legislation affording a federal claim to victims of racial discrimination, which was originally designed to remedy the states' failure to protect African-Americans and other racial minority groups from race-based violence and other forms of discrimination. Advocates of VAWA drew upon the racial analogy to argue that the states had similarly failed to protect women against widespread sexual violence, principally rape and domestic violence. They argued that a federal civil rights remedy was necessary to stem the tide of violence against women and to make equality a reality for women who were often deprived of jobs, education, friends, and family relationships as a result of the violence directed at them.

Resistance to the civil rights remedy came from those, including Chief Justice Rehnquist of the United States Supreme Court, who believed that the federal courts were a "precious national resource" which should be protected from "domestic relations" matters said to be better handled locally.[118] Opponents of VAWA distinguished civil rights violations involving racial discrimination by characterizing violence against women as personal, not political, in nature, and as "the product of private relationships, not public discrimination."[119] Despite the politicization of domestic violence that had accompanied legal reforms at the state level for nearly a decade, old notions of gender violence (as qualitatively different from other kinds of violence) surfaced to make passage of the federal legislation extremely difficult. For some, violence in the home was still more a matter of family than a denial of equal rights.

In this round of cultural struggle over the meaning of domestic violence, concerns about federalism emerged as the rhetoric to minimize the extent and seriousness of domestic violence. Opponents

---

[118] *See* Judith Resnik, "Naturally" Without Gender: Women, Jurisdiction, and the Federal Courts, 66 N.Y.U. L. Rev. 1682, 1688 (1991).

[119] Nourse, supra note 114, at 4.

maintained that federal courts were too important to be devoted to matters of gender and family. In response, scholars such as Judith Resnik carefully documented how federal courts were already very much in the business of regulating gender and the family, and questioned why matters connected to women and family should be devalued as too trivial to occupy the national courts.[120]

In the end, VAWA was enacted into law after some tightening of the proof required to show that the crime was motivated by the victim's gender. Plaintiffs bringing civil suits must now prove that the criminal acts were "due at least in part, to an animus based on the victim's gender," a provision that promises to spark further disputes as to whether "ordinary" rapes and wife-battering qualify for federal protection. The animus requirement is likely to be the new site where the contest between "domestic violence as private relationship" versus "domestic violence as public discrimination" is played out. It is ironic that at the end of this century, feminists must convince the courts that domestic violence is really about gender to (literally) make a federal case out of it.

Siegel and other legal historians provide a historical perspective on domestic violence that is both disquieting and empowering. It is sobering to realize that because of the capacity for systems of male domination to revive themselves in updated forms, two generations of feminists one century apart were unsuccessful in mobilizing political forces to put an end to wife-battering. However, it is possible that feminist insights about the rhetoric of privacy and the "veil of relationship" have begun to change the public's understanding of the nature of domestic violence. The new writings certainly have enabled feminist advocates to speak out against domestic violence with renewed clarity and conviction, and to take the issue to federal as well as state court.

D.   LEGAL PROHIBITIONS ON SAME-SEX MARRIAGE

Much of the feminist legal scholarship on rape, sexual harassment, and domestic violence implicitly recognizes that the law has

---

[120] Resnik, supra note 118, at 1721-29 (describing federal laws of the family).

harmed women through inaction—whether it be the failure to crimi-nalize marital rape, the failure to guarantee a non-hostile working en-vironment, or the failure to enforce laws against battery and assault when the victim lives with her assailant. In these contexts, the theory is that sexual subordination of women is accomplished through permit-ting private—that is, nongovernmental—male violence to go unpun-ished. The more recent feminist writings emphasize that women's continued vulnerability to violence and exploitation is produced as much by cultural images and discourses, as it is by deficiencies in legal doctrine. Nevertheless, short-term solutions most often include calls for more law, for increasing the range of criminal, civil, and ethical prohibitions and sanctions.

However, the sexual subordination of women is not always accom-plished through failure to punish sexual exploitation. There is a smaller body of applied feminist legal scholarship that primarily ad-dresses the state's *suppression* of women's sexuality and sexual free-dom, rather than the state's failure to protect against sexual violence. Important work has been done by writers in gay and lesbian studies who have explored how the state's selective support for heterosexu-ality and its de-legitimation of same-sex relationships perpetuates sexism.[121] Here, deregulation or the lifting of legal restrictions is sometimes the preferred strategy to increase legal acceptance for non-traditional couples, families, and other intimate relationships.

In the postmodern era, simultaneously advocating for more law and for less law is a "contradiction" to which activists have grown ac-customed. The debates of the 1990s tend to be less abstract, and cen-ter on selecting the wisest course of action for the moment.

1. *Legal Climate for Same-Sex Marriage*

The issue of same-sex marriage has become the focal point for a lively debate among feminists and within the gay and lesbian commu-nity about the transformative possibilities of legal change. For many years, the legal climate for same-sex marriage was exceedingly hostile. In the early 1970s, several same-sex couples mounted legal challenges to the states' refusal to issue marriage licenses to them, only to be sum-

---

[121] See discussion of gay and lesbian studies, supra pp. 157-70.

marily rebuffed by courts who treated marriage "by definition" as a union of a man and a woman.[122] The judicial opinions were so curt and lacking in depth that they conveyed the impression that it was ludicrous for same-sex couples even to assert a constitutional right to marry.

Despite the stunning losses, the issue of same-sex marriage did not die. Thousands of gay and lesbian couples participated in marriage ceremonies to proclaim their commitment to one another and to protest the lack of legal recognition. When the most virulent forms of discrimination and harassment against gay men and lesbians began to abate in some places, it became possible to approach same-sex marriage as a real possibility and to debate its merits more openly. Particularly after several municipalities enacted "domestic partnership" laws according some marriage-like benefits to registrants, it was no longer unthinkable that the states might ultimately open marriage to same-sex couples.

The high-water mark to date came in 1993 with *Baehr v. Lewin*,[123] in which the Hawaii Supreme Court held that the state could not constitutionally limit marriage to opposite-sex couples without proof of a compelling reason to do so. Not surprisingly, however, this one decision did not end the controversy, even in Hawaii. The fate of same-sex marriage in Hawaii is still an open question, depending on whether opponents will ultimately succeed in overturning the judicial ruling by passing a state constitutional amendment.

Meanwhile, the backlash to the Hawaii decision has been swift and intolerant. Sixteen states quickly passed legislation barring recognition of Hawaii same-sex unions, and in 1996, Congress passed the Defense of Marriage Act,[124] banning recognition of same-sex marriage for federal purposes (such as income tax law) and purporting to relieve states of their constitutional obligation to accord "full faith and credit" to same-sex marriages when and if they are recognized in other states. The negative emotions evoked by same-sex marriage were apparently so powerful that they crowded out not only possible constitutional objections to the new law, but also the usual conservative sentiments for

---

[122] *See, e.g., Baker v. Nelson*, 191 N.W.2d 185 (Minn. 1971); *Jones v. Hallahan*, 501 S.W.2d 588 (Ky. 1973); *Singer v. Hara*, 522 P.2d 1187 (Wash. Ct. App. 1974).

[123] 852 P.2d 44 (Haw. 1993).

[124] 28 U.S.C. § 1738C (1996).

local control and states' autonomy that had driven recent public policy debates in welfare and other family-related matters.

2. Feminist Responses to Same-Sex Marriage

Among feminist legal writers, there is general agreement that same-sex couples ought to be given the option to marry, particularly now that the issue has become an active political controversy. This support for same-sex marriage as a legal option, however, has not always translated into enthusiastic support for marriage as an institution, even assuming that the current gender restrictions were lifted. Instead, many radical and lesbian feminist writers have sharply questioned the desirability of marriage and whether a campaign for same-sex marriage ought to be a high priority. Among gay and lesbian scholars, moreover, the most passionate arguments for same-sex marriage have come from men, most notably William Eskridge, who has marshaled historical evidence to show that marriage-like unions between members of the same sex have occurred throughout human history.[125]

Feminists historically have objected to marriage on the grounds that it is a sexist institution that perpetuates the economic and sexual subordination of women. Their basic claim is that marriage institutionalizes gender hierarchy, and that the legacy of coverture lives on despite widespread changes in formal legal doctrine. Feminists often question whether women can retain their sense of independence and self-worth once they become part of this historically patriarchal institution. Particularly in the early 1970s, young women so strongly doubted the value of marriage that many preferred to enter less formal "live-together" arrangements, resulting in a huge rise in the number of unmarried-but-cohabiting heterosexual couples. The feminist critique of marriage is much more muted today. For the most part, the issue tends not to be discussed, leaving doubt as to whether the newer generation of feminists (who show no sign of abandoning marriage) share the skepticism of their mothers.

Mary Dunlap's summary of the reasons feminists are ambivalent toward marriage is representative of much of the radical and lesbian

---

[125] William N. Eskridge, Jr., *The Case for Same-Sex Marriage: From Sexual Liberty to Civilized Commitment* (1996).

feminist literature. She argues that "the basic validity of feminist criticisms of marriage has not disappeared" despite the "waves of reform, in and out of law," that marriage has undergone. Her list of defects highlights some of the economic, sexual, relational, and ideological features of heterosexual marriage.

> Women who get married still widely lose their birth names in favor of those of their husbands, a tradition that seems to epitomize the loss of personal distinction and identity that marriage too often brings. Domestic labor and childrearing remain primarily the enclave of women (both married and otherwise), and these tasks remain uncompensated and free of any provisions for job security or retirement. While growing consciousness of the seriousness of domestic violence has appeared in recent years, the problem continues, partly through the stony, ancient concept of ownership of women by men. Whatever the societal variations of this chauvinistic model of marriage, the legal foundations of the model of marriage do not appear to have been revolutionized yet.[126]

The burning question of late has been whether changing marriage to include same-sex couples could somehow "cure" these defects by transforming the social meaning of marriage. No one disputes that marriage currently carries with it a host of tangible and intangible privileges—from health care coverage to the right not to be compelled to testify against one's spouse in court—that would be of enormous benefit to same-sex couples. And to a large extent, the movement to establish domestic partnership laws constitutes an effort to import some of these privileges to unmarried couples. Rather, the issue that has generated a split of opinion among commentators is whether same-sex marriage would upset the hierarchical structure of marriage itself, for heterosexual as well as gay and lesbian couples. As Catharine MacKinnon framed the issue, it "might do something amazing to the entire institution of marriage to recognize the unity of two 'persons' between whom no superiority or inferiority could be presumed on the basis of gender."[127] For William Eskridge, the hope is that when gender is no longer always available as a proxy for status

---

[126] Mary C. Dunlap, The Lesbian and Gay Marriage Debate: A Microcosm of Our Hopes and Troubles in the Nineties, 1 Law & Sex. 63, 69-70 (1991).

[127] Catharine A. MacKinnon, Not by Law Alone (1982), in *Feminism Unmodified: Discourses on Life and Law* 27 (1987).

D. Legal Prohibitions on Same-Sex Marriage

within a marriage, this will increase the prospects for developing egalitarian models of marriage and might even become a "means to impel a general redefinition of masculinity and femininity."[128]

Along these lines, Nan Hunter has reasoned that the sex of the partners is the only formal element remaining that currently defines marriage, now that official rules enforcing relations of dependence and authority between the spouses have been abolished. If the availability of same-sex marriage were to "destabilize" the gendered constructs of "husband" and "wife," the entire foundation supporting marriage as a hierarchy might fall. Taking up the familiar taunt directed toward same-sex marriage posed by the question, "Who would be the husband?" Hunter speculated that the positive impact of same-sex marriage would likely be felt beyond the gay and lesbian community:

> Who, indeed, would be the "husband" and who the "wife" in a marriage of two men or two women? Marriage enforces and reinforces the linkage of gender with power by husband/wife categories, which are synonymous with the social power imbalance between men and women. Whatever the impact that legalization of lesbian and gay marriage would have on the lives of lesbians and gay men, it has fascinating potential for denaturalizing the gender structure of marriage law for heterosexual couples.[129]

The most forceful voice of dissent from these optimistic predictions continues to be that of Paula Ettelbrick, who first expressed her qualms about same-sex marriage as part of a 1989 debate with Tom Stoddard, when they were both directors for the Lambda Legal Defense and Education Fund, a public interest organization for promoting gay, lesbian, and bisexual rights. In a highly influential essay entitled Since When Is Marriage a Path to Liberation? Ettelbrick took the position that the campaign for same-sex marriage would harm the movement. She believed that to obtain the right to marriage, activists would have to emphasize how gay and lesbian couples were just like heterosexual couples and would "end up mimicking all that is bad

---

[128] Eskridge, supra note 125, at 61.

[129] Nan D. Hunter, Marriage, Law and Gender: A Feminist Inquiry, 1 Law & Sex. 9, 17 (1991).

about the institution of marriage in our effort to appear to be the same as straight couples."[130]

At the core of Ettelbrick's argument is her fear that same-sex marriage would have a de-radicalizing effect on our society. Her vision of lesbian identity starts with affirming difference, not emphasizing sameness. Very much in tune with the feminist turn toward difference in the 1980s, Ettelbrick believes that "[j]ustice for gay men and lesbians will be achieved only when we are accepted and supported in this society despite our differences."[131] Rather than seek to assimilate gay men and lesbians into the current institution of marriage, Ettelbrick wants to undermine the "two-tier" system of relationships that currently privileges marriage and discredits other kinds of intimate relationships. Ettelbrick asserts that marriage must be deregulated in order to establish the validity of "relationships of choice," whether the relationship in question is between two sexual partners or whether it consists of a family-like relationship in which there is no sexual connection. This libertarian strain of feminist politics emphasizes that taking away the power of the state to regulate primary relationships creates an opportunity for women to define their own relationships, on their own terms.

Ettelbrick's concerns about same-sex marriage have more recently been amplified by Nancy Polikoff, who analogizes the strategic dilemma currently facing lesbian activists over the issue of same-sex marriage to the politics and rhetoric surrounding the campaign for legalizing abortion. Polikoff notes that early abortion-rights activists embedded their arguments within the larger struggle to end male domination, emphasizing women's liberation, the right of women to use their bodies as they wished, and women's entitlement to sexual fulfillment. When the movement became more mainstream, the rhetoric shifted to "pro-choice" and advocates emphasized women's privacy rather than women's liberation. In their effort to win lawsuits, advocates downplayed women's sexual freedom and became reluctant to challenge the more conservative view that, at best, abortion was a necessary evil. As a result, the link between restrictions on abortion and male domination gradually became invisible. Polikoff claims that

---

[130] Paula L. Ettelbrick, Since When Is Marriage a Path to Liberation?, in *Lesbian and Gay Marriage: Private Commitments, Public Ceremonies* 20, 23 (Suzanne Sherman ed., 1992).

[131] *Id.* at 22.

D. Legal Prohibitions on Same-Sex Marriage

the initial radical energy behind the movement so dissipated that "'abortion on demand' is no longer the call of abortion supporters but the specter brought forth by antiabortion voices."[132]

For the moment, the two sides on the issue of same-sex marriage seemed to have "agreed to disagree":[133] The campaign to recognize same-sex marriage still has momentum, as does the movement for domestic partnership and other legal initiatives designed to facilitate and validate nontraditional relationships. Interestingly enough, the backlash over the Hawaii decision may have pushed the national dialogue a bit to the left. Some opponents of same-sex marriage may now be softening their opposition to other legal reforms that would benefit gay men and lesbians, such as amending Title VII to prohibit discrimination based on sexual orientation. The irony is that the same Congress that rushed to pass the Defense of Marriage Act is close to enacting national laws to protect gay men and lesbians against job discrimination. Placing same-sex marriage on the national agenda may itself have had a progressive impact, regardless of the cultural reverberations such marriages might have if they ultimately are permitted.

One important, yet undeveloped, theme of the scholarship on same-sex marriage is the need for feminists to re-examine the nature of marriage. The recent debate reveals that feminist ambivalence toward marriage runs deeper than the concern that heterosexual marriage tends to lock men and women into a traditional division of labor and gender roles. Instead, the basic structure of marriage as an inherently *sexual* union between adults is being called into question by the controversy. Mary Dunlap, for example, speculates that lesbians and gay men may well use the right to marry to preserve and legitimate intimate relationships, involving co-parenting and long-term companionships, that are not grounded on sexual activity. She argues that "[t]he buried premise of most discussions of marriage, that marriage must involve sex, should be unearthed and, insofar as government is concerned, rejected."[134]

Much of the mainstream discussion of marriage presumes that the purpose of marriage is to provide a legal limit upon and sanction of

---

[132] Nancy D. Polikoff, We Will Get What We Ask For: Why Legalizing Gay and Lesbian Marriage Will Not "Dismantle the Legal Structure of Gender in Every Marriage," 79 Va. L. Rev. 1535, 1542 (1993).

[133] *See* Dunlap, supra note 126, at 90.

[134] *Id.* at 87.

sexual activity and that sexual activity is a prerequisite for marriage, even though it is obvious that many married couples do not frequently engage in sexual activity or do not regard sex as the core of their relationship. That marriage in the law is frequently conceived as primarily a sexual institution, rather than as a situs for important emotional and intimate relationships, is a form of gender bias that has not received as much attention in the legal literature as one would expect, given the ubiquity of marriage and its importance in people's lives. Uncoupling gender from marriage by envisioning same-sex marriage allows us to focus on the other ways in which marriage is a gendered institution. Women need to ask themselves what they consider to be the defining experiences of marriage and how they want the law to reflect their views.

The applied scholarship on same-sex marriage echoes the 1980s equality/difference debate, undertaken a decade later when understandings about the social construction of law and social institutions are more sophisticated. Although it is still vexing to struggle with the question of whether to emphasize sameness to achieve short-term results or to underscore difference for the sake of the long term, feminist scholars now have more tolerance for multiple strategies and are aware that there is no way to control the cultural impact of social interventions. In the next wave of feminist scholarship on marriage, it will be important to develop a deeper appreciation for women's diverse experiences of marriage, including the reasons why women still get married, and to use this knowledge to counter the narrow, sexualized idea of marriage that continues to dominate legal doctrine and discourse.

CHAPTER 9

Applied Feminist Scholarship— Motherhood and Reproduction

It was not until the wave of women who entered law school in the 1970s joined the profession and began to populate law faculties that women secured a presence in areas other than family or domestic relations law, the one enclave where women had been encouraged to practice and teach. Like the larger society, the organization of the legal academy and the practicing bar was influenced by separate spheres thinking. Women were thought to be specially suited to handle legal matters relating to households and children—areas which, not coincidentally, were often derided as lacking intellectual challenge or not warranting high levels of compensation. While men taught high-status courses in constitutional law and jurisprudence (as well as every other subject in the law school curriculum), women tended to be confined to teaching family law and, perhaps, trusts and estates, devalued subjects that held less promise of leading to high-profile careers.

By the time feminist academics began to compile materials for courses on "Women and the Law" and "Sex-Based Discrimination" in the early 1980s, it was not surprising that they gave more prominence to constitutional law principles of equality and to women's status in nontraditional sites, principally the workplace, than to family law. Downplaying women's status as mothers and wives fit in well with the movement for equality, as feminists tried to rid the concept of "woman" of its inevitable ties to motherhood, nurturing, and domestic roles. Feminist analyses of the family, moreover, often criticized gender differentiation of roles within the family—the new ideal became the egalitarian family where a mother and a father equally shared child care and household work and both had careers outside the home. Gender-neutral language describing family roles also emerged—the discourse shifted to refer to "spouses," rather than "husbands and wives"; "parents," rather than "mothers and fathers." Feminist scholars were most interested in exploring the intersection of work and family, asking how women could "have it all" by combining work and family, in much the same way men had been given social support to combine their roles as fathers and workers. The 1980s debate over pregnancy leave was emblematic of this feminist focus: Motherhood was most often discussed in relation to its effect on wage work.

It is true that applied feminist legal scholars never lost interest in the "classic" family law topics, developing a voluminous literature on such topics as no-fault divorce, standards for determining child custody, and distribution of marital property. The building blocks of feminist legal theory, however, tended to be located in debates over constitutional and statutory anti-discrimination cases, rather than in discussions of family law precedents. For example, the struggle over anti-essentialism found expression in feminist critiques of the reasonable woman standard in Title VII cases; the pornography controversy, which required feminists to examine competing theories about the sexual subordination of women, was played out in the context of a proposal to amend civil rights laws. Even theorists such as Robin West who, in developing her theories about the gendered nature of jurisprudence, placed considerable importance on women's role in reproduction, did not focus much on the legal treatment of motherhood and the image of mothers that the law projected.[1]

Recently, Martha Fineman, a major feminist commentator on motherhood and the family, has charged that feminist legal theorists have neglected the family. She sees this as a major flaw in feminist legal theory, arguing that the family remains "the most gendered of our social institutions."[2] Fineman's assertion may be an overstatement, especially when one considers the importance cultural feminists place on relationships that model that of mother and child, and more recent applied scholarship by writers such as Joan Williams[3] and Reva

---

[1] *See* supra pp. 67-68.

[2] Martha Albertson Fineman, *The Neutered Mother, the Sexual Family and Other Twentieth Century Tragedies* 149 (1995).

[3] *See* supra pp. 195-97.

Siegel,[4] who have addressed the family as central to their analysis of the economic and sexual subordination of women.

In any event, Fineman's challenge comes at a time when there is considerable public interest in the plight of poor women, particularly mothers who receive Aid to Families With Dependent Children (AFDC), a topic that clearly deserves more attention from feminist legal scholars. In 1996, Congress enacted sweeping measures "to end welfare as we know it," after persistent campaigns to cut back on expenditures and change the way welfare recipients purportedly behave. Feminist legal scholars are now increasingly weighing in on the "welfare debate," hoping to have some impact on national discourse and policy.

This is an area of law that seems particularly impervious to feminist and critical race perspectives. The mainstream discussions, emanating from both conservative and liberal quarters, have thus far proceeded without questioning whether the categories and terms of debate are fatally infected by sexist and racist assumptions and stereotypes. Feminist scholars have set about deepening their analysis of how the law has constructed mothers and motherhood and have intensified their critique of the dominant ideology and cultural images of the family that seem to drive current public policy. In particular, the most recent feminist scholarship bears a close relationship to the scholarship on "white privilege,"[5] showing how certain types of families have been labeled as "normal" and receive hidden privileges and subsidies, while other nontraditional families are cast as "deviant" and "dependent." This literature also takes an intersectional approach, starting from the proposition that privileged families derive their status and are deemed worthy of subsidies because of the gender, race, and class positions of the "heads" of the family.

Closely connected to the feminist analyses of motherhood is a considerable body of literature on reproduction and reproductive rights. The beleaguered status of *Roe v. Wade*[6] has prompted many feminist legal writers to seek a more sure footing for constitutional protection of a woman's decision to terminate her pregnancy, and to delve more deeply into the reasons why *Roe* has been so controversial. Beyond restrictions on abortion, various recent attempts by government to con-

---

[4] *See* supra pp. 193-95, 260-63.
[5] *See* supra pp. 107-12.
[6] 410 U.S. 113 (1973).

trol the behavior of pregnant women have generated a feminist critique on topics ranging from "fetal protection" policies which exclude women from certain toxic workplaces[7] to the prosecution of pregnant drug addicts for exposing their fetuses to crack cocaine. Particularly in the last decade, feminists have also responded to changes in reproductive technology and the culture surrounding these practices, and have participated in the debates over such topics as in vitro fertilization, posthumous procreation, and surrogacy.

One important way that much of the feminist work on reproductive rights differs from more mainstream treatments of these highly contested issues is its emphasis on women as mothers or potential mothers. For example, feminists are more likely to approach legal restrictions on abortion as regulations designed to pressure or force women into motherhood. Feminist discussions of abortion and related issues typically reject the common tendency to discuss the fetus as a physical being separate from the mother, with interests that are often antagonistic to the mother's. These writings tend to emphasize the relational and social context in which women make decisions about reproduction, as compared to the more medicalized discourse that dominates law and popular culture.

Although abortion rights remain a high priority within feminist legal scholarship, writers are now paying more attention to legal obstacles facing women of color and poor women who wish to become mothers. The literature debates forced sterilization, criminal penalties for giving birth to a baby exposed to crack, and economic disincentives for having children while on welfare as restrictions on reproductive freedom that disproportionately affect less privileged women. Reproduction is a context in which the burdens faced by different groups of women may be quite different, but few women escape the oppressive effects of gender on their choices and life prospects.

This chapter discusses a small, but very important, slice of the feminist legal literature on families and reproduction: that which focuses most directly on motherhood, including legal restrictions that have the effect of compelling women to have babies or impose penalties upon them for giving birth. As in so many other areas, the recent literature is as much concerned with dissecting the complex meaning

---

[7] See Sally J. Kenney, *For Whose Protection? Reproductive Hazards and Exclusionary Policies in the United States and Britain* (1992).

embedded in discourses and cultural constructs as it is with examining legal doctrine. To borrow a phrase from Joan Williams, much of the feminist legal literature on motherhood and reproduction employs "the model of lawyer as persuader in the realm of social discourse and focuses on how to reframe existing rhetorics to achieve feminist goals."[8]

A.   MOTHERHOOD AS AN IDEOLOGICAL CONSTRUCT

A common thread in much of the feminist scholarship on motherhood is the observation that "motherhood" is not simply a descriptive term. Instead, the term is loaded with normative content and may subtly convey an ideological message beyond the simple fact that a particular woman gave birth to a child or is currently raising and nurturing a child. Like the term "woman," "mother" is often modified to designate something special about the context in which mothering takes place. In everyday discourse, for example, there is much talk about "single mothers," "working mothers," and "welfare mothers." Always on the lookout for hidden norms, feminist scholars have directed attention to the default term suggested by these modifications, asking: Just who is the "normal" mother who needs no further explanation to be appreciated and understood?

Despite the immense variety of contemporary contexts in which women mother children in the United States, feminists argue that "mother" still has the capacity to evoke a far narrower image or prototype, which serves as a measure by which real-life mothers in all their diversity are judged. The dominant image of the "mother" is first and foremost that of a married woman. Notably, the term "married mother" is almost never used—rather, it is simply assumed that a mother will be married, carrying the further tacit assumption that a mother is heterosexual, given that it is legally impossible for one woman to marry another woman. From this perspective, the "single

---

[8] Joan Williams, Gender Wars: Selfless Women in the Republic of Choice, 66 N.Y.U. L. Rev. 1559, 1562 (1991).

mother" stands out as deviating from the norm, lumping together never-married women, divorced women, and widows into this one politically charged category. Most significantly, the absence of a man in the household is highlighted by the modifier "single," suggesting that it is problematic to be engaged in mothering without the involvement of a man.

Despite the increasing number of mothers of young children who participate in the labor force, the category "mother" probably also still connotes a "housewife" or a woman who is not employed outside the home. Instead, the modified phrase "working mother" is commonly understood to mean a mother who works outside the home. There is no analogue in "working father": Men simply "are" simultaneously parents and wage workers. As noted in the discussion about the economic devaluation of housework,[9] this model of the (nonworking) mother carries the judgment that work done in the home does not qualify as real work. It is also a handy way to signal that a woman's primary identity comes through being a mother—we do not commonly speak of "maternal worker" to indicate that an employee is also a mother, perhaps because the identity of mother overwhelms that of wage worker when the two (presumably incompatible) terms are used together.

Finally, for at least the last decade, there has been a continuous public debate about "welfare mothers." This term has acquired a very specific meaning, such that being on welfare has now come to be synonymous with receipt of AFDC benefits. The phrase "welfare mother" is defined by contrast to the "normal" mother, who presumably does not rely on AFDC to support herself and her family. One of the prominent themes of the new feminist scholarship on welfare is that terms such as "welfare mother" tend to cut off debate and understanding. They hide the ambiguity in the meaning of "welfare," diverting attention from the myriad forms that subsidies take in a complex economy. Thus, we are not apt to consider a woman who receives survivors' benefits under Social Security or who gets the benefit of the home mortgage deduction to be a "welfare mother," even though such public subsidies may be critical to her family's maintenance. Instead, the unmodified "mother" is presumed to exist within a self-sufficient family,

[9] *See* supra pp. 190-95.

A. Motherhood as an Ideological Construct

a privatized entity that is seen as contributing to, rather than taking away from, the larger society.

Even this brief discussion of the implicit assumptions lurking within the common-sense meaning of "mother" suggests the normative and ideological dimensions of the word. The unmodified or default term "mother" does not simply connote the typical mother, but functions much as an implicit male norm does in other contexts: It sets the standard by which mothers are judged, regardless of whether most mothers are capable or desirous of meeting such a standard. This is why Martha Fineman regards motherhood as a "colonized category," by which she means a social construction that was "initially defined, controlled and given legal content by men." She claims that "[m]ale norms and male understandings fashioned legal definitions of what constituted a family, of what was good mothering, who had claims and access to children as well as to jobs and education, and, ultimately, how legal institutions functioned to give or deny redress for alleged (and defined) harms."[10] The point is that even though society tends to restrict mothering to women, women's experiences have not been the starting point for our understanding of what constitutes "motherhood" or what separates a "good" mother from a "bad" or "deviant" one.

Because so many women do become mothers at some point in their lives, the importance of the category "mother" to feminism and feminist legal theory is unquestioned. What is also well recognized by many feminist scholars is how cultural constructions of motherhood affect all women, even women who have never been mothers or will never be mothers. Despite the 1970s push for individual equality which resulted in the eradication of most explicit gender categories in the law, cultural constructions of "Woman" are still inextricably tied to motherhood. Fineman argues, for example, that regardless of any woman's individual decision not to bear or raise children, "women *will* be treated as mothers (or potential mothers)" because "social construction and its legal ramifications operate independent of individual choice."[11] There is widespread recognition that formal equality and gender neutrality in the law has not meant that women now live gender-neutral lives. To the contrary, the new motherhood scholars

---

[10] Fineman, supra note 2, at 38.
[11] *Id.* at 51.

tend to embrace Fineman's assertion that women live "gendered lives" that mark and confine them as women, in part because they cannot escape the effects of oppressive and totalizing social constructions, such as the ideal of motherhood, on their daily lives. Thus, young women may be treated as less employable simply because they might someday become mothers, while infertile women often undergo painful, expensive treatment to help them bear children, in part because our society still stigmatizes childless women as "unwomanly."

The feminist reexamination of motherhood appears to have at least two implicit goals. The first is to provide more social support for real mothers and their children. Carol Sanger, for example, describes our society as "encouraging childbirth and disregarding real children."[12] Despite the continued valorization of motherhood in the culture, it seems increasingly difficult to be a mother, as evidenced by the media's preoccupation with the harm that employment of mothers allegedly causes to children, coupled with the contradictory expectation that mothers should work for economic reasons. Swimming upstream from the dominant view that places paramount importance on "putting men back into the home" and maintaining "intact" families, many feminists want to make it possible for mothers to raise their children "alone" (that is, without a husband) and to legitimize the "female-headed" family.

The second goal relates to freeing women from the strictures of motherhood. This means not only making motherhood less burdensome for women, but allowing women, mothers and nonmothers alike, to develop and express identities that do not conform to the narrow model of the ideal mother. Arguing that a woman's status as a mother is not the only status she has, Sanger warns against the tendency to reduce women to the experiences they have as mothers—to mistake motherhood for "the whole show."[13] Indeed, the very use of the term "motherhood," as opposed to more active terms such as "mothering" or "mother work,"[14] may reinforce this tendency to look upon moth-

---

[12] Carol Sanger, M is for the Many Things, 1 S. Cal. Rev. L. & Women's Stud. 15, 46 (1992).

[13] *Id.* at 31.

[14] For example, philosopher Sara Ruddick uses the terms "mothering," "maternal work," and "mothering work" to reinforce the idea of mothering "as practice or work," rather than as a "fixed biological or legal relationship." Sara Ruddick, *Maternal Thinking: Towards a Politics of Peace* xi (revised ed. 1995).

erhood as a status that overwhelms the other aspects of a woman's identity. The revival of interest in motherhood is as much about changing the cultural meaning of "mother" as it is about expanding tangible benefits to mothers.

The influence of the law in shaping the institution of motherhood is not as clear as it seems to be in other areas of feminist legal inquiry. One striking feature of the recent feminist scholarship on welfare, for example, is how much attention it devotes to cultural images and political rhetoric, rather than to the specifics of statutes, constitutional principles, or other, more characteristically legal analysis. The law in this area seems to have less of a life of its own. It tends to reflect, rather than to construct, dominant cultural attitudes and ideology. The relative lack of importance of legal categories might also suggest that families—or at least families headed by women—are not considered important enough to warrant principled application of the law. Although legal categories can certainly oppress women, their absence hardly guarantees equitable, or even compassionate, treatment.

B.   CONSTRUCTING DEVIANCY: RACE, PATRIARCHY, AND SINGLE MOTHERHOOD

The law no longer places explicit restrictions on single motherhood and seems to make it possible for a woman to raise her child without living with the child's father or some other man. Many of the formal restraints on divorce have been lifted with the adoption of no-fault schemes and the most punitive treatment of "illegitimate" children has been declared unconstitutional, thus taking away some of the stigma that attaches to never-married mothers. It is true that with the demise of "maternal preference" rules in custody disputes[15] and greater recognition of the rights of unwed fathers, single mothers can no longer be confident of being designated the custodial parent. However, there is still no major trend toward the single-father household: When the parents are not together, it is far more likely that the mother will take on responsibility as the primary parent.

[15] *See* supra at p. 41.

Chapter 9.   Applied Feminist Scholarship—Motherhood and Reproduction

Despite this seemingly more liberal legal environment, feminist scholars uniformly protest that single mothers, particularly if they are poor and black, are regarded as "deviant" in our culture and that their contributions as mothers are dramatically devalued. Much of the recent feminist literature on welfare reform aims to delineate how such denormalization and devaluation is accomplished and why single motherhood, despite its prevalence, is treated as suspect, taking as its framework the triple intersection of race, sex, and class.

Feminist scholars contend that poor single mothers do not benefit from the positive cultural associations of motherhood to nearly the same degree as other mothers. The law often treats them as if they were qualitatively different from other mothers, had different desires for their children, and required legal coercion to ensure that they acted like "good" mothers. In her analysis of the specifics of many state "reform" welfare policies that were the precursors to the federal reform, Lucy Williams describes them as programs of "behavior modification."[16] Without solid empirical support for the proposals, some states embarked on incentive schemes to induce welfare mothers to act in conformity to the model mother. Welfare mothers were given a monetary bonus if they married the father of their child ("bridefare"), had their welfare payments cut off or reduced if they gave birth to a child while receiving AFDC benefits ("family caps"), and were threatened with termination of benefits if their children missed more than a specified number of school days ("learnfare").

These behavior modification programs were not designed to help women make the transition to paid employment by developing work-related skills or training, but were aimed at influencing personal decisions women made and changing how they related to children and sexual partners. The learnfare program, for example, assumes that welfare mothers need encouragement to monitor their children's behavior. The state steps in as "the strong arm" to make sure the children go to school, presumably because the mother is too weak or lacks motivation to get her children to do what they are supposed to do. Feminist critics have pointed out, however, that children of women receiving AFDC do not miss appreciably more days of school than other children (one study found a difference of only three days more

[16] Lucy A. Williams, The Ideology of Division: Behavior Modification Welfare Reform Proposals, 102 Yale L.J. 719, 721 (1992).

B. Constructing Deviancy: Race, Patriarchy, and Single Motherhood

per year), and that there is little reason to suppose that threats to punish the mother will affect a strong-willed or troubled teenager who refuses to attend school.[17]

In a fairly transparent way, the behavior modification programs operate as a substitute for the traditional authority of the father and husband. Under learnfare, the discipline of a stern father is replicated by the state's threat to cut off funds. Bridefare tells the single mother that she will be better off with a man to head the household, while family caps take away a single mother's reproductive autonomy by penalizing her decision to bear a child. Single welfare mothers are thus not permitted to act as the heads of their own households with the same authority and dignity as other custodial parents.

Women on welfare also lose much of their privacy. They are often required to reveal details of their sex lives as part of paternity proceedings designed to reimburse the state for welfare expenditures by extracting child support from biological fathers. They are subjected to supervision and regular visits by bureaucrats and social workers. The surveillance of welfare mothers and their families is so prominent a feature of these programs that scholars call these families "public" families, stressing that receipt of AFDC funds converts the private family into an overregulated entity in which it is presumed appropriate for the state to intervene. This system informally discourages single motherhood by way of punitive "incentives" that make it too costly for a single mother to exercise independent judgment about the most important matters in her life. It operates as a powerful mechanism to maintain the deviant status of single motherhood.

Feminists explain these updated forms of stigmatization of single motherhood as grounded in patriarchy, in the perceived need to maintain male control of families. While in the past, male control was effected by reposing virtually all significant legal rights in the father alone—including entitlement to the custody of children—the contemporary era is marked by a domination through cultural symbols and informal means. Fineman's major thesis is that the dominant conception of the family is built upon the sexual union between a man and a woman and that this imagery of "the sexual family"[18] takes precedence over the tie between a mother and her child. By so naturalizing

---

[17] *Id.* at 732-34.
[18] Fineman, supra note 2, at 145-47.

the "horizontal intimacy" between heterosexual adults, the dominant paradigm assumes that men are essential to complete families and that families without men are deficient, deviant, and dysfunctional. Fineman argues that the power of the sexual family as a cultural symbol has been so compelling that even critics of the traditional family, such as gay and lesbian activists, often tend to press for reforms that mimic the family as a sexual entity, rather than call for the abolition of privileges associated with traditional marriage.

Feminist explanations for the culturally constructed deviancy of single motherhood are also rooted in race, specifically what Dorothy Roberts regards as the historical devaluation of black motherhood.[19] Prior to the 1960s, the hostility toward "welfare mothers" was not as intense as it is today. Under the original federal program, support was given mainly to widows with children, a predominantly white group who were considered among the "deserving poor." The history of AFDC is also a history of racism: Before the federal government increased its control over the discriminatory exercise of discretion by state welfare officials, large numbers of African-Americans were effectively excluded from benefits. In a review essay examining recent books on welfare policy, for example, Sylvia Law reminds us that state policies were often "arbitrary and explicitly racist,"[20] noting a Georgia plan which denied benefits to African-American women during cotton chopping season, under the presumption that black women could always find "appropriate" work in the fields. The localized rules that guided welfare administrators were also often highly moralistic: Women were systematically taken off the rolls for being "immoral," an amorphous category variously interpreted to include behavior that ranged from cohabiting with a man during the previous six months to giving birth out of wedlock. This blend of conventional morality and racial bias severely limited the extent of relief, in what one commentary described as the "tradition of searching out the deserving few among the many chiselers."[21]

[19] Dorothy E. Roberts, The Value of Black Mothers' Work, 26 Conn. L. Rev. 871 (1994).

[20] Sylvia A. Law, Ending Welfare As We Know It (Review Essay), 49 Stan. L. Rev. 471, 478 (1997).

[21] Nancy Fraser & Linda Gordon, A Genealogy of Dependency: Tracing a Keyword of the U.S. Welfare State, 19 Signs: J. of Women in Culture & Soc'y 309, 321 (1994).

B. Constructing Deviancy: Race, Patriarchy, and Single Motherhood

The current hostility toward welfare mothers is a product of the late 1960s, when the states were pressured to abide by federal requirements that made it far more difficult to exclude black women. Early on, limited work requirements were imposed on this new group of AFDC beneficiaries. The common understanding that it was appropriate to support widows to stay home while they cared for their children did not extend to "welfare mothers," who were increasingly associated in the popular mind with poor, black, never-married women. The insistence that recipients be made to work to remain eligible for benefits has culminated in the massive contemporary workfare program, which exempts only women who have children under one year of age. Dorothy Roberts theorizes that these harsh work requirements have become part of the "new consensus" about welfare policy because of racist assumptions that, as caretakers, black women have little positive to offer to their children and that black women do not suffer as much as other women when forced to separate from their children.[22] For Roberts, the legacy of the slave woman who saw her children sold or auctioned off or the "Mammy" who was required to leave her children each day to work in a white family's household, lives on in cultural beliefs that have had a major influence on contemporary public policy.

This racialized negative image of the "welfare mother" has evolved, but nevertheless persisted, over the last thirty years. As a factor in the demonization of black single mothers, scholars frequently cite the famous report written in 1965 by Daniel Patrick Moynihan, then assistant secretary of labor. The Moynihan Report drew a causal link between the "breakdown" of the black family, the increasing number of black families on welfare, and the prevalence of families headed by women. Rather than tracing problems in the family to poverty, the cognitive move was to attribute the cause of poverty to "deviant" family structures not dominated by men. A common narrative emerged describing a "culture of poverty," through which welfare mothers transmitted bad values to their children and reproduced dependency in the next generation. The sense of moral degeneracy, lack of a work ethic, and distance from middle-class virtues is captured by the image of the "welfare queen," presumably a woman who lives royally "off the dole" and acts as if she is entitled to support. The most famous invocation of the stereotype of the "welfare queen" came during the

---

[22] Roberts, supra note 19, at 874.

testimony of Clarence Thomas at his Senate confirmation testimony. Thomas described his sister, who apparently received AFDC, as being caught up in the culture of poverty, claiming that "[s]he gets mad when the mailman is late with the welfare check. That's how dependent she is . . ." and that "her kids feel entitled to the check, too. They have no motivation for doing better or getting out of the situation."[23]

With the immense publicity in recent years surrounding the problems of "crack babies" and the frequent lament about "children having children," the image of the AFDC mother may have shifted from "welfare queen" to "black, dependent, teenage mother," who is dependent both on drugs and on welfare. These two intensely negative images of "welfare mother" effectively shift the focus away from the concrete situations facing women who receive welfare—the particulars of their lives—to the psychology of the women themselves. As Regina Austin explains it, the dominant view assumes that the problems of poverty can be cured by changing the "motivation and aspirations" of poor people and heightening the visibility of "role models," particularly middle-class blacks who have made it.[24]

Critics of the psychological approach warn that this process of addressing poverty as a pathological condition not only makes "welfare mothers" a less sympathetic group, but renders invisible the ways in which AFDC families are similar to "working poor" or middle-class families. In the public debate over welfare policy, feminists have used a straightforward strategy of attempting to counter the power of the negative image of "welfare mothers" with statistics showing that the image bears little resemblance to reality. Sylvia Law, for example, has charged that the belief in the culture of poverty or intergenerational transmission of dependency is a "myth" because over 80 percent of daughters who grew up in "welfare" homes are not dependent on welfare themselves.[25] Causal attribution is particularly important here: Because poor people are more likely to have children who are poor, it is not surprising that children from welfare homes have a greater likeli-

---

[23] The Thomas quote is cited and discussed in Wahneema Lubiano, Black Ladies, Welfare Queens, and State Minstrels: Ideological War by Narrative Means, in *Race-ing Justice, En-gendering Power: Essays on Anita Hill, Clarence Thomas, and the Construction of Social Reality* 323, 362 n.6 (Toni Morrison ed., 1992).

[24] Regina Austin, Sapphire Bound, 1989 Wis. L. Rev. 539, 575.

[25] Law, supra note 20, at 476.

B. Constructing Deviancy: Race, Patriarchy, and Single Motherhood

hood than middle-class children of being poor as adults and needing public assistance. The critical question is whether poverty (and economic class) is treated as the cause of welfare dependency, rather than the "culture of poverty" as presupposed by current policy.

Perhaps most importantly, the data call into question the common belief that there is a clear demarcation line between "welfare mothers" and "other mothers" with respect to the sources of support they receive for their families. Interviews with welfare mothers and surveys of women on AFDC show a common cyclical pattern in their lives: Women frequently go on and off welfare, between intervals of paid employment.[26] This makes "welfare mothers" look much more like other mothers, who also frequently engage in part-time or temporary employment.

The prototype of the "welfare mother" as a black, unmarried teenager with several children is also not descriptive of the typical woman receiving AFDC. Fewer than 40 percent of AFDC recipients are African-American.[27] Most mothers receiving aid are adults: Only approximately 8 percent of recipients are teenage mothers, and more than half of that group are age 18 or 19.[28] The average family on welfare is not made up of a woman with the large brood of children, but includes fewer than three persons, counting the adults.

The striking incongruity between the dominant image of the "welfare mother" and the current realities has prompted speculation among feminist scholars as to why this image has so much capacity to influence the public mind and does not seem to dissipate in the face of contrary evidence. Martha Minow, a prominent commentator on this issue, takes the position that the latest welfare reforms, particularly the harsh work requirements for welfare mothers, probably "serve the symbolic and psychological interests of those who never will be subjected to them."[29] The stigma imposed on welfare mothers through the current system is not designed solely to influence the behavior of this relatively small group of women. It also underlines societal approval of traditional marriage, white racial privilege, and the male-dominated workplace. Contempt for the "welfare mother" subtly

---

[26] Id.

[27] Williams, supra note 16, at 744.

[28] Law, supra note 20, at 482.

[29] Martha Minow, The Welfare of Single Mothers and Their Children, 26 Conn. L. Rev. 817, 834 (1994).

reinforces the belief that women should be controlled by men and that it is appropriate to place a higher value on white families in our culture. It also serves as a way of deflecting attention away from poverty and the material effects of racial subordination by scapegoating black, single mothers who become "the synecdoche, the shortest possible shorthand, for the pathology of poor, urban, black culture."[30] The dominant discourse on welfare trades on supposed causal links between welfare and poverty and welfare and racial tensions, assuming that the elimination of welfare will have a positive impact on these other larger social ills. Many feminist critics would like to invert this causal chain and to approach welfare as a product of sexism and racism, rather than its cause. This difference in causal attribution is perhaps the most telling distinction between progressive and dominant discourses on the topic.

C.   EXPLORING THE RELATIONSHIP BETWEEN "DEPENDENCY" AND "PRIVILEGE"

One key word that appears repeatedly in discussions on welfare policy is the word "dependency," often used to describe the situation of AFDC recipients who cannot find a way to change their lives and get off welfare. Labeling a person "dependent" in our society is usually pejorative: It suggests an addiction, as in the phrase "drug dependency," that takes away the person's ability to make rational judgments and separates that individual from self-reliant persons capable of acting in their own interest. Particularly because women have long been characterized as "dependents," it is not surprising that the recent debate over welfare has sharpened feminist interest into the larger, cultural meanings of "dependency."

Much feminist scholarship is directed at showing how "dependency" is a political and ideological concept and not simply a statement about receiving an economic subsidy. The literature tries to blunt the distinction between groups recognized as receiving public subsi-

---

[30] Lubiano, supra note 23, at 335.

C. Exploring the Relationship Between "Dependency" and "Privilege"

dies—notably AFDC recipients—and the vast majority of Americans who benefit from hidden subsidies as a result of taxation schemes, regulation of businesses, and laws affecting economic transactions. Martha Fineman, for example, starts her analysis of recent welfare reforms with the assertion that "we all live subsidized lives," noting that "the fact of subsidy is not remarkable. The question is why we stigmatize some subsidies, but not others."[31]

In much the same way that writers on "white privilege" have attempted to show how the material advantages of being white have been hidden from view, feminists have investigated the features of the "welfare state" that have benefitted the middle and upper classes, yet do not render these groups "dependent" in the same sense as receiving benefits does to welfare mothers. The structure of the system of social supports we have today has been described as a "two-track welfare system."[32] The first-track programs, such as old age insurance, unemployment, and benefits for families of veterans, are not generally called "welfare" and carry little stigma or dishonor. Designated as entitlement programs from the beginning, they were "constructed to create the misleading appearance that beneficiaries merely got back what they put in."[33] Significantly, there are no onerous work requirements attached to receipt of these benefits—the surviving spouse of a veteran, for example, is entitled to receive benefits for her children, regardless whether she is employed or is a homemaker. First-track benefits thus function as privileges of citizenship. They are the invisible benefits of living in a modern welfare state.

In contrast, second-track benefits, like AFDC, are highly visible and politically volatile programs by which government takes on what was once the function of private charity. Because these benefits were funded from general tax revenues, rather than earmarked wage deductions, the impression was created "that claimants were getting something for nothing."[34] As noted earlier, as a condition of receiving aid, recipients of second-track benefits were closely supervised to ensure that they were truly needy and behaved in ways that did not offend the moral sensibilities of government officials.

---

[31] Martha Albertson Fineman, The Nature of Dependencies and Welfare "Reform," 36 Santa Clara L. Rev. 287, 288 (1996).

[32] Fraser & Gordon, supra note 21, at 321.

[33] *Id.* at 321.

[34] *Id.* at 321-22.

From an economic standpoint, there is no bright line between first-track and second-track benefits—each constitutes a public subsidy through which the government redistributes wealth. In the 1997 debate over tax reform, for example, there was a dispute as to whether the proposed $500-per-child tax credit should be given to low-income families whose tax liability was less than that amount, that is, whether poor families should receive a refund for the amount of the subsidy given to more affluent families. Those who opposed such a refund argued that it constituted a form of "welfare" rather than tax relief, implying that there was a qualitative difference between the two kinds of public subsidies. However, it would be just as logical to argue that the $500 credit was a form of welfare to all but the poorest families. It is this rhetorical distinction between welfare and other subsidies—between what is perceived to create "dependency" and what is regarded as an "entitlement"—that has been a focal point of feminist inquiry.

In a historical article that traces changes in the understanding of the word "dependency" from preindustrial times to the present, Linda Gordon and Nancy Fraser provide the most extensive treatment of the cultural meaning of the word. The authors contend that "dependency" is an ideological term which, as applied in the contemporary context to single mothers on welfare, connotes an individual problem, one that "registers" as moral/psychological, in the sense of "an individual character trait like lack of will power or excessive emotional neediness."[35] This usage of the term, however, first developed only in the late Nineteenth Century to describe what was then known as "pauperism."

Earlier uses of the term had been directed more toward describing social structures. Fraser and Gordon explain that in preindustrial England, the most common meaning of "dependency" was that of "subordination," describing, for example, the relations of a servant to the master, or a peasant to the lord. The term then was understood to describe a social hierarchical relationship, one that was considered normal for most men and women. By the Eighteenth and Nineteenth centuries, a new, specifically gendered meaning of the term "dependency" emerged to signify a married woman's relationship to her husband. The "housewife" was then invented as an "icon" of dependency, describing a "sociolegal status" rather than a psychological trait. De-

---

[35] *Id.* at 312.

C. Exploring the Relationship Between "Dependency" and "Privilege"

pendency also had a distinctively political and racial dimension in the industrial era, referring to the subordinate status of the "colonial native" and the "slave."

At this time, moreover, a rhetorical shift occurred which moved the labor of white workingmen outside the realm of relationships characterized by domination and subordination. Fraser and Gordon contend that "the language of wage labor in capitalism denied workers' dependence on their employers, thereby veiling their status as subordinates in a unit headed by someone else."[36] Ironically, the workingman's structural dependence on the employer was recast as the epitome of self-sufficiency, a linguistic usage that survives to this day. This set the stage for attaching a gendered and racialized meaning to "dependency" that fits with the new model of "dependents" as comprising mostly women and racial minorities.

With the abolition of formal systems of political and legal subordination—the end of slavery and coverture—came the ascension of the psychological meaning of dependency and, Fraser and Gordon stress, the "disappearance of 'good' dependency."[37] In its contemporary usage, dependency is associated with pathology and stigma, negatively affecting not only those who are dependent but those who care for dependents. In its contemporary feminized and racialized form, welfare dependency is embodied in the image of the black, single welfare mother.

Feminist critiques of welfare policy often resist this use of "dependency" to refer to an individual psychological trait and seek instead to recapture some of the structural dimensions of the term, to locate "dependency" once more in social relationships. Thus, instead of asking how women on welfare can become self-sufficient through training, workfare, or incentive programs, more feminists are questioning the very meaning of dependence and independence. One inquiry, for example, asks whether the only route to "independence" should be wage labor, particularly given that low-wage jobs seldom offer workers autonomy and flexibility. Another recurring question is whether it makes sense to require all mothers with young children to work outside the home, knowing that someone must be "assigned" to care for dependent children. Manipulating the multiple meanings of dependency,

---

[36] *Id.* at 319.
[37] *Id.* at 323.

Martha Minow recently framed the critical question as whether "single mothers on welfare [are] properly to be viewed as dependent people who should become economically self-reliant, or as people upon whom children depend, and people upon whom society depends to raise those children successfully?"[38]

Feminist writers generally favor providing greater economic support, perhaps in the form of guaranteed income, to mothers and others who perform the work of caring for children, elderly parents, or disabled family members who depend on them. Arguments in favor of economic support for mothers to stay home and care for children might seem strange coming from feminists who pushed to expand women's employment opportunities and to free mothers from discrimination in the workplace. The contemporary scholarship on welfare, however, has begun to draw a distinction between the right to work outside the home and "coerced work"[39] which serves principally to make the labor women already perform in their homes invisible and does little to enhance the material position of most poor women. Like other mothers, some welfare mothers may find it best to work only part-time or to spend part of their lives at home caring for others. The main issue is whether the political tide can turn so that such a choice will be accepted as responsible and thought of as consistent with leading an independent life.

D.   FORCED MOTHERHOOD: GENDER EQUALITY AND ABORTION RIGHTS

For many feminist writers, any re-examination of motherhood must necessarily include the legal and social environment in which a woman decides whether to become a mother in the first place. Perhaps the most central item in the agenda of the women's liberation movement of the late 1960s and early 1970s was the push for "abortion on demand," a slogan that has since been appropriated by oppo-

[38] Minow, supra note 29, at 822.

[39] Heidi Hartman & Roberta Spalter-Roth, Reducing Welfare's Stigma: Policies that Build Upon Commonalities Among Women, 26 Conn. L. Rev. 901, 905 (1994).

nents of abortion to dramatize what they regard as the radical nature of feminist claims to reproductive rights. In its historical context, however, "abortion on demand" was not meant to signal that abortions were so insignificant that women should feel no compunction about aborting for any reason. Rather, the demand grew out of an assessment that because motherhood had such a profound impact on the lives of women, every woman, regardless of financial means, should have a right not to be forced to become a mother against her will. "Abortion on demand" was designed to remedy a very unequal situation in which only women who could afford to travel abroad or to the few states with liberal laws had access to safe abortions. Other women—typically young women with little money—faced the many risks associated with illegal abortions as their only option to forced childbearing.

The right secured by the *Roe v. Wade* decision in 1973, however, fell considerably short of "abortion on demand." The Supreme Court held that the right to privacy prohibited state interference with abortions performed in the first trimester of a woman's pregnancy. Essentially, the new right protected the privacy of the medical decision, which was regarded as being made jointly by the pregnant woman and her doctor. Notably, *Roe* gave no right to demand an abortion from an unwilling physician. Nor was a woman guaranteed that abortion would be a service available in public hospitals or clinics. Instead, subsequent cases made it clear that the right of privacy did not prohibit the government refusing to fund abortions for poor women, even "therapeutic" abortions deemed necessary to protect women's physical or mental health.[40]

In the years following *Roe*, opponents of the decision gained strength and succeeded in convincing Congress and state legislatures to restrict public funding of abortions and discourage abortions from being performed in public hospitals. The irony was that twenty-five years after *Roe*, access to safe, legal abortion still depends on whether a woman has the money and the social support to seek out a physician, often located far away or in another state, who would be willing to perform the procedure.

---

[40] *See Harris v. McRae*, 448 U.S. 297 (1980) (upholding denial of funding for medically necessary abortions, excepting only those procedures which threatened the mother's life); *Webster v. Reproductive Health Serv.*, 492 U.S. 490 (1989) (upholding ban on non-life-saving abortions in public facilities even for women willing to pay full cost).

Moreover, with respect to late-term abortions, *Roe* allowed states to restrict or prohibit the procedure in the interest of promoting and protecting "potential life." This interest in the fetus became the focal point for the pro-life movement which successfully lobbied for a variety of new restrictions designed to discourage abortions, obstacles such as 24-hour waiting periods, parental notification, and a requirement to supply graphic descriptions of fetal development to women desiring abortions. By the mid-1990s, the discourse on "fetal rights" had become so prominent that many predicted the Supreme Court would overrule *Roe* and return the issue of abortion to state legislatures. Instead, the Court reaffirmed the basic constitutional right in 1992,[41] but authorized states to set limits on a woman's right to terminate her pregnancy, provided only that those restrictions did not constitute an "undue burden" on the right to choose. The new "undue burden" test, in practice, can severely curtail access to abortion as the states employ a variety of strategies to make it costly for physicians to perform abortions, and burdensome and humiliating for women to seek them. In the 1990s, the image of the back-alley abortion has been replaced with that of the picketed, understaffed abortion clinic—formal legalization has not entirely erased the stigma of abortion, nor eliminated the practical obstacles to obtaining one.

This experience with *Roe* has led pro-choice feminists to question why there is still so much resistance to abortion rights and whether legal doctrine and discourse can somehow be retooled to strengthen women's access to safe, affordable procedures. On a doctrinal level, many feminists have argued that a woman's right to terminate her pregnancy should be anchored in the Equal Protection Clause, either as a substitute for *Roe*'s constitutional right to privacy or to supplement the privacy rationales of the Supreme Court precedents. In an early article, for example, Sylvia Law argued that the constitutional equality principle should be invoked whenever the state restricted abortion because, by doing so, "both nature and the state impose upon women burdens of unwanted pregnancy that men do not bear."[42] More recently, Anita Allen has called for recognition of the right to abortion as nothing less than a precondition to full, "first

---

[41] *Planned Parenthood of Southeastern Pa. v. Casey*, 505 U.S. 833 (1992).

[42] Sylvia Law, Rethinking Sex and the Constitution, 132 U. Pa. L. Rev. 955, 1016 (1984).

D. Forced Motherhood: Gender Equality and Abortion Rights

class" citizenship for women.[43] Although the content of their constitutional analyses differs, each emphasizes the life-altering effects of pregnancy and motherhood on women, and how formal access to the public sphere means little if the responsibilities of child care make it practically impossible for women to participate in the workforce, politics, or other public settings on an equal basis with men. In recent years, discussion of abortion as an issue of women's equality has tended to be eclipsed by a medicalized discourse which centers on the morality of killing a fetus. Without dodging this aspect of abortion, several feminist writers have sought to reorient the discussion back to equality by offering a more explicit and thorough account of the connection between the right to abortion and women's status in society.

Reva Siegel's historical study of abortion regulation[44] best exemplifies this line of feminist scholarship. Siegel squarely rejects the trend toward discussing abortion as if it related only to the issue of childbearing, as opposed to child rearing. The debates about "choice" often seem to focus exclusively on the moment of birth: Should the woman terminate her pregnancy or give birth? The decontextualized quality of the discussion makes it appear as if the woman can then freely choose whether to raise the child or give it up for adoption. Abortion restrictions may be regarded as forcing women to remain pregnant, but they are less often looked upon as forcing a woman to become a mother.

Siegel argues that it makes sense, however, to reconnect abortion to motherhood, for the simple reason that the vast majority of women who bear children also raise those children. Only 6 percent of all babies born to unmarried women between the ages of 15 and 44 in 1982 were placed for adoption.[45] Thus, when a woman decides whether to have an abortion, this is often tantamount to deciding whether she can and should become a mother—a relational decision with important implications for at least the next two decades. Siegel stresses that the choice is far from being unconstrained for most women in our society.

---

[43] Anita L. Allen, The Proposed Equal Protection Fix for Abortion Law: Reflections on Citizenship, Gender, and the Constitution, 18 Harv. J.L. & Pub. Pol'y 419 (1995).

[44] Reva Siegel, Reasoning from the Body: A Historical Perspective on Abortion Regulation and Questions of Equal Protection, 44 Stan. L. Rev. 261 (1992).

[45] *Id.* at 371 n.434, *citing* Christine A. Bachrach, Adoption Plans, Adopted Children, and Adoptive Mothers, 48 J. Marriage & Fam. 243, 449-50 (1986).

Hypothetically, a woman compelled to bear a child she does not want could give it up for adoption, abandon it, or pay someone to care for the child until maturity. In this society, however, these are not options that women avail themselves of with great frequency for the simple reason that few women are able to abandon a child born of their body. That society as a whole, or some women in particular, may judge it morally preferable to give a child up to adoption rather than abort a pregnancy is beside the point. Once compelled to bear a child against their wishes, most women will feel obligated to raise it.[46]

Identifying the sources of this obligation to "take on" motherhood is an important feminist inquiry. Siegel mentions the emotional bonds that many women feel toward their child as the pregnancy progresses, as well as the "intense familial and social pressure" that is brought to bear on women to raise the child they carry. Interestingly, pressure to keep the child is often most pronounced for less privileged women upon whom motherhood imposes the most severe material burdens. Thus unmarried black mothers, for example, are less likely to place their babies for adoption than are unmarried white mothers. Moreover, only very rarely do married women place their children up for adoption—such a decision seems not to be a socially acceptable method of "family planning" in the contemporary United States. Siegel's basic point is that when legislatures place restrictions on abortion, they are well aware of the constraining force of these gender norms and "both desire and expect that most women will raise the child they are forced to bear . . ."[47]

Nevertheless, the impression of the abortion decision that emerges from legal cases, and increasingly from popular discussion, often seems far removed from the social institution of motherhood. Commentators have remarked that the sonogram-like image of the fetus in the womb that has captured the popular imagination depicts a being who is virtually autonomous.[48] In this familiar visual image, the mother is either invisible or peripheral to the central figure of the floating fetus. Siegel argues that this tendency to miss the significance of the mother's role in gestation and child rearing is not limited to

---

[46] *Id.* at 371-72 (footnotes omitted).

[47] *Id.* at 372.

[48] *See* Rosalind Pollack Petchesky, Fetal Images: The Power of Visual Culture in the Politics of Reproduction, 13 Feminist Stud. 263, 268 (1987).

visual depictions—the discourse of the law also treats procreative choice as if it were unrelated to social conceptions of motherhood.

This tendency to "erase" the woman is not simply a function of analyzing abortion under the right to privacy rather than the right to equal protection. It is more likely traceable to deeper structures of legal rhetoric that would affect analysis and thinking, regardless of the constitutional peg upon which a decision is based. According to Siegel, the "physiological framework" or "physiological paradigm"[49] by which the Supreme Court reasons about the abortion decision figures heavily in its failure to accord more weight to the wishes and needs of the pregnant woman. The legal decision is driven by an account of medical facts about gestation and reproduction. Categories established by the "trimester framework" and the "point of viability" have dominated the discussion, suggesting that the proper legal conclusion will follow from getting the science right. This medicalized account of pregnancy conjures up an image of the autonomous fetus and obscures the social context of interdependency in which a potential mother must make a decision that inevitably will also affect her life.

At first blush, the Supreme Court's medicalized approach to abortion may appear acceptable because it seems to be based on objective, scientific fact. Siegel criticizes the physiological mode of reasoning about abortion, however, not because it is inaccurate, but because it is "objectively incomplete."[50] By selectively focusing on certain facts relating to the physical development of the fetus, the discourse systematically ignores the social and cultural dimensions of childbearing and child rearing, including, of course, the impact that becoming a mother has on a woman's personal identity and life prospects. Siegel also claims that the selective focus makes it easier to hide the gender stereotyping and traditional assumptions about women and motherhood that frequently underlie the enactment of restrictions on abortion. Simple recitation of the "interest in fetal life" has the tendency to prevent further inquiry into whether gender bias may have led the legislature to embark on a course of "fetal life saving by compelled pregnancy."[51]

To unearth the gender bias beneath restrictions on abortion, Siegel traces modern "habits of reasoning" about abortion to the

---

[49] Siegel, supra note 44, at 265.
[50] Id. at 290.
[51] Id. at 362.

Nineteenth Century campaign against abortion led by obstetricians and gynecologists. At that time, physicians attempted to persuade the public that the medical profession—as opposed to midwives and other women lacking professional stature—should control the process of childbirth. Discussing abortion and fetal development in scientific terms fit well with this new concept of childbirth as a medical procedure requiring medical expertise. Specifically, doctors set about discrediting the importance of the older concept of "quickening"—the moment when a pregnant woman first feels the baby move—and substituted conception as the pivotal point in the reproductive process. Prior to the physicians' campaign, criminal penalties were not generally imposed if abortions were performed before quickening. By the end of the Nineteenth Century, however, most state laws had outlawed all abortions, save for the unusual case when the procedure was deemed necessary to save the woman's life.

In addition to promoting the professional objectives of the medical profession, the Nineteenth Century campaign against abortion also had wider social objectives that spoke more directly to gender and motherhood. Up to the middle of the century, abortion had been increasingly used by middle-class, married women as a method of birth control to limit the size of their families. Abortion opponents decried this practice, arguing that married women had a duty to reproduce. They were particularly concerned with abortion as a method of birth control among "native" American women, meaning white, non-immigrant women, and even maintained that interrupting the "natural" processes of reproduction would damage women's health.

These arguments supporting a marital obligation to reproduce were in direct opposition to feminist claims of the time for "voluntary motherhood."[52] Nineteenth Century feminists were not avowedly "pro-choice" in that they did not campaign openly for abortion as a method of birth control. Instead, their demand for voluntary motherhood was grounded in a wife's right to refuse her husband's demands for sex, a precursor of the contemporary movement against marital rape. Siegel contends that the Nineteenth Century feminists had a vision of women's "self-ownership in marriage"[53] that focused attention on the conditions under which women became mothers and how

[52] *Id.* at 305.
[53] *Id.*

D. Forced Motherhood: Gender Equality and Abortion Rights

motherhood dramatically affected their lives. Thus, in this earlier struggle, opponents of abortion countered feminist critiques of marriage and compulsory motherhood with medicalized arguments focusing on fetal development, threats to women's health, and the political implications of permitting birth control among the more privileged classes.

The import of Siegel's research is that the fusion of the medical and sociopolitical arguments against abortion accomplished in the Nineteenth Century campaign are with us today, although in muted form. The habit of reasoning about abortion in physiological terms is very much in evidence in contemporary case law and popular debate. It may be that few would openly argue today that white married middle-class women have a duty to reproduce and have no right to contest their husbands' demands for "unprotected" sex. Contemporary arguments against abortion tend to focus exclusively on protecting unborn life. Nevertheless, the "gender codes" that put pressure on women to become mothers, to keep and raise their children, and to subordinate their professional and personal interests for family have not disappeared. Joan Williams has argued that the idea that women should be "selfless" when it comes to motherhood remains a very strong component of contemporary gender ideology; public opinion polls, for example, indicate that most Americans believe that it should be illegal for a woman to have an abortion if the decision is based on her desire to pursue or maintain her career.[54] Although the Supreme Court rulings on abortion restrictions do not discuss them as markers of traditional values about women and motherhood, it is well known that pro-life groups tend to attract traditionally minded women, while feminist, professional women are more heavily represented in pro-choice groups.

In contexts other than reproductive rights, the Court will not permit states to justify gender-based restrictions by reference to stereotypes and habitual assumptions about how women should behave, including the assumptions that women have an obligation to become mothers, to be the primary caretakers for children, and to discharge most domestic responsibilities. Although reproductive rights are central to women's lives, they have not been confronted in law as an issue of gender equality. The Twentieth Century feminist movement may

[54] Williams, supra note 8, at 1583.

have discredited the notion that motherhood is women's destiny to the extent that it is now assumed that motherhood is voluntary. The new feminist writing on abortion, however, recapitulates an earlier feminist concern for examining the social and material conditions under which women exercise "choice," both in the context of abortion and with respect to motherhood more generally. The distinctively contemporary feature of this new scholarship is its ability to tease out the gender bias in neutral modes of argumentation, particularly in showing how the "objective" discourse of science and medicine can obscure sexist attitudes and sever the conceptual connection between restrictions on abortion and compulsory motherhood.

E.   LIMITATIONS ON THE RIGHT TO CHOOSE MOTHERHOOD

One continuity between the Nineteenth Century campaign against abortion and the current controversy over abortion rights is that, in each historical period, the arguments were primarily directed at white, middle-class women and seemed to have the most immediate relevance for that group. In the earlier era, abortion opponents played on nativist fears that, as middle-class wives gained more autonomy to limit the size of their families, the population of lower, immigrant classes would swell in comparison to the more "refined" classes. Today, some writers question whether the issue of abortion rights has been so high on the feminist agenda in part because white, middle-class women have dominated advocacy groups such as NOW and Planned Parenthood.

As Dorothy Roberts explains it, emphasizing abortion rights over other potential issues relating to reproduction tends to put the experience of relatively more privileged women at the center of the women's movement, and carries the risk of neglecting the needs of poor women, particularly poor women of color. Roberts theorizes that:

> The primary concern of white, middle-class women are laws that restrict choices otherwise available to them, such as statutes that make it more difficult to obtain an abortion. The main concern of poor women of color, however, are the material conditions of poverty and oppression

E. Limitations on the Right to Choose Motherhood

that restrict their choices. The reproductive freedom of poor women of color, for example, is limited significantly not only by the denial of access to safe abortions, but also by the lack of resources necessary for a healthy pregnancy and parenting relationship.[55]

In many contexts, of course, the diverse priorities of different groups of women are not in opposition to each other. For example, securing fuller abortion rights probably will not harm poor women of color, especially given that many poor women may have a special need to avoid the burdens of motherhood. What has sometimes been difficult for white feminist scholars to appreciate is that what may constitute oppression for one group—for professional women, forced motherhood—may seem relatively benign to those women who have been "deemed not even worthy of the dignity of childbearing."[56] The danger is not so much that interests among women will clash as that reproductive freedom will not be conceived broadly enough to encompass the experiences of less privileged women.

In this decade, feminist scholars have developed a body of literature addressing reproductive rights from the perspective of women of color. As with the writing on abortion, the themes of compulsion and lack of respect for women's agency are prominent. However, these works typically examine the ways that women of color are denied the right and opportunity to be mothers, exploring how the state and other social forces enforce judgments about which women "deserve" to bear and raise children.

Patricia Williams, for example, has written eloquently about the many formidable obstacles to reproductive freedom faced by African-American women from the era of slavery to the present. In an autobiographical essay entitled On Being the Object of Property,[57] Williams reflected on the plight of women in her own family. A central theme of the essay is how vulnerable African-American women have been to having their children taken away from them. The essay opens by mentioning Sophie, Williams's great-great grandmother, who was purchased as a slave when she was only 11 years old and immediately

---

[55] Dorothy E. Roberts, Punishing Drug Addicts Who Have Babies: Women of Color, Equality and the Right of Privacy, 104 Harv. L. Rev. 1419, 1461 (1991).

[56] *Id.* at 1458.

[57] Patricia J. Williams, *The Alchemy of Race and Rights: Diary of a Law Professor* 216 (1991).

impregnated by the slaveowner. Her child, Mary, was subsequently taken away from her and raised as a house servant. Because slave mothers had no legal right to keep their children, taking Mary from her mother was not a legal violation. Williams's description of the severing of this mother-child relationship also suggests that class distinctions— here, the difference in social status between slaves who worked in the master's house and field slaves—also destroyed family ties.

Throughout the essay, Williams recounts other ways that mothers were separated from their children. We are told about Marjorie, Williams's godmother, who was given away by her light-skinned mother when she was six to be raised with her darker-skinned cousins. Because her mother had decided to marry a white man and "pass" for white, she could not raise Marjorie without disclosing her heritage and jeopardizing her marriage. Although the institution of slavery had long since been abolished, enforcement of the color line, sometimes reinforced by anti-miscegenation laws, still made it practically impossible for interracial families openly to live in peace. The choice made by Marjorie's mother may have been less circumscribed than Sophie's, but race and class still significantly hampered her ability to fulfill the role of a mother. Because Marjorie did not look like her mother, she was sent to a more "appropriate" family to be raised, insuring that racial segregation would continue to seem natural rather than socially constructed.

Juxtaposed with the telling of the stories of women in her family, Williams describes the cases of black and Hispanic women who took legal action against their doctors for subjecting them to sterilization without first securing their informed consent. A typical pattern was for a doctor to perform a tubal ligation, or even a hysterectomy, on an indigent woman who had just given birth, sometimes without telling the woman beforehand. Williams also recites statistics that indicate an extraordinarily high rate of sterilization among Native American and Puerto Rican women, with the procedure often performed in public hospitals. In sharp contrast to the unwillingness to provide public funding for abortions, sterilization as a method of birth control for women of color has been subsidized.

As I interpret the essay, by connecting the instances of separation of mother and child to the compulsory sterilization of women of color, Williams enables the reader to reflect on the low value society places on motherhood when the mothers are poor women of color. The women who were pressured or tricked into being sterilized were in ef-

E. Limitations on the Right to Choose Motherhood

fect "separated" from the children they might have had in the future and denied the right to choose motherhood. In the more contemporary setting, the methods of separation are less explicit and more privatized: The law now gives women legal rights to their children, but poverty, race, and the power of the medical profession still makes reproductive freedom an illusion for some women. Williams's essay illuminates why African-American feminist scholars might be less inclined to dwell on the burdens of motherhood and the denial of abortion rights, and instead look for ways to help poor women with child-bearing and child rearing.

Williams's approach to reproductive rights emphasizes the socially constructed aspects of even the most "natural" of human relationships, the connection between a parent and a child. Perhaps the most discussed part of her essay is her musings on the famous "Baby M" case,[58] in which Mary Beth Whitehead, a surrogate mother, resisted giving up her infant pursuant to a contract she had signed with William Stern, the father of the child. In commenting on the trial judge's decision to enforce the surrogacy contract, Williams was appalled at how readily the law can subordinate a woman's relationship to her child to the demands of contract law.

Because all the parties in the litigation were white, the Baby M case does not directly illustrate the obstacles faced by women of color in their role as mothers. Instead, Williams used the case to show how "social constructions are conceived and delivered up into the realm of the real as 'right,' while all else is devoured from memory as 'wrong.'"[59] She analogized the contract awarding Baby M to the Sterns to the "heavy-worded legalities by which my great-great-grandmother was pacified and parted from her child."[60] Williams's equation of Whitehead's situation to Sophie's makes the point that the power of the law, combined with poverty, can defeat the rights of motherhood. From this perspective, the individual's "choice," so celebrated in contract law and in the case law of reproductive rights, pales in significance to the compulsion of collective forces by which children are assigned to socially "appropriate" parents. Although several feminist writers have taken a more favorable view of surrogacy contracts—in

---

[58] *In the Matter of Baby M*, 525 A.2d 1128 (N.J. Super. Ct. Ch. Div. 1987), *rev'd*, 537 A.2d 1227 (N.J. 1988).

[59] Williams, supra note 57, at 225.

[60] *Id.*

fact, the legal and moral status of such arrangements is hotly debated in the feminist literature—Williams's treatment of surrogacy poignantly illustrates her major theme of motherhood as a cultural construct and institution that can be facilitated or undermined by law. Her richly textured stories suggest that, more often than not, poverty and racism operate to discourage women of color from being mothers and make them particularly vulnerable to losing the children they bear.

Supporting Williams's view of the precarious position of mothers of color, Dorothy Roberts has argued that "[r]ace has historically determined the value society places on the individual's right to choose motherhood."[61] The meager supports that have been offered to white women in their role as homemakers and mothers tend to be denied when the prototypical recipient is black and poor, as evidenced by recent welfare reforms.[62] Moreover, Roberts asserts that black women are more likely to be punished for their reproductive choices, even to the extent of imposition of criminal penalties.

The most dramatic example of such a punitive response to the exercise of reproductive choice can be seen in recent prosecutions of drug-addicted mothers for having babies. Roberts's study of these cases indicates that the law has targeted procreation as the act that triggers criminal penalties—pregnant women charged with such crimes as child abuse or distribution of drugs to a minor can avoid prosecution by having an abortion, which reveals that it is not simply the use of drugs which warrants punishment.[63] Even when there is no evidence of actual harm to the fetus, an addict who exposes her fetus to such a danger faces prosecution. Roberts sees the social judgment behind these prosecutions as expressing the view that such women do not deserve to be mothers. This judgment is apparently so pronounced that it can transform what would otherwise be a constitutional right to procreate into an occasion for direct governmental coercion.

Roberts does not deny that the exposure of babies to crack can have tragic effects and that the mothers of such babies bear some measure of responsibility for their actions. What she questions is why the government would choose to punish drug-addicted mothers for having babies, rather than to provide assistance to these women, such as

---

[61] Roberts, supra note 55, at 1463.

[62] *See* supra at pp. 281-88.

[63] Dorothy E. Roberts, Unshackling Black Motherhood, 95 Mich. L. Rev. 938, 938 n.1 (1997).

increased funding for drug rehabilitation programs or prenatal services. The choice she examines is society's decision to punish women for their conduct during pregnancy, instead of increasing the chance of healthy pregnancies through more direct means. Particularly when the likelihood that pregnant addicts will avoid seeking prenatal care for fear of detection is factored in, the governmental response appears self-defeating.

Roberts explains the punitive response as stemming from the devalued status of black motherhood. Approximately three-fourths of all prosecutions of drug-addicted mothers have been brought against women of color,[64] mostly because such women are more often treated in public hospitals, and these facilities are more likely to report substance abuse to the authorities. For example, Roberts cited one study in the New England Journal of Medicine indicating that black women were ten times more likely than white women to be reported to the public health authorities for substance abuse during pregnancy.[65] The racially disproportionate impact of the criminal penalties gives the law a racially selective meaning—the message is that abortion (or sterilization), not motherhood, is the socially preferred course of action for this group of women. Roberts doubts that such a punitive response would have occurred but for the class and race of the prototypical defendant, claiming that "[i]f prosecutors had instead chosen to prosecute affluent women addicted to alcohol or prescription medication, the policy of criminalizing prenatal conduct very likely would have suffered a hasty demise. Society is much more willing to condone the punishment of poor women of color who fail to meet the middle-class ideal of motherhood."[66]

Roberts's scholarship emphasizes the threat that government intervention poses to the reproductive freedom of poor women of color. She is principally concerned about the processes of devaluation, particularly legislative and administrative judgments that only certain women have the right to reproduce and that there is nothing problematic about pursuing a public policy of discouraging poor people from having children. Taking the perspective of poor women of color, Roberts places the right to be a mother at the top of the agenda for reproductive rights.

---

[64] *Id.* at 938.
[65] Roberts, supra note 55, at 1453.
[66] *Id.* at 1436.

Much of the feminist scholarship on abortion rights also centers on devaluation. However, in this context, the analysis centers on how women are devalued when they are forced to be mothers, rather than denied the right to be mothers. Denying a woman the right to terminate an unwanted pregnancy has significant economic and social repercussions in part because of the confining constructions given to motherhood in our culture. Compulsory motherhood continues to be a central mechanism of some women's subordination.

The emphasis of these two strands of feminist scholarship is admittedly different—the primary evil for one is compulsory sterilization, while the other is more occupied with forced motherhood. The apparent tension between arguing for the right to be a mother and the right not to be a mother, however, dissipates to some degree when the focus is placed on the conditions under which women become mothers. The hope of much of the new feminist scholarship on motherhood and reproductive rights is that women will find common ground in their advocacy for greater social support for mothers, regardless of their diverse social positions.

CHAPTER 10

Conclusion

It is often said that we live in a post-feminist age. The conventional wisdom is that gender discrimination is largely a thing of the past and that feminism, as we have known it, can provide little help to those women trying to cope with the debilitating effects of sexual bias. I hope that this book refutes both contentions. If there is one theme that emerges most prominently from the eclectic body of research we call "feminist legal theory" it is that gender has permeated thinking in the law, affecting basic doctrinal categories, legal discourses, and the structures of legal institutions. Using gender as a way to organize life and law, moreover, has most often worked to the detriment of women. In a variety of contexts, legal feminists have demonstrated that gender is often inseparable from hierarchy—that "male" functions as a code word for superior, while "female" still carries associations of inferiority. The works discussed in this book pose a formidable challenge to the idea that gender is "complementary" in our culture. In matters of sex, difference still seems incompatible with equality.

As this century ends, it is clear that contemporary law has been influenced by feminism, but that influence is difficult to assess. In some specific areas, the law has been inspired by feminism and has evolved in a decidedly progressive direction. The development of the claim for sexual harassment in the realm of employment, for example, has given some women the very important option of staying in their jobs and resisting, rather than simply quitting because of an intolerably hostile environment. Overall, however, I think it is fair to say that the effects of feminism on the law have been sketchy, less than transformative, and not invariably beneficial to women. In my opinion, this has more to do with the virulence of sexism in our legal culture than the inadequacy of feminism as emancipatory theory and practice. The longer we investigate gender bias in the law, the deeper we find its roots. There is still more feminist writing examining how women are subordinated by law than laying out strategies for liberation. Law and legal discourses continue to be so saturated with gender bias that it is hard to envision another kind of future. After studying feminist legal theory, few students seem satisfied with the status quo. Many leave the course with a will to resist, however, even if they feel pessimistic about the prospects for radical cultural or legal change.

The maturation of feminist legal theory that this book traces also suggests why the subject is crucial to progressive social change. In particular, the critique of objectivity that feminist scholars often bring to their analysis of law is empowering for students who sense that something is unfair, but hesitate to challenge what has been enshrined as "reasonable." Even a cursory study makes it apparent that there is no quick fix for the deep-seated gender bias that feminist scholars have identified—neither grand theories of equality, nor a steadfast commitment to reason and principle, can show the way out of the innumerable double binds that epitomize the predicament of women in relation to the law. Most feminist theorists have, of necessity, also become pragmatists who devise provisional strategies to make things somewhat better, knowing that their strategies are also likely to make things somewhat worse. To choose a good strategy, feminists need first to acquire a deep understanding of how specific biases operate in context, and how bias resonates in contemporary culture. This is where feminist legal theory can prove invaluable.

To some extent, the concerns that animated women's liberationists in the late 1960s and early 1970s represent the unfinished business of feminist legal writers today. Second-wave feminists emphasized dangers that they regarded as endemic to being a woman, especially the marginalization that followed marriage and motherhood and the likelihood of being targeted for sexual violence or abuse. They saw the twin images of women—as "Mothers" and as "Sexual Subordinates"—as stultifying, and at times defamatory, and struggled for women to be accepted as individuals. Nothing revolutionary has happened on this score. I find that even women who resist the label of "feminist" often acknowledge the unequal status of women in these important realms, and feel an urgency to discuss such topics as date rape, pregnancy leave, and sexual disparagement by co-workers. For all the significant differences among women, which the scholarship of the last decade has so amply documented and debated, common ground can still be found in the very pervasiveness of gender discrimination, which touches most women at some point in their lives. Unless we are to hold women solely responsible for their own oppression, the conventional wisdom that gender discrimination is no longer prevalent simply does not square with the common understanding that in the late 1990s it is extremely difficult for a woman to be both a "good" mother and a "valuable" employee and to live her life in safety, free from sexual violence, abuse, or denigration.

Feminist historical studies, such as Reva Siegel's, in which she explains how patterns of gender discrimination are reproduced over time in updated versions, are particularly useful to understand the contemporary feminist paradox: Things seem to have changed a lot for women, yet strangely have remained the same. Popular culture often reports and exaggerates the changes, but neglects the continuities. As a middle-aged feminist who remembers the days before the women's movement, I marvel at the resiliency of the basic structures of male domination in the face of remarkable changes in the situation of women.

The developments in feminist legal theory described in this book provide considerable insight into the forces that reproduce gender discrimination and show how the law has both contributed to the (re)construction of an unequal society and has been a powerful catalyst for change. The complex and contradictory character of the influence of law, however, only reinforces law's importance as a field for feminist inquiry. The field of feminist legal theory is just old enough to benefit from a retrospective view, which I offer in closing.

During the nearly thirty years of feminist scholarly writing covered in this book, the legal construct used most consistently to address gender discrimination has been "disparate treatment," supplemented at times by disapproving references to "gender stereotyping." Although specific legislation or judicial interpretation of particular governing standards at times may seem to embody a different principle, the ban against disparate treatment goes a long way toward explaining the law's basic approach to claims of sex bias. In its simplest formulation, the ban against disparate treatment requires that women be treated the same as men, at least in those circumstances in which men and women are similarly situated. The concept is comparative at its core: The standard by which the equity of the treatment of women is judged is through comparison with the situation of men. The legal penchant for formulating hypothetical questions typically comes into play when the legal issue boils down to whether a particular woman would have been treated differently if she had been a man. In such cases, the male standard is made explicit and the person charging sex bias must come up with probative evidence that a man in "her" situation received better treatment.

Compared to the prohibitions against disparate treatment based on gender, prohibitions against gender stereotyping are less uniformly imposed and the law is less certain as to what qualifies as gender stereotyping. In its narrowest sense, gender stereotyping refers to the use of unfounded generalizations about women as a group, such as "women are not good drivers," that are then used against an individual woman whose behavior does not conform to the stereotype, to place her at a disadvantage. Particularly in constitutional jurisprudence, the courts have repeatedly stated that gender stereotypes and habitual ways of thinking about women do not provide sufficient justification for the imposition of a different rule for men than for women. In these situations, however, the distaste for gender stereotyping tends principally to supplement the mandate against disparate treatment. It is not often the case that a "neutral" rule or standard applied equally to men and women is struck down as discriminatory because it finds its justification in stereotypes about men and women. The current legal disapproval of gender stereotyping rarely is sufficient to prohibit the use of "implicit male norms," without some further showing of hostility or animus against women.

Clearly, the ban on disparate treatment, even augmented by some restrictions on gender stereotyping, is not nearly expansive enough to respond to the varieties of gender bias that feminist legal theorists have exposed and critiqued since the early 1970s. When matched against the three stages of feminist legal theory described in this book, for example, the prohibition against disparate treatment seems well suited only to address issues of attaining access for women in male-dominated settings, characteristic of legal controversies at the forefront of the Equality Stage. Though it is not the only measure of equality or justice, a legal right to equal access does remove one important obstacle for a woman pursuing a nontraditional life.

However, when women are subordinated in contexts in which marked differences between men and women are most salient, notably with respect to laws relating to reproduction and sexuality, we cannot rely upon the ban on disparate treatment to produce just results. The struggle of "equal treatment" feminists to construct a compelling analogy between the situation of pregnant working women and other temporarily disabled employees is only the best known example of the difficulty of straining all controversies into the comparative framework required by a disparate treatment approach. Although analogies are often useful as arguments, there is always a danger that the analogy will hide the specificity of women's situation, for instance, missing the importance of the social meaning of pregnancy by emphasizing its similarity to a physical disability. The preoccupations of feminist writers during the Difference Stage thus typically had little to do with the disparate treatment of men and women and require a different set of concepts to comprehend gender-linked injuries such as rape, domestic violence, and sexual harassment, which are faced predominantly by women.

Finally, the disparate treatment principle seems to have virtually no capacity to address issues of diversity among women. As the concept of disparate treatment has developed in the law, gender discrimination in single-sex groups is hard to fathom. For example, the proposition that women of color might experience discrimination due to their gender, as well as race—even in cases in which white women are not also discriminated against—simply does not "compute" under conventional legal analysis. Intersectional analysis does not lend itself readily to the comparative framework. It has also been an uphill battle to convince the courts that bias against gay men and lesbians is a form of sex discrimination, because such bias does not fit into the conventional disparate treatment mold. Often attempts to enlarge the concept of gender stereotyping to cover the kinds of bias that have surfaced in feminist writing in the Diversity Stage have not been successful, because litigants are unable to connect the stereotyping to concrete instances of disparate treatment of men and women.

Particularly in the past decade, feminist scholars have been developing new concepts of gender bias that go well beyond disparate treatment. As I see it, the most important of these new constructs is what I have called "devaluation." Unlike disparate treatment, devaluation as a process does not principally involve comparing the treatment of one individual to another "different" individual, or even comparing the treatment of different social groups. Instead, devaluation is largely a cognitive process which links certain activities and conduct to gender in a hierarchical fashion. What is devalued is an entire category, whether it is housework, part-time work, emotional harm, or feminine behavior. The source of the devaluation is linked only indirectly to individuals or groups. For example, the association of a category with women—the gendering of a category—often derives from a female image of the *prototypical* worker, victim, or other actor. It is important to realize that the effects of gender devaluation are felt disproportionately by women. Nevertheless, men as well as women may be harmed by gender devaluation, insofar as men follow "female" patterns, such as being a primary parent or displaying feminine (or effeminate) qualities.

As a form of bias, gender devaluation may not seem as stark as disparate treatment because individuals of either sex may sometimes avoid its harshest effects by leading a "male" life, for example, by working full-time in a male-dominated profession, or by adopting a competitive, aggressive style of personal interaction. Nonetheless, I believe that in contemporary society, gender devaluation as a form of bias is as prevalent as, if not more prevalent than, disparate treatment. For this reason alone, it should be addressed by law. To my mind, moreover, gender devaluation is no less pernicious than disparate treatment. I see no reason the mental image of "things female" should convey a meaning of inferiority, deficiency, or lack of value, unless one refuses to accept the most fundamental tenet of feminism, that women are as fully human as men. That devaluation operates in the realm of ideas does not diminish its practical significance because socially constructed reality is nonetheless real. The recognition of gender devaluation as actionable bias in the law could provide a way to challenge some particularly resilient structures and habits of thoughts that have contributed to women's economic and sexual subordination.

In the future, feminist scholarship will likely continue to grapple with various kinds of cognitive bias, in addition to gender devaluation. A considerable body of the most recent feminist applied scholarship has examined the harmful effects of narrow prototypes in contexts principally involving the treatment and status of women. We have seen how scholars have critiqued the narrow image of the ideal mother and how it tacitly excludes unmarried, lesbian, or minority mothers, and have expressed concerns that the prototype of the battered woman does not take account of the strong women who resist their abuse by means other than fleeing from their homes. The prototype of the "stranger rape," particularly the combination of white victim and black offender, has also probably prevented a fuller response to intraracial and acquaintance rapes.

In each of these examples, the prototypes are not simply too narrowly drawn; they have a normative dimension as well. The white woman attacked by a black stranger is cast as innocent, suggesting that other rape victims are partly to blame for their injuries. The domestic violence victim who defies the image of the abject battered woman by fighting back may be denied support because she did not leave when she had the chance. Welfare mothers who "refuse" to marry the fathers of their children may receive a lower amount of support.

The social and legal disadvantages experienced by women who do not fit the prevailing prototypes seem intricately connected to sexism and racism. On their face, of course, the prototypes are neutral as to gender and race. The bias comes into play, however, when we tease out the implicit rationales supporting a belief that the prototypes depict reality. Behind the prototypes lie judgments of value that, feminist writers contend, reinforce patriarchy and white privilege. They argue that the ideal mother is depicted as married, not because the average mother is married, but because of the preferred status of male-headed households, and that the prototype of the stranger rape draws upon a white victim/black offender scenario, not because most rapes follow this pattern, but because depicting black men as sexually dangerous serves to justify white male control over both white women and black men. As I describe them, the prototypes are not primarily descriptive but normative, serving as justifications for existing power distributions in society.

In one sense, the gender- and race-laden prototypes amount to a form of stereotyping, insofar as they function to deny protection to "nonconforming" women. However, the traditional legal understanding of stereotypes as generalizations that saddle individuals with assumptions about the group does not capture the more complex processes that produce and reproduce the prevailing prototypes. There is not yet a term in the legal vocabulary for the cognitive bias described here.

Perhaps most importantly, it is far from clear how the law might respond to "biased" prototypes. It is probably not possible to "ban" their influence on the law, precisely because they operate on a subconscious cognitive level and because we all need to simplify the world by constructing bounded categories and images. The challenge for feminist scholars of the future will be to continue to expose the underlying normative judgments embedded within the most biased prototypes, and find ways to promote the development of more diverse images of women's experiences and of women's victimization, in the hope of loosening the hold of these narrowing constructions. This kind of feminist legal analysis takes us far afield from comparative, disparate treatment analysis. The bias in the legal responses to date rape, domestic violence, and single motherhood cannot be understood by examining how a comparable group of men are treated, because there is no comparable predominantly male group. In the next decade, the law undoubtedly will continue to confront gender bias that affects a predominantly female group. To do this, we need legal concepts that express how basic categories of thought can be so contaminated by gender bias that they make it seem reasonable and just to deny legal protection to vast numbers of women.

Finally, in the next wave of feminist legal theory, I predict that even more attention will be paid to the deconstruction of what passes for individual choice. In a variety of contexts, feminist writers have probed behind women's choices to examine the social conditions under which women make critical decisions relating to reproduction, motherhood, sexuality, and work. The recent feminist scholarship examining the false dichotomy between agency and victimization is only the most explicit effort to develop a richer version of women's subjectivity, one that regards women as strategic actors but also acknowledges the importance of constraints on choice. Similar attempts to show the coercion behind choice and the choice exercised even under coercive conditions characterize much of the recent applied feminist scholarship, treating such diverse topics as consent in sexual relationships and the work/family dilemma. This body of work emphasizes the recurring theme that it makes more sense to treat "choice" as operating on a continuum, as being more or less constrained, rather than simply as a binary condition that is either present or absent. Moreover, feminists writing about matters of choice tend to recognize that there is no escape from making difficult political judgments. The key issue frequently boils down to *which* constraints are so unacceptable or unfair that they *should* undermine the moral and legal significance of individual choice. When it comes to deconstructing individual choice, I see less need to develop new concepts, and suspect that feminist scholars will continue to try to persuade their readers that the conventional wisdom both overestimates the freedom of women's choices and underestimates women's capacity for resisting and coping with oppression.

This book opened with a discussion of what it means to "think like a feminist" in matters relating to the law. Like the skill of "thinking like a lawyer," it provides a distinctive way of framing questions, with few definitive answers. "Thinking like a feminist" is frequently taxing because it requires a skeptical attitude toward even the most conventional legal categories to a degree that often makes conventional legal analysis seem superficial in comparison. Feminist thinking can be depressing because it so often leads to a conclusion that the much-touted progress in gender equality is illusory or at least far less comprehensive than is advertised. It also makes women doubt their own choices. To my mind, however, feminist legal theory is the most exciting and empowering way to approach law. It has allowed me to teach law and address those topics and questions that matter most to me as a woman, a simple luxury that was denied to earlier generations of female academics.

On the first day of one of my feminist legal theory classes, a very astute graduate student from a discipline other than law asked me whether it was possible to think like a lawyer and a feminist at the same time. I should have let her answer that question for herself after she had finished the course and reflected on the scholarship discussed in this book. Instead, I could not resist saying that I believed that feminist analyses greatly enriched the study of law, and that I wanted to reframe her question to ask whether it is possible to think like a lawyer *without* giving sustained thought to gender and to the lives of women.

Index

Index

Index

Index

Index